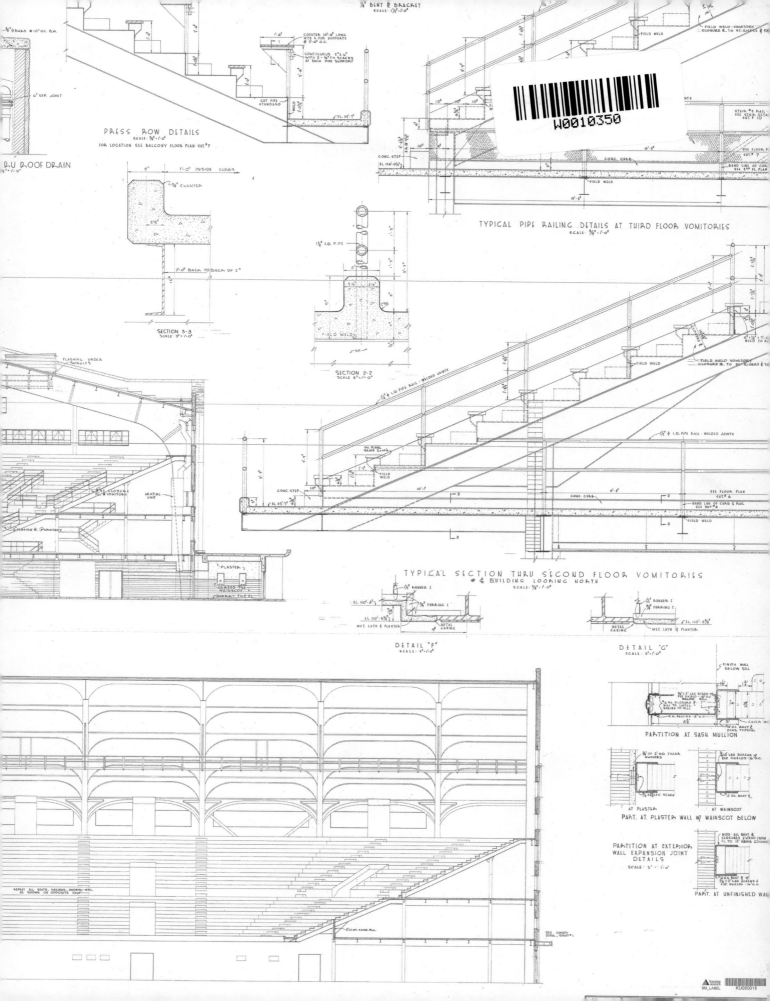

BEWARE OF THE PHOG

50 YEARS OF ALLEN FIELDHOUSE

Doug Vance

Jeff Bollig

Officially Licensed by the University of Kansas

SP
SPORTS
PUBLISHING
L.L.C.

www.SportsPublishingLLC.com

ISBN: 1-58261-718-X
       1-58261-884-4 (leather edition)
       1-58261-885-2 (collector's edition)

Publisher: Peter L. Bannon and Joseph J. Bannon Sr.

Senior managing editor: Susan M. Moyer

Acquisitions editor: Bob Snodgrass

Developmental editors: Kipp A. Wilfong, Doug Hoepker

Art director: K. Jeffrey Higgerson

Book layout: Kerri Baker, Dustin Hubbart and Innerworkings, L.L.C.

Book design: Dustin Hubbart

Dust jacket design: Dustin Hubbart

Project manager: Kerri Baker

Imaging: Kerri Baker, Dustin Hubbart, Christine Mohrbacher and Heidi Norsen

Research/Assistant editor: Janelle Martin

Copy editor: Cindy McNew

Photo editor: Erin Linden-Levy

Vice president of sales and marketing: Kevin King

Media and promotions managers:

       Jonathan Patterson (regional marketing manager)

       Randy Fouts (national marketing manager)

       Maurey Williamson (print marketing manager)

Printed in the United States

Sports Publishing L.L.C.
804 North Neil Street
Champaign, IL 61820

Phone: 1-877-424-2665
Fax: 217-363-2073
Web site: www.SportsPublishingLLC.com

To Sue, Cory and Stuart, whose patience, understanding and inspiration long ago exceeded my expectations.

—*Doug Vance*

To Laurie, Courtney and Kyle, who give me reason to smile every day.

—*Jeff Bollig*

...and with deep gratitude to those loyal Jayhawk fans everywhere.

CONTENTS

Telling the story of a building can be a challenge. What does one say about a conglomeration of bricks, steel, wood and glass? In a sense, a building is actually not that much different than the human body. There is the physical aspect and there is the spiritual aspect. It is the symbiotic relationship of the two that allows one to tell the story of Allen Fieldhouse. But it is not something one person can do alone. The story of Allen Fieldhouse is best told by those who created the memories for all to enjoy.

Larry Brown—Head Men's Basketball Coach 1984-88: "I spent five of the greatest years of my life in this building. There is no better place to go to school. There is no better place to play. I am honored to have coached at a place that understands the value of history, tradition and sportsmanship. It's no secret that we enjoyed an advantage in Allen Fieldhouse. It's a special place."

Nick Collison—Men's Basketball Letterwinner 2000-03: "I remember most vividly the times we would go on monster runs against teams as the most fun I had. The noise just escalates until there is an eerie level where you can't hear anything. And in a weird way it seems almost quiet. There were so many times when it would be a six- or eight-point game and then all of the sudden we would go on a run like 20-4. And just like that, the game was over."

Danny Manning—Men's Basketball Letterwinner 1985-88: "To this day, I have never been in another gym with as much enthusiasm, electricity and as much love as the fans gave to me. That is an awesome feeling."

Ted Owens—Head Men's Basketball Coach 1965-83: "One of the most memorable moments would have to be the Bud Stallworth game in 1972. That was the 20th reunion of the 1952 national championship team. Having the 1952 team back and having such a great performance against Missouri was very special. People who have cared all their life about Kansas basketball want to be buried around Kansas basketball. That's where I want to be."

Wayne Simien—Men's Basketball Letterwinner 2002-05: "Being a Kansas native, I have grown up in Allen Fieldhouse. I have seen the floor, players and coaches go through metamorphoses. Through all the changes one thing has stayed constant—the walls and structure that breathe the rich history of Kansas basketball."

Bob Timmons—Head Men's Track Coach 1964-89: "Oh, it was a zoo. Everyone was practicing at once. The basketball court was ringed with a curtain. At the same time, we had our team running around the track and upstairs under the stands the weight men were throwing the shot against a wall and the javelin into a bale of hay. The baseball team was using a batting cage and a few of the football players were playing catch in the area between the court and track. I don't know how anyone could concentrate. We were actually ahead of our time, however. No one else had a facility that served as many purposes."

Jo Jo White—Men's Basketball Letterwinner 1966-69: "I'm humbled by the recognition. But I can't accept this alone. Every night I gave you everything I had. And in return, you cheered me on and gave me everything you had. That's what I call a relationship. That relationship I will cherish forever. "Rock, Chalk, Jayhawk""

Roy Williams—Head Men's Basketball Coach 1989-2003: "As a coach and as a player, you felt the incredible energy and passion that came from the atmosphere in Allen Fieldhouse. We fed off that. The fans were so knowledgeable and appreciative of the effort and the focus on team play. It was truly an honor to be a part of that. There may be other arenas that have all the bells and whistles, but there are none better than Allen Fieldhouse."

Lynette Woodard—Women's Basketball Letterwinner 1978-81: "I had always loved basketball, but I didn't know anything about basketball. It was instinctual. I always compared it to a piano player who could play by ear but did not know the notes. This (Allen Fieldhouse) is where I learned the notes. Kansas basketball means life to me. It was a great place to play the game I love. It's given me so much in my life, wonderful friends, a great education and a great job. Everything I find important in life I've been able to hone at Kansas."

Dedication to teamwork was the hallmark of many memorable Jayhawk teams that were born, nurtured and celebrated in Allen Fieldhouse.

Appropriately, teamwork also made it possible for this book to become a reality.

The challenge of chronicling the 50-year history of a storied building that has been home to so many significant moments also required the true spirit of cooperation among many people who have been associated with the heritage of athletics at the University of Kansas.

The old adage—"If these walls could talk ... the stories they would tell"—comes into play when writing about bricks and mortar. Obviously, we couldn't interview the building or the seats inside. But we did find many people who were devoted to what the building represents, who played a meaningful or small role in its history and were eager to share their story.

Let the record show that teamwork is how we were able to fill the pages ahead and tell the story of legendary Allen Fieldhouse.

It started with a pair of former KU sports information staffers who collaborated to assemble the facts, figures and history of Allen Fieldhouse in sharing the role of author. While it was important to tell the basic history of the building, it was our common goal to go beyond the scores, the records and moments of victory and defeat, and bring to life the emotions that were ignited throughout its existence.

The pages ahead would not be easy to fill without the cooperation of many of the coaches, administrators, players, fans, media and admirers of what Allen Fieldhouse represents. If it were possible, we would assemble all of those who contributed to this book on the Allen Fieldhouse floor and ask for the typical home game capacity crowd to offer a show of appreciation.

Since we will not have that opportunity, the authors would like to say thanks by acknowledging those who added so much spirit to our task.

First and foremost, we want say thanks to Sports Publishing, L.L.C. and in particular to our athletic director and head coach on this project, Bob Snodgrass and Kipp Wilfong.

We also would like to acknowledge the many hours of hard work and devotion from Janelle Martin, who became a regular in local Lawrence and KU campus libraries doing research on the project and uncovering much of the forgotten past of Allen Fieldhouse. Janelle is one of the unsung heroes of this project.

Every book that depicts a history needs an anchor source of information, and ours was the media relations office at KU. Former media relations director, Mitch Germann, his replacement, Chris Theisen, along with assistants Beau White, Mason Logan, Laura Lesko and Candace Dunback should be saluted for going beyond the call of duty in helping us find facts and figures. Of course, we also want to thank athletics director Lew Perkins, associate athletics director Jim Marchiony and head coach Bill Self for their assistance and agreeing to partner in the production of this book.

The great photo images you will find throughout the upcoming pages are the product of several talented photographers. KU athletics department staff photographer Jeff Jacobsen was the primary source of the images throughout the book. Many of the historic pictures you will see came from Rich Clarkson, and from the *Lawrence Journal-World*.

We would also like to thank Barry Bunch, Kathy Lafferty and the staff at the University of Kansas Archives for their great cooperation. University Archives proved to be an invaluable source of history for this project.

Beyond those individuals and groups, the following people were also instrumental in bringing back to life the history of this great Kansas landmark:

Warren Corman, Keith Lawton, Judy Morris, Max Falkenstien, Bob Timmons, Monte Johnson, Curtis Marsh, Bob Frederick, Floyd Temple, Richard Konzem, Larry Hatfield, Darren Cook, Nick Collison, Kevin Pritchard, Darnell Valentine, Bud Stallworth, Tim Jankovich, Norm Stewart, Johnny Orr, Jerod Haase, Ryan Robertson, Kelvin Sampson, Rick Pitino, Kim Anderson, Jerry Waugh, Maurice King, Eddie Sutton, Rick Wulkow, Stanley Reynolds, Scott Thornley, Mark Freidinger, Ed Hightower, Doug Beene, Howard Hill, D.W. Acker, Blair Kerkhoff, Jay Kutlow, Pete Goering, Bob Davis, Rick Plumlee, Tom Hedrick, Fred White, Mark Janssen, Jim Ryun, Doug Knop, Bob Lockwood, Cheryl Burnett, Curtis McClinton, Katie Armitidge, Bob Porter, Tom Stidham, Todd Gilmore and Mike Gentemann.

We hope you enjoy the book as much as we enjoyed putting it together.

Doug Vance and Jeff Bollig

Lew Perkins
Athletics Director

You might say that intercollegiate athletics have been my life.

For more than 40 years, my progression from student-athlete to coach to administrator has taken me to every corner of the nation, to hundreds of campuses and to more arenas, stadiums, gymnasiums and ballparks than I care to count.

But until my appointment at Kansas, I had never been to Allen Fieldhouse. Sure, I knew all about the place—at least I thought I did. As a basketball player at Iowa, I played for legendary Kansas basketball and football standout Ralph Miller. We were constantly regaled with stories of the Phog Allen days and the history of Kansas basketball.

Later, as athletic director at Wichita State, my Jayhawk "friends" would not miss an opportunity to share with me their experiences of "The Phog." Hey, I grew up in Boston. I knew all about great arenas such as Fenway Park and the Boston Garden. While impressed with the passion of the Jayhawkers, deep down I didn't think a 50-year-old basketball gymnasium in the middle of the plains could hold a candle to the homes of the "Green Monster" and "Parquet Floor."

Allen Fieldhouse was quiet that midsummer day when I first stepped foot in the building. But I could tell instantly the place was special. Though large even by today's standards, the proximity of the bleachers to the court created a certain coziness. The lack of soft theater seats told me that elbowroom was not included in the season ticket. And the banners — they just kept going and going and going.

I thought to myself, if only these walls could talk.

What would they say about Wilt Chamberlain's 52-point, 31-rebound debut against Northwestern? Did they really throw the javelin into hay bales on the third floor? What did it sound like when the fans chanted 'Sit down, Norm'? Tell me of the passion Bobby Kennedy possessed in that speech? 150 points...versus Kentucky...really? Batting cages and a golf driving range underneath the stands? Students camping out for a week before a game for which they *already* had tickets? An October practice session...drawing 16,300 fans...at midnight?

I could not wait for my first basketball game in Allen Fieldhouse. As much as I had seen on television and as much as I had heard from others, the actual experience turned out to be even better. I now consider myself among the fortunate to have experienced Allen Fieldhouse.

Nothing can match being there, but *Beware of the Phog* may be the next best thing. The combination of anecdotes, photographs, statistics and drawings paint a colorful, yet reverent history of this jewel. At times you will be humored, saddened, intrigued and amazed—but most of all you will be proud.

Certainly, time has taken a bit of a toll on this grand old building. We must be diligent in making sure it remains highly functional. But we will not do so at the expense of tradition and history.

Those walls might not be able to talk, but don't tell me I didn't hear the "Rock, Chalk, Jayhawk" chant that summer day.

How Cool

"I JUST SAT DOWN. IT WAS TOO LOUD. YOU CAN'T COACH DURING THE GAME. NO ONE CAN EVER HEAR YOU."
— Bill Self after coaching his first game in Allen Fieldhouse

Upon heading to work on his first day as head basketball coach at the University of Kansas, Bill Self could not hide the sense of awe that overcame him as he drove up Naismith Drive and approached Allen Fieldhouse.

Self's coaching career had taken him on a journey that has led him to the Mecca of college basketball. He would have the opportunity to coach from the same seat as Phog Allen, Dick Harp, Ted Owens, Larry Brown and Roy Williams. He would patrol the sideline of the same court where the likes of Chamberlain, White, Robisch, Valentine, Manning, LaFrentz and Collison collected trophies and hung banners.

"I thought to myself, 'How cool is this?' It just doesn't get any better."

Anyone who follows college basketball knows of the prowess and tradition of the Kansas program. Self had witnessed it first-hand as a student-athlete at Oklahoma State (1981-84) and as a graduate assistant coach for the Jayhawks under Brown (1985-86). But even those experiences did not impress upon him the magnitude of the opportunity that had come his way.

Bill Self was introduced as head coach at KU April 21, 2003.

"I thought I knew what the Allen Fieldhouse experience was," he said. "But when you are blessed—and I mean that literally—to be the head coach or play for the University of Kansas, you truly are part of something special. I got goose bumps the first time I came out of the locker room and walked through the tunnel to all of those fans."

Self's Allen Fieldhouse experience began with the customary midnight practice session—"Late Night in the Phog," played to a sellout crowd of 16,300 on October 17. The doors opened at 6:40 p.m., but were closed almost two hours later when all the seats were filled more than three hours before practice began. Though he had been there before, Self was awestruck as he walked onto the court to address the crowd.

"You guys have already spoiled me," he told the Jayhawk faithful. "It gave me goose bumps. I didn't expect this. It's better than I thought it would be."

Self's return to Kansas came full circle that evening with the return of former Jayhawk head coach Larry Brown and the 1988 NCAA national championship team to join in the festivities. It was Brown who had brought Self to Kansas as a graduate assistant coach in 1985-86. It was a proud moment for the both the teacher and the student. Brown was emotional as he addressed the crowd:

"I've never had a chance to properly thank you all from the bottom of my heart. I am so proud to have sat on that bench. God bless you all. Go KU."

After two exhibition wins, Self joined every one of his predecessors by winning his first "official" game at Allen Fieldhouse, a 90-76 win over Tennessee-Chattanooga,

Larry Brown made Kansas No. 1 in 1988.

Photo provided by Jeff Jacobsen

November 21. Four days later, a sold-out crowd was whipped into a frenzy as third-ranked Michigan State visited Lawrence. The Jayhawks withstood a late Spartan rally to win 81-74. The game and the atmosphere left quite an impression on both coaches.

"It (Allen Fieldhouse) was awesome and every bit as good as I heard," Michigan State head coach Tom Izzo said. "The fans are great out here. I loved playing here, and I really enjoyed the experience."

"I don't know if I have ever had more fun coaching," Self said. "The Fieldhouse was great tonight. There is no better place to coach. It is the reason you want to coach at a place like this."

Self's first year in Allen Fieldhouse was full of drama and excitement as his team won 13 of 14 games. The lone blemish would be a last-second 69-68 loss to a feisty Richmond team on January 22. An NCAA Tournament qualifier, the Spiders won when Tony Dobbins hit a 10-foot leaner in the lane with :01 remaining. The only other game that was in doubt in the final seconds was a heart-stopping, 90-89 overtime win over Iowa State. Down five points late in regulation, the Jayhawks sent the game into the extra period with Keith Langford's three-point bucket from the top of the key with :27 left.

Self's 13-1 record in his first season as a head coach raised Kansas's all-time record in Allen Fieldhouse to 551-101 (.845) in 49 full seasons. That includes 47 seasons of .500 or better play and 13 undefeated campaigns (full schedule). In the last 20 years, Kansas is 271-21 (.928) at home. That includes a school-record 62-game winning streak that began with a 106-62 victory over Colorado February 26, 1993, and ended with an 85-81 loss to Iowa on December 8, 1998. That eclipsed a 55-game string from March 3, 1984, to January 30, 1988.

Despite the presence of new facilities popping up on college campuses across the nation, Allen Fieldhouse has stood the test of time for 50 years. While upgrades have been made in several areas, the character of the facility has essentially remained the same since it hosted its first sporting event March 1, 1955. There has never been any level of significant support to mothball the structure in favor of a new arena—much to the chagrin of opposing coaches.

Since attendance records were kept beginning in the 1964-65 season, the Jayhawks have drawn a total of 7,778,837 in 561 games for an average of 13,866 per game. Seating capacity was 15,800 until the 1995-96 season, when it was increased to 16,300. On a season ticket basis, Kansas has been sold out for every game since the start of the 1985-86 season.

It would be quite a stretch to credit a mass of limestone, mortar, steel and glass for the success of any sports franchise. It is doubtful Yankee Stadium would hold its place in history without the presence of Ruth, Gehrig, DiMaggio and Mantle. The Boston Garden would have been just another arena without the likes of Russell, Cousey, Havlicek and Bird. As more than one coach has said, a building has never beaten anyone.

But the story of Allen Fieldhouse, like any great sporting venue, is more than just a collection of box scores. Structures such as Wrigley Field, Augusta National Golf

On game nights, Allen Fieldhouse becomes a place of worship for Jayhawk fans.

Photo provided by Jeff Jacobsen

Club and Lambeau Field achieve a virtual shrine-like status through the synergy created by athletes, coaches, fans, architecture and time. The facility becomes the place of worship where thousands of fans share a common bond.

A great sporting venue is measured by more than just success. If winning were the only criteria, then you would not see fans flock to Wrigley Field and Fenway Park as consistently as they do. The Cubs and Red Sox haven't played in the World Series in years but that does not diminish the historical significance of their home playing fields.

Paul Pierce is among many former Jayhawks who experienced net gains during their KU careers.

Phog's Phantasy

Phog Allen's influence extended far beyond the boundaries of Mt. Oread.

Known as the "Father of Basketball Coaching," his on-court strategies and motivational methods were copied by coaches from all corners of the globe. In fact, many members of the Allen coaching tree still employ some of his philosophies and terminology in their work. Ironically, the person who invented the game and would serve as Allen's head coach at Kansas, Dr. James Naismith, thought of basketball only as an activity for students to keep them physically fit between the fall and spring sports season. Coaching the sport was not something Naismith thought of as a requirement. In serving as the Jayhawks' first coach, Naismith in reality operated as a manager and would engage in such activities as making sure the facility was ready for play and officiating the game. He would go on to become the only Jayhawk coach to have a losing record (55-60 in nine seasons, 1898-1907). To be fair, Naismith dedicated most of his energies as the University's Director of Chapel and an instructor in the Physical Education Department.

Phog Allen coached just one season in the building named in his honor.

An osteopath, Allen was a firm believer in the power of massage and liniments to treat a variety of ailments. He contended his teams had an advantage because they were in better physical condition and healthier than their opponents. To his athletes, peers and friends, Allen was known as "Doc" in reference to his "other" occupation. Some doctors looked upon Allen's methods with disdain, but athletes came from all over the world to have him work miracles on them. His patients included Hall of Fame pitcher Grover Cleveland Alexander, New York Yankee first baseman Johnny Mize, Boston Bruin defenseman Eddie Shore and a number of college athletes from KU and other schools, including archrivals Kansas State and Missouri.

"He was a proponent of keeping the body hydrated. If you look at the old photos of Doc coaching, you noticed he had several bottles of water under his chair," said Jerry Waugh, a former player and assistant coach for the Jayhawks. "He was a firm believer

An early practice session on the Allen Fieldhouse court in 1955.

Photo provided by KU Sports Information

that a person should drink a lot of water to keep the muscles and joints loose and the throat clear."

An example of Allen's almost obsessive dedication to his players' physical well-being came at halftime of the 1953 NCAA title game between Kansas and Indiana. The head coach/osteopath spotted Jayhawk center B.H. Born rather unsuccessfully trying to clear his throat by gargling alum water. According to longtime Kansas broadcaster Max Falkenstien, Allen stopped his chalk talk and spent the next several minutes showing Born and his teammates how to properly gargle.

"Try and picture it," Falkenstien said. "It's halftime of a national championship game and the coach is taking 10 minutes to teach his center how to gargle. He's telling Born to throw his head back and gargle deeper in his throat."

The Jayhawks played well in the second half, especially Born with a clear windpipe, but unfortunately lost the game 69-68. The only consolation was that Born earned NCAA Tournament MVP honors.

In addition to his coaching duties, Allen served as Kansas's athletic director from 1919 to 1937, and was a volunteer for several amateur sports organizations. Despite his occasional battles with university administrators and athletic governing bodies, Allen was instrumental is starting and/or strengthening a variety of high-profile events. In 1923 he gave rise to the Kansas Relays, one of the nation's top collegiate track and field events. In 1930, he began a crusade to have basketball included as an Olympic sport—as an honor to Naismith. His goal was to have it part of the 1932 Los Angeles games. Politics delayed its inclusion until the 1936 Berlin games.

The NCAA Tournament is among the nation's most popular sporting events, and it is no surprise that Allen had a hand in its success. As the founder of the National Association of Basketball Coaches (NABC) and first president in 1927, Allen was intent on strengthening the game. The National Invitation Tournament had been highly successful, but Allen believed the proceeds were not going back to the institutions. He and a few other coaches felt the NCAA should have its own tournament to raise funds for its members and the NABC. The inaugural NCAA Tournament in 1939 lost $2,521 and was in peril of extinction. However, Allen convinced organizers to move the Western championship and national title game to Kansas City where he would serve as tournament manager the next year. The tournament netted nearly $10,000.

The University of Kansas physical plant also has Allen's imprint on it. In 1920, with Allen serving as basketball coach and athletic director, he took on the added chores of a one-year stint as football coach. On November 13, with powerful Nebraska visiting for homecoming, Allen led his charges back from a 20-point halftime deficit to emerge with a 20-20 tie. On the following Monday, Allen and the team were feted to a 10-minute ovation and the band played fight songs. Allen announced that a new stadium would be built to replace the dilapidated wooden bleachers of McCook Field. Within two weeks, the students and faculty raised $200,000. On May 10, 1921, students armed with hammers and axes began demolishing the old stadium. School administrators served refreshments and hot dogs.

The new stadium was part of a larger project to honor those who fought in World War I. It would seat 38,000 and be combined with the drive to build the first student union west of the Mississippi River. Allen would serve as the chairman of the fundraising project. He wasn't the only basketball coach to have a hand in the construction of the Kansas football stadium. Legendary UCLA coach John Wooden spent one summer traveling the Midwest in search of work. Allen offered him a job working on Memorial Stadium and encouraged the future Purdue hoops All-American to remain in Lawrence to pursue his degree. Wooden accepted the job but declined the invitation to stay and play for Allen.

When Allen first appeared on the Kansas campus as a student in 1905, basketball was played in the basement of old Snow Hall, which stood to the immediate north of where Watson Library is located today. The building was named after the school's first professor of natural science and its fifth chancellor, Francis Huntington Snow. (He was best known as an expert on Darwin's theory of evolution. At first he vehemently opposed the teachings, but later he was able to reconcile evolution with his strong belief in Christianity.) The west portion of the basement, known as "the large room," was where Naismith introduced the game to students as part of the physical education curriculum. The actual games were played in downtown Lawrence at the armory, skating rink or YMCA, whichever was available.

© KU Sports Information

Allen's teams won 84.3 percent of their games over 29 seasons in Hoch Auditorium.

In 1907, the physical education department moved to Robinson Gymnasium, on the site where Wescoe Hall stands today. The facility was named in honor of the first governor of the State of Kansas, Charles Robinson, a Republican from Lawrence who served from 1861-63. The quarters were still tight as portable bleachers were brought in to accommodate a capacity of 900 fans. The building, which was designed by Naismith based on the Springfield, Massachusetts YMCA structure, had outgrown its ability to host official games. The facility was regarded the best of its kind west of the Mississippi River at the time of its opening.

The team would continue to practice there, but games would move to Hoch Auditorium. Built for $350,000 and dedicated October 14, 1927, the facility was actually a stately performing arts center that allowed for a basketball court to be squeezed in between the seating and the stage. Nicknamed "The Opera House," Hoch seated 3,800 for basketball but did not offer great sightlines. It was named for Edward Wallis Hoch of Marion, Kansas, who served as Kansas governor from 1905-1909. The tapering of the walls near the stage left no out of bounds area. Netting behind the baskets protected glass chandeliers. Kansas defeated Washburn 29-26 January 6, 1928, in the first game played in Hoch.

From Allen's perspective, Hoch was anything but a home for Kansas basketball. Practices were still conducted at Robinson Gymnasium, with the team dressing there before games, followed by the walk to Hoch. Allen would not practice at Hoch except on an occasional basis because the wooden floor sat directly on concrete. Players would complain about painful shin splints and opposing teams would often skip practices the next day due to tired legs. Both Kansas and opposing players had less complimentary names for the auditorium, calling it "Horrible Hoch" and "House of Horrors." In addition, the basketball team had to compete with other groups such as orchestra, band and organ practices, speeches, plays, Christmas vespers, etc. It was not surprising Allen wanted a new facility shortly after his teams started playing there.

As the Kansas News Bureau noted in a January 13, 1955 report, Allen was blunt in his appraisal of Hoch: "Talk about a home-court advantage. Our home-court advantage is a joke, compared with other home-court advantages. Some weeks we have practiced no more than our invading opponent for a given game. By that standard, our

Photo provided by Lawrence Journal-World

After his retirement, Allen (left) along with his great grandson, John (center) and son Bob, became fans.

home-court record shouldn't be as good as it usually is. Hoch was our reward for winning six consecutive (conference) championships from 1922 through 1927."

Despite his protestations to the contrary, Allen was nearly unbeatable at Hoch; his teams were 204-38 (.843) in 29 seasons. Allen's granddaughter Judy

Morris, who attended games there into her teens, took some exception to the contention that Kansas did not enjoy a home-court advantage in Hoch. Morris is the daughter of Milton "Mitt" Allen, who played for his father at KU from 1934-36.

"I know Phog didn't like Hoch, but he did have an advantage in one sense," Morris said. "On the stage side, the walls tapered at each corner of the court. The court basically ended at the wall. It created quite a visual illusion. Opposing players had trouble catching and shooting the ball."

Kansas' last season at Hoch came in 1954-55. It was not a vintage Jayhawk team as Allen had lost several talented players off the 1952 NCAA championship and 1953 NCAA runner-up squads. On February 19, 1955, a crowd of only 2,200 watched Kansas drop the final game in Hoch Auditorium, 66-55 to Nebraska. There was no ceremony or special mention of it being the last game at Hoch, most likely due to the fact that Allen Fieldhouse was not finished. Kansas would move into Allen Fieldhouse for the final two games of that season. The facility suffered its greatest indignity when lightning sparked a fire that gutted it in 1991.

Despite the presence of Hoch, records indicate that Allen first broached the subject of a new facility for basketball and other sporting events in October 1927. The University's *Graduate Magazine* reported of Allen's announcement that year "that plans are now being drawn up for a field house to cost between $350,000 and $400,000. It would seat about 14,000 people." It would be a multipurpose arena that could support all of the University's athletic teams. But the Great Depression had set in shortly thereafter, followed by World War II. He knew there was no way the University could justify such a structure during this time period.

Photo provided by KU Sports Information

Hoch Auditorium was known as the "House of Horrors."

New Digs
for the
Jayhawks

"YOU KNOW, I HAD ALWAYS UNDERSTOOD THEY DIDN'T NAME BUILDINGS AFTER MEN WHO WERE LIVING. IN THAT CASE, I WASN'T IN ANY HURRY TO HAVE THE FIELDHOUSE NAMED AFTER ME."
—*Phog Allen*

From high above, Allen Fieldhouse looked like a giant barn under construction.

World War II was over and Hoch Auditorium had outgrown its 3,800 capacity. Seating was so limited that a rotation was established that would allow only one-third of the 9,000-member student body to attend a game at a time. Tickets were divided into groups determined by alphabetical order. Allen thought the time was right to pursue the concept of a new arena again.

On October 7, 1946, the State of Kansas Board of Regents instructed KU chancellor Deane Malott to "initiate studies as to a site and possibilities of a bond issue to cover the major cost" of a new arena. As reported by the Kansas News Bureau, Malott noted growing enrollment had put a pinch on current facilities.

"A fieldhouse has long been in the building program. But a higher priority is being assigned to it because with doubled school enrollment, the need is much greater. Not only cannot all students at present witness basketball games, but the pressure for other uses of Hoch Auditorium is far greater than ever before."

In February 1947, Alfred B. Page, a state representative from Topeka, introduced a bill to the Kansas House that would appropriate $650,000 to build a
10,000-seat facility. The   plan was to have the school pick up the remaining
$500,000 of the predicted $1,150,000 price tag. Page was a 1931 graduate of
Topeka High School and played basketball at Stanford under Kansas All-American
John Bunn.

The ways and means committee killed the bill March 25, 1947. Page surmised
that it became the victim of a then-record $15,241,000 funding level for state educa-
tional institutions. Leading the opposition was the Kansas Council of Women, which
supported the construction of 10 dormitories at the five state institutions.

But University leaders remained undaunted. In 1949, plans were made for
another plea to the state legislature. It was announced that University officials would
pursue a drive for a fieldhouse. Some were opposed, mostly academicians, citing a
more pressing need for additional classroom space, libraries and dormitories. However,
that opinion was in the minority and solid support by the community leaders gave the
school some hope for success. How vital was the need? As one athletic department
spokesperson said, "The whole future of the athletic program is at stake" with the vote.

On March 17, a diverse contingent of University representatives visited the
state capitol. The small hearing room was packed as Allen, KU business manager J.J.
Wilson, athletic director E.C. Quigley and student body president Patrick Thiessen
spoke of the need for the facility. Also there were basketball players Claude Houchin
and Jerry Waugh; cheerleaders Dorothy Scroggy and Bernadine Reed; Louise Lamb,
president of the Jay Jaynes (the student pep club); football coach J.V. Sikes and alumnus Judge Harry Fisher, among others. Allen orchestrated the entire presentation.

There was concern that Allen Fieldhouse was built too far away from dormitories for students to attend games.

A report in *The Kansas City Star* quoted Allen's impassioned address to state legislators regarding Hoch Auditorium, "That floor was laid on concrete. It has no resiliency. The boys have sprains, bruises and shin splints. It's a hodgepodge, and it isn't good for basketball. I'm delighted, gentlemen, that Kansas State college got a fieldhouse, but we'd like some consideration, too. We feel the university is the pinnacle of education in the state and should have the proper physical education facilities." Later that spring, $750,000 was appropriated by the legislature for the facility.

At the time of those discussions, the intent was to add a gymnasium and a physical education unit shortly after the fieldhouse was constructed. Officials probably did not expect the delay to be some 40-plus years: It was not until 1999 that the Horejsi Family Athletics Center was built to the immediate west of the field-house. It provides practice facilities for the men's and women's programs, and serves as home of the volleyball team. Numerous other facilities such as athletic department offices, a baseball stadium, indoor workout facility for football and track, a strength center, football practice fields, tennis courts and a soccer field were added over time.

On December 8, 1949, the University announced that the state architect office under the direction of Charles L. Marshall had begun developing detailed plans that would allow for construction bids to be received in the spring of 1950. Allen orig-inally proposed a seating capacity of 20,000 and enough room to host a football game during inclement weather. Some university officials and legislators countered with a more modest figure of 12,500, matching Kansas State's new building (Ahearn Fieldhouse). A compromise was reached and the drawings were started. The specifi-cations called for a capacity of 16,000, which would be the nation's second largest university arena, trailing Minnesota's Williams Arena at 18,250.

It was the second collegiate fieldhouse that the state of Kansas would approve in less than 10 years. In 1943, the Kansas State Legislature earmarked $750,000 for a new arena on the Kansas State University campus in Manhattan with plans to seat 10,000. Tiny Nicholls Gymnasium was bursting at the seams, necessitating more classroom space and seating to support a basketball program that was challenging the quality of its neigh-bor to the east in Lawrence. When it opened in 1950, the Kansas State Fieldhouse seat-ed just over 11,000. Allen was intent on making sure his fieldhouse would be bigger than the one his rival Wildcat head coach Jack Gardner had built.

As was his mode of operation, Allen relied on a heavy dose of persuasion and logic to lobby for a bigger arena than Kansas State. In his testimony before the

Senate Ways and Means Committee, he noted that 1.5 million people lived within an 80-mile radius of Lawrence, compared to only 300,000 in the Manhattan vicinity.

"There was no way he was going to let it be smaller than what Kansas State had," Waugh said. "He was determined to see that it would be bigger. Of course Doc (Allen) and Jack Gardner had quite a rivalry going, so they were both always looking to one up each other."

One factor that led to the approval of funding was the multipurpose nature of the building. Among the other features were a six-lane, one-eighth-mile oval track and a variety of rooms for offices and classes. At the time, head track coach Bill Easton was conducting indoor practices under the east side of Memorial Stadium. In addition to athletics, the fieldhouse would be used for physical education classes, commencement ceremonies, ROTC drills during times of war and for centralizing enrollment, which had previously been spread out through campus. As a means to keep costs down, the vast majority of the seats would be of the bleacher variety (612 stadium seats with hinged bottoms were installed on the east side balcony) and the floor of the arena would be an even mixture of sand, silt and clay.

The announcement left much to be answered because the remaining source of funds was in question. The early estimates pinned the cost at approximately $1,250,000 including the initial appropriation. That rough estimate was based on possibly delaying certain items, such as the installation of some of the bleachers.

The steel framework was started in February 1954.

The exact location had not been nailed down by the time of the appropriation. Early on, the most prominently mentioned site was across from where the student union stands today. But attention quickly shifted to the intramural fields south of 16th and Michigan streets (where the computer center and the "new" Robinson Gymnasium are located today). Wilson and Professor of Architecture George Beal traveled to the University of Minnesota, Swarthmore (Pennsylvania) College and Hershey, Pennsylvania, to visit facilities and generate ideas for Kansas' new arena.

Just as the project had gained strong momentum, the outbreak of the Korean War gave rise to fears that it would be delayed. The National Production Authority (NPA), the federal wartime regulatory agency, had the power to divert materials that were needed by the military. In early 1950, the NPA suggested a material shortage was likely to occur. Nonetheless, initial approval for the steel was secured November 10, 1950, three days after a request from Chancellor Malott was delivered in Washington, D.C. Making the plea was Wilson and the chair of the building committee, School of Engineering dean T. DeWitt Carr, a retired naval officer who was well connected on Capital Hill. The effort came on the heels of extensive lobbying by a variety of individuals in Kansas and Washington, D.C.

The architect who did the actual drawings was Frank Johnson, who was assisted by a small team that included 25-year-old Warren Corman. Just out of the Navy, Corman was working part time while he was pursuing his architecture degree from KU.

According to Corman, the positive result of the trip to the nation's capital required the state architect staff to modify the original drawings. That threatened to put an unexpected delay in getting the project out for bid on time.

"We had to make several changes because we needed to reflect the military uses for the building. The plans were drawn on starched linen with India ink and were about four feet by six feet in size. Just days before the project was put up for bid, a secretary working in the office knocked over a bottle of ink on the plans. We had to work night and day to redraw some of our work and to meet our deadline. We could have killed her," Corman chuckled.

Combining the input of Marshall's staff and the University committee leading the project, the bid procedure began January 17, 1950. The contract with Bennett Construction of Topeka was signed October 5, 1951, with the goal to have the building completed August 24, 1953—900 days after ground was to be broken. University officials settled on an area southwest of campus just west of Michigan Street on what was pasture land. There were no dormitories nearby and the University buildings were all located on the "hill." There was serious concern that the facility would be located too far for students and residents to attend games.

On February 22, 1951, the Kansas House of Representatives approved the remainder of the funds for the project. It was part of a $5,006,646 educational building fund bill for all institutions of higher education in the state that passed by a 106 to seven margin. The new estimate of the cost of the fieldhouse was pegged at $2.5 million.

But approval of the request for steel did not equate to delivery. Bennett scoured the nation for the materials but to no avail. The fieldhouse required four times as much steel as a building of comparable size, adding to the challenge. On February 23, 1952, Marshall wrote a letter to John T. Thomas of the Federal Security Agency, again requesting that structural steel needed for the arena be released by the NPA. A strong appeal was made, emphasizing the use of the building for ROTC purposes. Approval was gained for a second time, March 5, 1952.

Even though the request was granted, finding the materials was no easy task. Pouring of the more than 900 concrete pilings began March 15, 1952, but they were not utilized for the rest of that year and all of the next. In late 1953, athletic director Dutch Lonborg, Bennett, Marshall and Keith Lawton, special assistant to Malott, traveled to Chicago to meet with representatives of the Allied Structural Steel Company.

Photo provided by Jeff Jacobsen

Allen Fieldhouse was built on what was once pasture land.

According to Lawton, the meeting was not going particularly well until one of the principals of the firm later entered the room.

"Dutch! Dutch Lonborg! What are you doing here?" the man bellowed.

Lonborg introduced the Kansas contingent to Harry Crowley, a top-level Allied Structural Steel executive who just happened to be one of the famous "Four Horsemen" of Notre Dame. Lonborg, a three-sport letterman at Kansas [including a basketball All-American in 1919), was a coach for 23 years at Northwestern prior to returning to Kansas as athletic director in 1950. It was during his tenure at Northwestern that he and Crowley forged their friendship.

After reminiscing for a while, Lonborg resumed a presentation that had taken on a decidedly more positive tone. Crowley indicated he could get his hands on an order of reclaimed steel from Pittsburgh. The other Allied Steel Company representatives sat mostly tight lipped. Upon returning to Lawrence, Bennett had secured the order of steel from Crowley. The materials arrived via railroad, and construction resumed in February 1954, when the first piece of the steel structure was put in place.

The series of delays caused some friction between Allen and those involved in the construction of the facility. In a January 8, 1952 speech to the Topeka Lions Club, Allen questioned what he called "unnecessary delays," contending that the contractor who also built Kansas State's Fieldhouse "is not showing the same enthusiasm for us as he did for them."

Marshall shot back, saying that Wildcat coach Jack Gardner had visited the construction site nearly every day, while Allen was only seen occasionally at his. Allen took exception to the characterization, but he would soon become a daily visitor to the grounds. Size also played a factor in the extended time needed to build the arena. Kansas State's Fieldhouse seated about

Former AD Dutch Lonborg (left) and then current AD Clyde Walker visit with Allen after his retirement.

Photo provided by KU Sports Information

11,000 and covered approximately 90,000 square feet, approximately half that of the arena being constructed in Lawrence.

The construction process did not provide for a significant feature of the building. For whom would the facility be named? There was strong public sentiment for naming it after Allen, but Naismith's contributions could not be ignored. In the autumn of 1954, a poll by the student newspaper, the *University Daily Kansan*, supported Allen. He earned 924 votes, while 10 voted for Naismith and another 30 for a combined naming of the two coaching legends. The matter was complicated, however, by the fact that Board of Regents policy dictated the naming of state buildings for individuals who were retired. There had been some precedent for bypassing the rule as the physical sciences building had been named for Malott, who had moved on from Kansas to Cornell.

There was much lobbying on Allen's behalf, although none of it orchestrated by the Jayhawk head coach, according to his granddaughter, Judy Morris. Lonborg, track coach Bill Easton, assistant basketball coach Dick Harp, former Jayhawk All-American and Wichita State head coach Ralph Miller and governor Harry Woodring all voiced public support for Allen. Missouri coach Wilbur "Sparky" Stalcup announced at a Kansas basketball banquet that "he had become the self-appointed mouthpiece of Big Seven coaches" in the effort.

Former Kansas governor and 1936 presidential candidate Alf Landon wrote to the Regents, "If this is a tradition, let's kick a hole in it for the man that deserves it more than anyone I know to have the new building named for him."

Chancellor Franklin Murphy suggested that the Regents set aside the rule and name the facility in Allen's honor. The Regents concurred in a vote taken in October 1954, but they did not announce the decision until December 17 that year. Naismith earned recognition as Michigan Street, which ran North and South in front of the Fieldhouse, would be re-named in his honor in November 1954. The playing surface

Allen Fieldhouse contains 2,700 tons of structural steel.
Photo provided by KU Sports Information

of the arena would bear his name beginning in the 1997-98 season. That action came as part of a series of events that marked the 100th anniversary season of Kansas Jayhawk basketball.

Upon learning the news, Allen was moved by emotion. "Again, let me say I feel extremely humbled at the honor. It's just terrific."

The facility took on a few unofficial descriptors over the year, most notably "The Monarch of the Midlands," and after Wilt Chamberlain appeared on campus, "The House that Wilt built." The Big Dipper's arrival on Mt. Oread served to increase attendance and revenues considerably. Many years later, Jayhawk fans added Allen's nickname "The Phog," to the list of monikers. Even with the simplicity of the "official" name, those in the media and some associated with the University made factual and grammatical errors in referencing the arena. Neither Allen's first name "Forrest" nor his nickname were included when the name was approved. The term "fieldhouse" is correct as one word; however, many references separated it into two. It has been surmised this occurred because the lettering on the east side of the building is separated by pillars, appearing visually as "Allen Field House."

The final bill for Allen Fieldhouse came in slightly above the $2.5 million estimate that was revised when plans were completed. The price tag was $2,613,167, although that figure was closer to $3 million by the time the various infrastructure costs and miscellaneous expenses were incurred. The per-square-foot cost was $14.22. Today, arenas are being built at cost of $300 per square foot.

Allen Fieldhouse
Original Construction Facts

Outside Dimensions:
344 feet by 254 feet

Height:
Sidewalls 60 feet high raising to a roof peak of 85 feet high

Arena Span:
252 feet by 341 feet

Dirt Area:
134 feet by 341 feet

Track:
1/8th mile lap (220 yards). Six lanes.

Photo provided by KU Sports Information

Seating Capacity:
17,000 (65 percent in the balcony)

Entrances:
East and West Lobby, plus six others (42 doors)

Exits:
13

Materials:
2,700 tons of structural steel; 700,000 bricks; 1,625 tons of stone; 52,000 haydite blocks; 4,500 gallons of paint (would cover 550 five-room houses); 245,000 board feet of lumber for roof (would frame 40 five-room houses). The amount of elctricity to run the lights could power 55,000 clocks.

NOTE: If the steel were drawn in a wire, it would build a fence four feet high and stretch from San Francisco to New York with enough left over to fence the entire state of Kansas.

Solid as a Rock

While Allen Fieldhouse has shown its age in a few areas, former state architect Warren Corman says no one should question its structural soundness. He noted that over the years, many design firms have approached the University with plans for adding everything from video boards, suites and wider concourses to the venerable fieldhouse.

"They made sure when it was built that it would be well above what was required. That building will last forever as long as you put a new roof on it every 20 years or so. To make some of the changes that have been proposed will take some additional support, but the building itself is solid."

"The building will last forever as long as you put a new roof on it every 20 years or so." – Warren Corman

Photo provided by Kenneth Spencer Research Library

What's in a Number?

In April of 1952, the specifications for Allen Fieldhouse listed a capacity of 16,000. However the "official" capacity was subject to much debate. The reason for the confusion? The temporary bleachers at the north and south ends on the lower level had a greater capacity than architects had envisioned.

So, when the official attendance for the dedication game was listed at 17,228, there were a few who were more than a bit skeptical of that number. In fact, there were numerous other games in subsequent years that the announced attendance hit or eclipsed the 17,000 mark. Therefore, that became the listed capacity.

"Those old bleachers in the endzones were thin wooden planks, with no leg room whatsoever—much less than the bleachers upstairs," John Novotny said. "People were packed in there pretty tight. And in those days, you didn't have a fire marshal worried about being over capacity. I know they packed the aisles that night."

Novotny was a student at Kansas during the Wilt Chamberlain era and then served in many capacities in the Jayhawk athletic department from 1966-81 (except for a two-year stint in 1976-77 at Southern Illinois). During Clyde Walker's tenure as KU's athletic director (1973-77), every effort was made to maximize revenues from Allen Fieldhouse. An extra row of folding chairs was placed immediately in front of the first row of permanent seats on the upper level, while two rows were added behind the last row of permanent seats at the top of the building. That pushed listed attendance figures for certain games over the 17,000 mark.

"We didn't do it for every game," Novotny said. "But when Kansas State, Missouri or a ranked team came in, we set up the chairs. It was a good move, except when I placed chairs in front of the chancellor's seats. He had trouble seeing. I learned real quick to leave that space empty."

The sidewalls of Allen Fieldhouse went 60 feet, rising to a roof peak of 85 feet high.

The north and south end zone bleachers used from the dedication game until the 1973-74 season were dismantled each year and moved back and forth from the south end zone of Memorial Stadium. When the tartan surface was laid down over the dirt floor prior to the 1974-75 season, new portable end zone bleachers were installed. Kansas officials lowered the official capacity to 16,000.

According to then Jayhawk business manager Doug Messer in a December 9, 1974 article in the *Lawrence Journal World,* "In truth Allen Fieldhouse never held 17,000 to begin with. Depending upon the amount of portable bleachers in use, the capacity was probably closer to 16,500."

But the official capacity would continue to fluctuate as various seating configurations and improvements were implemented. Prior to the 1980-81 season, the

An inside view of the Fieldhouse during its early construction phase.

media was moved from its working area that was located on the lower section of the west balcony seats at midcourt to the east side floor level opposite the team benches. Approximately 204 chair-back seats were added to the area that the media had vacated and in surrounding rows. Capacity was revised to a 15,129 officially but was published at 15,200.

In August of 1985, then-athletic director Monte Johnson announced plans to remove the lower-level wooden bleachers on the east and west sides and replace them with those of aluminum construction prior to the start of the basketball season. The new bleachers were to be retractable and would be raised five inches off the floor to allow fans to see over the media and team benches. The north and south endzone bleachers were to be stationary. This new seating structure was facilitated by the construction of the Anschutz Sports Pavilion, just west of Allen Fieldhouse. The new indoor workout facility provided an area for all sports other than men's and women's basketball and volleyball to practice. A total of 610 seats were added, moving capacity to a listed 15,800. The price tag for the project was $250,000.

Subsequent renovations to bring the facility into compliance with fire and handicapped access codes raised the capacity to the present day figure of 16,300.

Allen Fieldhouse has been home to many sports, including volleyball.

Photo provided by Jeff Jacobsen

A Night for the Ages

"I'LL BE IN THE DRESSING ROOM BEFORE THE GAME AND AT HALFTIME AFTER THE DEDICATION. BUT I'M NOT TALKING. IT'S UP TO YOU, DICK."
—Phog Allen to Jayhawk assistant coach Dick Harp

There was never any question that the formal dedication of Allen Fieldhouse would be a gala extravaganza. After all of the political maneuvering, arm-twisting and waiting, the University had every right to celebrate its newest jewel. But left undetermined was the actual date of the dedication. If all had gone according to the original plans after the bids were taken in January 1951, the facility would have been ready for the 1953-54 season. But those prospects evaporated as obstacles mounted.

The delays and uncertainty also scuttled plans to welcome Kansas alumnus Adolph Rupp and his Kentucky Wildcats as the opponents for the first game in the facility. Rupp had built the Wildcat program into a national power and a matchup between the teacher (Allen) and the pupil (Rupp) would capture national attention. That game would have to wait as scheduling conflicts could not be overcome. Rupp and his Wildcats would not visit Lawrence until the 1958-59 season, a few years after Allen had retired.

In an August 27, 1954 meeting involving University administrators and athletic department officials, a tentative date of February 14, 1955 (versus

Allen in front of the building he helped inspire.

Oklahoma A&M), had been established as the first game for the fieldhouse. At issue, however, was the fact that it would be the Jayhawks' last home game of the season. Athletic director Dutch Lonborg and Allen both wanted more than one game played in their new facility that year. It was reported in the January 6, 1955 *Lawrence Journal World* that officials from Kansas and Kansas State agreed to trade home playing dates. Kansas would travel to Manhattan February 12, while Kansas State would return the favor in Lawrence March 1 for the dedication game.

One day after the newspaper report, Kansas announced that tickets for the game could be ordered at a price of $2, plus 25 cents for handling. The order was to be sent to Jayhawk radio announcer Max Falkenstien's father, Earl, who was the athletic department's business manager.

Oddly enough, the Kansas–Kansas State game that year in Manhattan also featured a dedication ceremony. Kansas State's new arena opened in 1950 and was known as "The Fieldhouse" or "The Palace." Speeches were made prior to the Wildcats' win over Utah State December 8, but the facility lacked a formal name. In October 1954, the Kansas Board of Regents approved the name "Mike Ahearn Fieldhouse and Gymnasium" after the longtime Wildcat coach and athletic director. Unfortunately, Ahearn passed away in 1948 as the building was being constructed. It would be the fifth largest collegiate facility when it opened.

Just as the Allen Fieldhouse opening would later include significant pomp and circumstance, so too did the dedication of Ahearn. Family members, local, state and national government officials and students participated in the activities. Kansas athletic director Ernest Quigley eulogized Ahearn, while Allen also spoke, saying, "You're never dead as long as you live in the hearts of friends. Mike lives here tonight."

Allen's presence that night added a bit of irony to the proceedings. When Ahearn stepped down as Kansas State athletics director in 1915, outgoing Wildcat football coach Johnny Bender encouraged Allen to apply for the position. Allen was coaching at Warrensburg Missouri Teachers College—now known as Central Missouri State—at the time. He did apply, but Z.G. Clevenger was selected. Four years later, Allen was brought on as athletics director at Kansas and the next year was appointed football and basketball coach.

The master of ceremonies for the evening was Howard Hill, former director of the Kansas State speech department. Ironically, Hill's son, Howard, Jr. would serve

Photo provided by Kenneth Spencer Research Library

103 former letter winners gathered for the dedication ceremony at halftime of the KU – K-State game in 1955.

as the public address announcer at Allen Fieldhouse from 1982 to 2004. The younger Hill was also the public address announcer at Kansas State for the 1970-71 campaign.

It was a less than vintage Kansas squad that came to Ahearn that night. The Jayhawks were 2-5 in the league, while the Wildcats were in the running for the conference title. Led by guard Dallas Dobbs' 36 points, Kansas upset Kansas State 78-68, to ruin the party for the overflow crowd that special night. As big as the win was for the Jayhawks, news back home in Lawrence was even better. Visiting the Lawrence campus that weekend was a high school senior from Philadelphia, Pennsylvania, by the name of Wilton Chamberlain. He had planned to attend the game in Manhattan, but NCAA rules prohibited entertaining prospects more than 30 miles from campus.

Allen Field House Dedication

University of Kansas
Vs
Kansas State College

March 1, 1955   Lawrence, Kansas

Official Souvenir Program
25¢

Photo provided by Jeff Jacobsen

While there was some competitive jealousy displayed on the Kansas campus because Kansas State built its new arena first, that timing actually worked in the Jayhawks' favor according to State of Kansas architect Warren Corman. Ahearn Fieldhouse was completed before plans were begun on Allen, therefore a model existed for comparison.

"Ahearn was designed as a classroom and an agricultural exhibition hall as much as anything," Corman said, "But when you put a basketball court in it, we found out there were some shortcomings. The only way to enter the upper level was by stairs from the floor. There was no upper concourse. We also saw there weren't enough entrances or toilets. We learned a bit from the design."

While there was much excitement and anticipation for the opening of Allen Fieldhouse, there were some nervous moments as well. Workers rushed to put on the finishing touches. As an article in the *University Daily Kansan* reported "the tasks of dusting, swabbing, window cleaning and many other things familiar to housewives were completed. The custom-built scoreboard, which had arrived only a week earlier, was tested only days before the game."

Produced by the Fairplay Scoreboard Co., it was donated by the Class of 1949 and was considered to be state of the art with a $5,500 price tag. It weighed 500 pounds and would hang from the center of the arena, featuring four sides that were six feet by eight feet long and five feet by two feet high. The unit had 1,064 light bulbs, including the capacity for triple digits in scoring. At the time, it was believed to be the only scoreboard in the nation with that capability. The most unique feature was a Jayhawk painted on each side that had a blinking eye activated by every Kansas score.

The wood playing surface was elevated 28 inches above the dirt floor. It was placed on risers, tied together by cables and took four and a half days to put together or take down at a cost of $1,500. It was comprised of 214, four-feet-by-eight-feet panels. For these reasons, the court would be put down each year in the fall and disassembled only once, that after the season. Due to changes in humidity and temperature, special attention had to be paid to making sure the surface remained level. The actual court dimensions were 50 feet by 90 feet, but the elevated area, including out of bounds areas, measured 60 feet by 114 feet. The wood court was identical to the one in Hoch Auditorium with a large "K" in the center jump circle. Welch Planning Mill of Midvale, Utah constructed the floor at a cost of $15,732.

A worker readies the new state-of-the-art scoreboard for the first game.
Photo provided by Kenneth Spencer Research Library

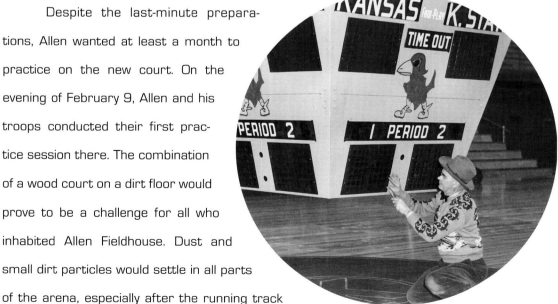

Despite the last-minute preparations, Allen wanted at least a month to practice on the new court. On the evening of February 9, Allen and his troops conducted their first practice session there. The combination of a wood court on a dirt floor would prove to be a challenge for all who inhabited Allen Fieldhouse. Dust and small dirt particles would settle in all parts of the arena, especially after the running track

The court was elevated 28 inches above the dirt floor.

was dragged for smoothing purposes. To keep players from slipping on the court, the surface had to be mopped before every practice and game.

Capacity of the arena was originally targeted at 16,000. After the drawings were made and after all of the seats were installed, capacity was essentially 17,000 according to Corman, who says he counted them about 10 different times during his career. For the dedication game, official attendance was listed at 17,228, which still stands as the school's single-game attendance record. While the fieldhouse was filled to more than capacity, it was constructed with comfort of the fan in mind. Rows were 29 inches apart compared to the standard 22 inches. Seats were 18 inches wide.

Newspaper accounts made it a point to emphasize the opportunity for fans to stretch their legs while sitting. There were 150 seats with tabletops at mid-court on the lower level of the balcony behind the benches to accommodate the media.

Perhaps the most nervous people in the house the night of the dedication were the coaches and players. Despite winning in Manhattan three weeks earlier, the Jayhawks were still underdogs. Kansas was 3-6 in the conference and had not won a home league contest that year. In a surprising move, Allen told assistant Dick Harp in pregame warmups that he was turning over the coaching responsibilities to him so as to "not put undue pressure on his team so they could concentrate on winning the game for the University, fans and themselves." Allen would sit on the bench and remain silent except for a pregame pep talk. His role that night was to lead the dedication ceremonies and to be "absent from their immediate consciousness though still present."

Asked what he said to his assistant, the longtime Jayhawk coach said, "I don't want to be in a position to ask the boys to do anything special for me. If they win, I want them to do so for the University. I'll be in the locker-room before the game and at halftime after the dedication. But I am not talking it up. It's up to you, Dick."

Harp, who did much of the scouting, went over the

Allen Fieldhouse nears completion.

Photo provided by Kenneth Spencer Research Library

defensive assignments before the game in the locker room. One thing he did not prepare for was the pregame speech. He learned well from his mentor, passionately exhorting the troops in dramatic style.

"Boys, as Doc told you, only a few are privileged to wear the colors of Kansas. You tonight, are among the chosen few. This is a great night—how great many of you won't realize until many years from now. Remember this. You want to do well tonight for a lot of reasons—for the University, your families, your friends, our followers and even for yourselves. But most of all, we have to win for Doc."

Kansas State center Roger Craft christened the fieldhouse to put the Wildcats ahead 2-0 (Craft's son Les would later play at Kansas State in the early 1980s). The lead would grow to 12-6 when Kansas countered with a run that put it up 19-16, punctuated by Bill Brainard's three-point play. The advantage would extend to 11 at halftime as Kansas led 44-33. Kansas State narrowed the gap to three points on three different occasions but could not overcome the double-figure scoring of Gene Elstun (21 points), Lew Johnson (20 points) and Brainard (16 points). All who donned crimson and blue expressed joy—and relief.

"I'm proud of many things this night, but I'm proudest, I think, of the way my boys came through after losing three in a row," Allen said.

"Imagine going down in history as the team that lost the game—to Kansas State—when they dedicated Allen Fieldhouse, with Phog Allen right there. We made up our minds that nobody was going to remember us like that," Elstun said following the game.

Harp did not downplay the challenge he and the players faced as Allen assumed the spectator role. "That (win) was important," Harp said. "Doc made his halftime speech, they had the skit and everyone thought the game was a nice occasion. It came off well and we thought it was magnificent. Yeah, we needed to win the game. That would have been a downer."

"I don't think any KU players have ever had the unique pressure those kids played under that night," said Bill Lienhard, a member of the 1952 Jayhawk NCAA championship team. "You just can't underestimate what a tremendous challenge they faced."

The dedication ceremony took place at halftime, which was extended from the standard 15 minutes to 35 minutes. There was considerable pageantry, with KU speech

Allen and assistant Dick Harp discuss strategy from the bench.

professor Allen Crafton providing a script under the direction of Gene Courtney and Harold Harvey that outlined the 64-year history of basketball. Special mention was made of the first women's game, while sophomore Marjorie Woodson carried an Olympic Torch, representing the sport's inclusion in the competition beginning in 1936. Those countries that participated in the Olympics were represented in the ceremonies by Kansas students who sported the countries native dress. Russell Wiley, professor of music, composed a march entitled *Mr. Basketball* that served as the background music for the oration.

Allen received the keys to a new Cadillac at halftime of the dedication ceremony.

Sheet music from Russell Wiley's new march for the halftime event.

A total of 103 former letterwinners took the court, including E.H. Owens, a member of the first Jayhawk squad in 1898-99. Chancellor Franklin Murphy, Governor Fred Hall, student body president Bob Kennedy and board of regents member Oscar Stauffer made speeches. At the end of the ceremony, the alumni association presented Allen with the keys to a new Cadillac. Granddaughter Judy Morris remembers that Murphy's kind and inspirational words about Allen's wife Bessie elicited an unexpected response.

"My grandmother stayed behind the scenes," Morris said. "But she had a huge impact on the success of Phog's career. She was a great writer. I am sure she did much of the writing for Phog's books. She also tutored most of his athletes. The honor was as much for her as it was for Phog. I'll never forget my grandfather crying as the chancellor talked about grandmother. It is the only time I ever saw him cry."

Allen made a brief speech, saying he could "humbly accept the fieldhouse as a tribute to all players past, present at the University." He walked off the court to the tune of "Auld Lang Syne," joined by his wife, three daughters—Mary, Jane and Eleanor—and two sons, Milton and Bob (both who played at Kansas for their father). The *Lawrence Journal-World* listed Mrs. Allen as the "Queen of the Dedication." She wore a blue suit with a pale pink French hat trimmed with flowers. She wore a pink and lavender orchid, as did her daughters.

Bessie Allen was the "Queen of the Dedication."

Photo provided by Kenneth Spencer Research Library

Allen and Chancellor Franklin Murphy visited the Jayhawk locker room before the halftime period ended. Allen said nothing other than a "Let's go," followed by a slap on the back. But Murphy reiterated much of what Harp said in the pregame speech.

"Boys, there is a big reason you must do your best tonight. His name is Allen and he's bigger than this fieldhouse. He is called Mr. Basketball because he is just that. Remember that you are playing before many of his All-Americans and you have it in your power to be All-Americans tonight. Let's really make this Dr. Allen's night."

In addition to University and government officials, several other dignitaries were in attendance, most

"I humbly accept the fieldhouse as a tribute to all players past, present at the University." – Phog Allen

notably Missouri head coach Sparky Stalcup and Colorado head coach Bebe Lee. Stalcup and Allen were close friends and frequently visited each other outside of basketball competition. The rival from the show-me state was duly impressed.

"The best thing about all this is that we won't have to go back to the damned Hoch Auditorium. It was a nightmare place to play. It's going to be great to come here and play on a real basketball court instead of in some made-over music hall where you get vertigo and the heebie jeebies because of those slanted walls. Brother, this is a basketball house like nobody has anywhere, and it's appropriate that the name of Allen is on it. I hate to play Phog's teams, but I sure love and admire that old guy beyond what words can express."

Allen's show of gratitude was punctuated by a postgame autograph session that lasted more than an hour. Police had feared that the game could bring a certain amount of misbehavior given the size of the crowd and the matchup with an archrival. Much to their delight, police reported no incidents and traffic problems were nonexistent as many walked or took public transportation.

As fans filed out of Allen Fieldhouse that night, there were plenty of good feelings. But looming in the future was another decision that would affect the future of the Kansas basketball program. Allen would turn 70 after next season and face mandatory retirement as dictated by state law. Talk had surfaced about the situation, but for this night at least, any further discussion would have to wait. Phog Allen, his team and his fieldhouse were the talk of the town.

A portrait of KU's first head coach—Dr. James Naismith—was presented to KU with members of his family on hand for the ceremony.

Kansas the Honored Guest for Many Openings

The dedication of Ahearn Fieldhouse was not the first time the University of Kansas had a role in the opening of a new collegiate arena. For Minnesota's Williams Arena opening February 4, 1928, Dr. James Naismith tossed the ball for the opening tip and served as an honorary referee. The largest collegiate arena at the time, it seated 18,250 and cost $650,000 to construct.

The Jayhawks were also the honored guests for the christening of Oklahoma State's Gallagher-Iba Arena, December 9, 1938. Kansas won the matchup between coaching legends Phog Allen and Henry Iba, 21-15. The facility was built at a cost of $1.5 million. Some 65 years later, the Cowboys are still playing on the original maple court, which was the most expensive court in existence when it was installed. Though the competition was heated between Allen and Iba, the two had the utmost respect for each other and were good friends. It was Allen who began the drive to get Oklahoma State admitted to the Big Seven Conference, something that did not occur until 1958-59.

The Invited and The Uninvited

The dedication of Allen Fieldhouse attracted 17,228 fans, a school record that still stands today. But Larry Hatfield is certain the turnstiles missed at least two who caught a glimpse of the building that much anticipated evening. Hatfield grew up in Lawrence, just south of the University of Kansas campus. He and his best friend, Jayhawk football All-American John Hadl, were determined not to miss the big event.

"Ever since we were in grade school, we went to the basketball games," Hatfield said. "I was a neighbor to Mitt Allen, so we got to know Dr. Allen and some of the players. We couldn't afford to go to the games, so Dr. Allen had us come to Robinson (Gymnasium) and then walk with the team to Hoch where we would go in with them and then find a seat. You had all these tall college athletes and two little kids in line with them. I am sure that looked a bit strange.

"But we couldn't do that when Allen Fieldhouse opened, so we had to try something else. We found out that we could scale the wall and find an unlocked window. With so much going on that night, I am not sure if anyone saw us or if anyone even cared we were sneaking in."

Hatfield and Hadl formed the state champion Lawrence High School football backfield, but on this one night Hatfield the quarterback called the wrong play for Hadl the running back.

"I was up looking through a window and noticed that about three windows down was a bathroom stall. I figured that no one would see John if he went through the window straight into the stall. He did that, but neither of us knew it was occupied. John didn't miss a beat. He went through the window and under the stall without knowing whether the person was surprised, scared or both."

One other time, the dynamic duo found itself in a pickle while seeking entry into the fieldhouse. As they scaled the wall and climbed through the window, they found themselves in the visiting team locker room, face to face with a policeman guarding the premises.

"We were caught redhanded," Hatfield said. "But I think the guard knew we weren't trying to steal anything. We just wanted to see the game. He told us to get out right away, and we were quick to comply."

Hatfield said he and Hadl were two of many children who found various means to watch Jayhawk athletic events. He said the size of Memorial Stadium and Allen Fieldhouse provided plenty of capacity. Ticket takers, he said, were more than willing on occasion to turn their head to allow a child to sneak in to watch the Jayhawks play.

Hatfield and Hadl no longer have to sneak into Allen Fieldhouse. A loyal supporter of the University, Hatfield has been a season ticket holder for more than 35 years. Hadl, meanwhile, is an associate athletic director for the Jayhawks.

The building's capacity was listed at 17,000 when it was first opened.

Photo provided by KU Sports Information

The Fifties
A Time of Transition

> "I'M DELIGHTED, GENTLEMEN, THAT KANSAS STATE COLLEGE GOT A FIELDHOUSE, BUT WE'D LIKE SOME CONSIDERATION, TOO. WE FEEL THE UNIVERSITY IS THE PINNACLE OF EDUCATION IN THE STATE AND SHOULD HAVE THE PROPER PHYSI-CAL EDUCATION FACILITIES."
>
> —*Phog Allen speaking to state legislators*

Photo provided by KU Sports Information

The long, illustrious career of a coach and a building, both staples of Kansas basketball, came to an end in the mid-1950s.

It was a decade marked by transition. Mammoth Allen Fieldhouse rose to replace outdated Hoch Auditorium and Phog Allen reached the state's mandatory retirement age. He was forced to relinquish his seat on the KU bench following the 1955-56 season, accumulating a 590-219 (.729) mark in 39 years.

Allen orchestrated KU's national championship in 1952 and brought inspiration for continued national success with the recruitment of seven-foot Wilt Chamberlain soon afterwards. However, Allen coached just one season in the building named in his honor, and was not on the bench when Chamberlain became eligible the following year.

Dick Harp, who had served as Allen's first assistant coach, ascended to the head coaching position in 1956-57 with a yearly salary of $7,500. The 38-year-old Harp was just the fourth head coach in school history. With Chamberlain in the lineup, Harp directed KU to the national championship game, where the Jayhawks lost in three overtimes to North Carolina, 54-53.

Photo provided by KU Sports Information

Dick Harp (left) was the natural choice to replace Allen as head coach.

It was a decade marked by a new building, a new coach and the arrival of a legendary player. Along the way, Cincinnati's sensational guard Oscar Robertson poured in an Allen Fieldhouse—record 56 points in an NCAA regional tournament game, and a 6-5 center for KU named Bill Bridges arrived on campus and established himself as one of the great rebounders in Jayhawk basketball history.

The first decade of Allen Fieldhouse closed with a special ceremony honoring legendary Kentucky coach Adolph Rupp when he brought his Wildcats to Lawrence in mid-December of 1959. KU had a 33-10 record at Allen Fieldhouse during the decade of the fifties under Allen and Harp.

Workers raced to complete Allen Fieldhouse in time for the dedication game March 1, 1955. Some minor details remained undone, but most of the finishing touches were made throughout the decade. Contrary to popular belief, the dirt surface was not one of the elements thought to be temporary in nature. In fact, the term "fieldhouse" was used because by definition it featured a natural surface.

Improvements were made to the exterior of the building. The Class of 1952 donated nine flagpoles that would fly above the entrance of the east lobby. The

American flag and those of each of the Big Eight schools would be flown on future

game days. They were installed December 14, 1959, and dedicated in a ceremony

just before tipoff of the Kansas-Kentucky game (won by the Wildcats 77-72). The

Class of 1953 donated the landscaping.

Allen (left) welcomed Adolph Rupp and his Kentucky team to Lawrence in 1959.

Photo provided by KU Sports Information

Allen's Influence in the Building of Other Basketball Programs

When 19-year-old Forrest Allen made his first appearance in a gymnasium at the University of Kansas in mid-October of 1905, it marked the beginning of a 50-year relationship that produced significant reverberations throughout the world of basketball.

But that should surprise no one. Allen was a dedicated student of the game and was exposed at KU to the man who hung the first peach basket, Dr. James Naismith.

Dean Smith and Roy Williams share in KU's rich basketball legacy.

Photo provided by Jeff Jacobsen

While Allen's lineage traces back to the inventor of the game, his hallmark as a legendary coach was born out of his creative interest and love of basketball.

His influence was carried forward across the basketball landscape by a trio of his former players who distinguished themselves as legends of the college game. Ralph Miller, Dean Smith and Adolph Rupp, like their college coach, had a basketball arena or playing surface named in their honor.

Miller, a starter on KU's 1940 NCAA Tournament runner-up team, coached 14 years at Wichita State, six seasons at Iowa and 18 years at Oregon State. A two-time national coach of the year, the home court at Oregon State's Gill Coliseum is named in Miller's honor.

The legendary Smith, a member of the 1952 KU team that won the NCAA championship, coached 36 years at North Carolina and compiled an NCAA record 879-254. UNC started playing its home games at the Dean Smith Center in 1986.

Bill Bridges battles for a rebound versus Kentucky.
Photo provided by Kenneth Spencer Research Library

Smith returned to Allen Fieldhouse just once as a coach at North Carolina. He was an assistant to Frank McGuire when the Tar Heels came to Lawrence and defeated the Dick Harp-coached Jayhawks, 78-70, December 17, 1960. Smith was named head coach at UNC the next season following McGuire's departure to coach in the NBA.

Rupp, a member of the 1922 and 1923 KU teams that won Helms Foundation National Championships, coached 41 seasons at Kentucky and compiled a record of 876-190 during his tenure.

Rupp passed Allen in 1966 as the all-time winningest college coach, and Smith later broke Rupp's winning mark in 1997.

Rupp, who won four NCAA championships at Kentucky, was born in Halstead, Kansas, a small frontier town along the Santa Fe Railroad in central Kansas a few miles north of Wichita. Rupp brought his Kentucky teams to Lawrence on two occasions (1959, 1971) and won both games against his alma mater.

On December 10, 1977, Kentucky played Kansas at Allen Fieldhouse on Adolph Rupp Night. Fans bowed their heads in a moment of silence for Rupp, who was back in

Lexington fighting a losing battle with cancer. Kentucky defeated Kansas, 73-66, but Rupp did not live long enough to hear the score of the game.

The University of Kentucky has been playing its home games in Rupp Arena, which has a seating capacity of 23,000, since 1976.

The name of another KU graduate during the Allen era is also enshrined at a collegiate basketball arena. In 1992, the basketball arena at Cleveland State was named in honor of John McLendon.

The first coach in history to win three consecutive national collegiate titles, McLendon graduated from KU in 1936, and was a student of Naismith's but did not play basketball for the Jayhawks since African Americans were not accepted on intramural or varsity teams at that time. McLendon, a member of the basketball hall of fame, had a 76-percent winning mark over his 25-year coaching career at both the collegiate and professional levels.

For the Birds

Allen Fieldhouse was always meant to be a venue for a variety of different events, but nobody thought the National Bird Watching Society would come calling.

During the construction process, sparrows made the vast facility their home. Workers at the facility would leave food scraps, thereby attracting the birds. However, it seems the fowl friends did not want to vacate the premises upon completion of the building. Once the issue was publicized in the *Lawrence Journal-World*, bird watchers flocked to the house of Phog March 8 for the final game of the 1954-55 season versus Oklahoma.

While Jayhawk fans were cheering their team to a 71-67 win, Society members were peering through binoculars at the huge beams that served as perches for the birds. Many options to rid the facility of the animals were considered. Air guns were ruled out because the ceiling was too high. Poisoned wheat was overruled because officials were fearful of the dead fowl falling on the court.

The newspaper solicited advice, directing people to address their letters to: "Strictly for the Birds." Many suggestions were immediately rejected, including sealing the building and asphyxiating the birds. Another solution was to enforce (with security personnel) that people not leave food after games. But eventually, the issue did not gain any additional publicity, indicating the birds eventually vacated the premises. However, as Allen Fieldhouse turns 50, it is not unusual to find a bird or two still flying through the Phog.

A Venue of Variety...Home of Concerts, Comedians, Commentary, Commencement and More

Madison Square Garden has been called the "World's Most Famous Arena" based on its variety of high profile events—both athletic and non-athletic—conducted within its confines. Allen Fieldhouse may not be on a par with The Garden on a national basis, but it, too, has a diverse history of hosting events. But then again, that should come as no surprise considering that the facility was designed as a basketball arena, indoor track venue and an ROTC training facility.

The fieldhouse, in its early years, was a popular stop for concerts; promoters brought many well-known performers to Lawrence. The concert series for Allen Fieldhouse was initiated by singer Harry Belafonte November 7, 1964, when he performed in front of 13,000 people. Belafonte returned for another engagement to kick off the start of school in September 1968.

While the fieldhouse is versatile, it wasn't constructed to be acoustically pleasing, as all performers came to learn. According to the *Jayhawker* Yearbook covering the performance by Henry Mancini and his orchestra, "Mr. Mancini was able to conquer the not too aesthetic acoustics of Allen Fieldhouse and kept KU scholars enthralled by such numbers as 'Dear Heart,' 'Mr. Lucky,' and the 'Theme From Peter Gunn.' Despite some competition from lighting difficulties and overly vigorous ventilating fans, the personable Mr. Mancini entertained the audience with various quips such as introducing 'The Stripper' as the national anthem for sorority girls."

Big-name crooners Robert Goulet (1965), Andy Williams (1968) and Roger Miller (1968) also performed in the facility. Goulet was a hit with the KU faithful as he attended the football game in the afternoon, where he led cheers in the Homecoming victory over Kansas State, 34-0, and then performed that night in Allen Fieldhouse. Trumpeters Al Hirt (1966) and Louis Armstrong (1967) ventured to KU, as did Ike & Tina Turner (1971), Elton John (1972), The Beach Boys (1973, 1975, 1977), ZZ Top (1977), The Doobie Brothers (1979) and Kansas (1981).

In another concert as part of the Homecoming festivities, Sonny and Cher wooed 14,777 fans October 13, 1973. Again, according to the *Jayhawker* Yearbook, "The largest audience, excluding athletics events and commencement (they forgot about Bobby Kennedy's speech, which drew an estimated 20,000 in 1968) in the history of the University of Kansas viewed a production spectacle which had been almost six months in the making. ...After the pair performed 'I Got You Babe' they took several bows, casually strolled down the specially constructed ramp, past the trailer which had served as a dressing room and into a waiting limousine. No autographs, no encore, no waiting for audience reaction."

The last singer to perform in Allen Fieldhouse was Roy Clark during Homecoming festivities October 22, 1983 (not counting a performance by the rock group Shooting Star at the 1990 Late Night festivities to tipoff the basketball season). In all, 30 professional musicians and/or acts have performed.

Many times the musical acts traveled with comedians. David Frye performed in Allen Fieldhouse along with the Ike & Tina Turner Review in 1971, while David Brenner opened for Sonny & Cher in 1973. Bob Hope made two stops at KU with his variety act, the first in 1971 and then 11 years later in October 1982. Funny man Flip Wilson used Allen Fieldhouse to shoot a commercial in September 1978.

Allen Fieldhouse was also used as a venue to express political statements to students and the community. Presidential candidate Bobby Kennedy spoke to an overflow crowd March 19, 1968, only three days after he declared his intention to seek the White House. Allen Fieldhouse nearly burst at the seams as students and community members alike packed the seats, aisles, crows' nests and basketball court to hear the popular easterner.

The *Jayhawker's* account of Kennedy's speech: "A crowd of 20,000 people, the largest group ever jammed into Allen Fieldhouse cheered as Kennedy pushed his way into the fieldhouse and began shaking hands. For the next 65 minutes, he delivered his speech, lampooning the administration's present policies and urging students to support his campaign."

Longtime resident and historian Katie Armitidge said, "I remember the fieldhouse was just absolutely packed. I picked up my two kids from school to take them and we were among the last to get there. I believe we sat on the top row of the fieldhouse. Bobby Kennedy looked so small. The crowd was all around. It was a very exciting and dynamic speech although I do not remember a thing he said that day, but I remember the atmosphere vividly. It was a tremendously dramatic occasion."

Late spring 1970 was a busy time for Allen Fieldhouse as it hosted four high-profile speakers in a six-week period. Within a week of the Kansas Memorial Union burning on campus in April 1970, activist and Chicago Seven member Abbie Hoffman took to the stage in Allen Fieldhouse.

"The most talked-about speaker of the year was Yippie leader and member of the Chicago Seven, Abbie Hoffman," said the *Jayhawker* Yearbook. In front of 7,000 people in attendance, he drew the ire of many by blowing his nose on what appeared to be the U.S. flag before departing with the words, "This place is a drag; I'm going to Dallas."

Democratic senator Edmund Muskie spoke to a partisan group in Allen Fieldhouse about a month after Hoffman. While the crowd was listening, many students—photographed by a *Lawrence Journal-World* cameraman—sat on the dirt floor of Allen Fieldhouse constructing a graveyard while Muskie spoke about Indochina and Kent State University.

One week after Muskie appeared in Lawrence, Apollo 13 astronaut James Lovell spoke at the All-University Convocation. Many Lawrence school children were allowed to come to the fieldhouse to hear the astronaut speak about his NASA experiences and nearly mobbed him on-stage.

Before the month of April ended, the national leader of the popular ecology movement, KU graduate Paul Ehrlich, warned students about the danger of the population explosion and its effect on the environment.

The Fieldhouse hosted a different sort of speaker in September 1974, when the Bill Glass Crusade came to town. Glass, a former college football All-American and NFL great, was on campus for a series of speeches over a one-week period. Glass started his evangelical speaking in 1969 when he founded the Bill Glass Ministries, which is now known as Champions for Life.

Former basketball coach Larry Brown conducted an impromptu press conference April 8, 1988, that met with the approval of Jayhawk fans everywhere. While sitting in the bleachers that surround the court in Allen Fieldhouse, Brown announced, "I'm staying" to the KU roundball faithful. The Jayhawks were fresh off winning the 1988 national championship when rumors of Brown's departure to UCLA began circulating.

The euphoria was short-lived, however, as weeks later Brown announced he was leaving to coach in the NBA and did not return for the 1988-89 season.

Nobel Peace Prize winner Desmond Tutu came to KU in April 1999 and participated in many campus activities, one of them a speech in Allen Fieldhouse.

Favorite son Bob Dole, former state senator and 1996 Republican nominee for president, has graced the stage in Allen Fieldhouse on three occasions. He participated in track and field and basketball during his KU days, so was quite familiar with the fieldhouse. He returned initially in August 1990 for a press conference dedicating the Bob Dole Humanities Building, which was built just east of Allen Fieldhouse on Sunnyside Avenue. He returned in April 1997 for what was called "A Tribute to Bob Dole" to announce that he was donating all of his papers to the soon-to-be-constructed Bob Dole Institute of Politics on the University's West Campus.

His most recent visit, May 21, 2004 included his friend and political adversary president Bill Clinton for the inaugural Robert J. Dole Lecture Series. Clinton was originally scheduled to speak at the Lied Center on West Campus, but high ticket demand forced his address to be moved to Allen.

In addition to the athletic, education and entertainment activities, miscellaneous other events have been staged in Allen Fieldhouse:

• The first Late Night to commemorate the start of men's basketball practice was actually conducted November 18, 1955, Wilt Chamberlain's freshman year.

• Commencement moved inside Allen Fieldhouse for the first time May 31, 1959, when inclement weather forced the move from Memorial Stadium. Both high schools in Lawrence have utilized the fieldhouse for the same ceremony.

• The Model United Nations opened April 1, 1960, in Allen Fieldhouse, following president Harry Truman's speech to the students just across campus in Hoch Auditorium.

• The first All-University Convocation convened in Allen Fieldhouse was August 1, 1969, when Chancellor Wescoe was forced to make his remarks inside due to inclement weather.

• The Kansas State Teachers organization conducted meetings in Allen Fieldhouse numerous times, the first occurring November 3-5, 1965.

• Mid-April 1966 was another busy time for Allen Fieldhouse, as KU students attended the Centennial Dance on April 16, 1966.

• The students returned April 20, 1966, to hear author Truman Capote read from one of his best-selling novels. Capote's *In Cold Blood,* a book based on real events occurring in a small Kansas town, was on top of the bestseller list at the time.

• The University's music department performed its Varsity Band Concert in Allen Fieldhouse May 9, 1969.

• On August 26, 1970, students for the first time traversed all three levels of Allen Fieldhouse for enrollment, a tradition that continued until Fall 1982. The burning of Memorial Union during the spring of 1970 caused the move to the fieldhouse.

• Perhaps the most unusual gathering came May 12, 1975, when 1,015 dogs roamed the floors of Allen Fieldhouse as the Lawrence Jayhawk Kennel Club sponsored the All-Breed Dog Show. It wasn't the Westminster Kennel Club's show, but the massive space did allow the first unlimited registration in the Jayhawk Kennel Club show's history.

• The National Sculpture Conference (8th Annual) brought sculptors from all over the country along with their designed pieces to Allen Fieldhouse March 24-25, 1974.

• The fieldhouse has been an official voting precinct site for Douglas County since the early 1980s.

• Hollywood came to Lawrence when the made-for-television movie *The Day After* was filmed at various locations in the area. On November 14, 1983, Allen Fieldhouse was used to depict a triage center for citizens injured by a nuclear bomb that hit the city.

• The Lawrence Red Cross and Sigma Alpha Epsilon fraternity conducted CPR training to interested KU students and faculty December 10, 1988.

• April 9-10, 1996, was the initial date for local blood drives to be conducted in Allen Fieldhouse.

• Another fire on campus—this one at Hoch Auditorium—forced another campus tradition into Allen Fieldhouse for two years. Holiday Vespers was performed December 8, 1991, and December 7, 1992, in Allen Fieldhouse.

• Allen Fieldhouse has welcomed thousands of friends through its doors over the years. It has also been the site of some sad goodbyes. There have been numerous "moments of silence" at sporting events in Allen Fieldhouse for members of the Jayhawk family who have passed. Additionally, the athletics department staff and coaches have attended memorials in the fieldhouse for longtime equipment manager Barbara Wilson (1997) and former women's basketball players Jackie Martin (1992) and Jennifer Trapp (1998).

NCAA Tournament Games in Allen Fieldhouse

Allen Fieldhouse provided the perfect venue to host NCAA Tournament games. In all, 37 NCAA postseason games were played there, including two by Kansas. In 1967, the No. 3-rated Jayhawks fell to No. 7 Houston, led by All-American Elvin Hayes, 66-53. The next day, Kansas won the consolation game over No. 2 Louisville, 70-68.

Perhaps the most impressive performance to come from an NCAA Tournament game in Allen Fieldhouse was the 56-point performance by Oscar Robertson in Cincinnati's 97-62 win over Arkansas March 15, 1958. That remains the building's single highest individual scoring mark. In addition to Robertson and Hayes, other standouts to play NCAA tournament games in Allen Fieldhouse include Kansas' JoJo White, Kansas State's Bob Boozer, Notre Dame's Adrian Dantley, DePaul's Dave Corzine, Indiana State's Larry Bird and Missouri's Willie Smith.

1956 – West Regional (March 16, 17)
SMU 89, Houston 74
Oklahoma City 97, Kansas State 93
Kansas State 89, Houston 70
   (third-place game)
SMU 84, Oklahoma City 63

1958 – Midwest Regional (March 14, 15)
Oklahoma State 64, Arkansas 40
Kansas State 83, Cincinnati 80 (OT)
Cincinnati 97, Arkansas 62
   (third-place game)
Kansas State 69, Oklahoma State 57

1959 – Midwest Regional (March 13, 14)
Kansas State 102, DePaul 70
Cincinnati 77, TCU 73,
TCU 71, DePaul 65
   (third-place game)
Cincinnati 85, Kansas State 75

1961 – Midwest Regional (March 17, 18)
Kansas State 75, Houston 64
Cincinnati 78, Texas Tech 55
Texas Tech 69, Houston 67
   (third-place game)
Cincinnati 69, Kansas State 64

1963 – Midwest Regional (March 15, 16)
Colorado 78, Oklahoma City 72
Cincinnati 73, Texas 68

Texas 90, Oklahoma City 83
   (third-place game)
Cincinnati 67, Colorado 60

1967 – Midwest Regional (March 17, 18)
Houston 66, Kansas 53
SMU 83, Louisville 81
Kansas 70, Louisville 68
   (third- place game)
Houston 83, SMU 75

1970 – Midwest Regional (March 12, 14)
New Mexico State 70, Kansas State 66
Drake 82, Houston 87
Kansas State 107, Houston 98
   (third-place game)
New Mexico State 87, Drake 78

1976 – Midwest First Round (March 13)
Notre Dame 79, Cincinnati 78
Missouri 69, Washington 67

1978 – Midwest Regional (March 17, 19)
Notre Dame 69, Utah 56
DePaul 90, Louisville 89 (2OT)
Notre Dame 84, DePaul 64

1979 – Midwest Regional (March 9, 11)
Arkansas 74, Weber State 63
Virginia Tech 70, Jacksonville 53
Indiana State 86, Virginia Tech 69

Largest Allen Fieldhouse Crowds

Crowd	Opponent	Date	Result
17,228	Kansas State	3-1-55	W, 77-66
17,200	Kansas State	3-6-74	W, 60-55
17,100	Notre Dame	1-22-74	L, 74-76
17,000	Kansas State	1-23-73	L, 70-91
17,000	Kansas State	2-1-71	W, 79-74
17,000	Missouri	2-20-71	W, 85-66
17,000	Nebraska	2-26-66	W, 110-73

NOTE: There were 17,000 fans in Allen Fieldhouse for the March 15, 1958 NCAA Tournament Midwest Regional Final won by Kansas State over Oklahoma State, 69-57

Away from competition, Henry Iba (left) and Phog Allen shared a mutual respect.

Photo provided by KU Sports Information

Allen
Fieldhouse
Moments

1950s

March 1, 1955 – Kansas 77, Kansas State 67

Dedication of Allen Fieldhouse versus Kansas State ... KU entered the game with a 9-9 record, but without a homecourt victory ... Gene Elstun scored 21 and Lew Johnson had 20 for the Jayhawks in the victory ... KU didn't trail in the second half, but KSU stayed close and were within three (65-62) with 7:42 remaining ... the Jayhawks opened a 71-64 lead and stalled away the final three minutes.

Homecoming Weekend (November 19), 1955 – Freshmen 81, Varsity 71

The Jayhawk varsity scrimmaged the freshman team in front of 14,000 fans at Allen Fieldhouse who turned out to see 7-0 freshman Wilt Chamberlain ... Wilt served notice of his impact, scoring 42 points in leading the newcomers to a victory over the veterans.

January 31, 1956 – Kansas 56, Oklahoma A&M 55

KU defeated the Cowboys on a last-second shot in the final meeting between coaching rivals Phog Allen and Hank Iba ... the win gave Allen an all-time 17-16 edge in the series with Iba ... Future OSU head coach Eddie Sutton played in the game for the Cowboys but did not score.

February 3, 1956 – First Indoor Track Meet

Kansas and head coach Bill Easton hosted the first indoor track meet in Allen Fieldhouse as the Jayhawks edged Oklahoma, 56-48, in a dual competition in front of 2,000 fans ... among those competing for the Jayhawks was sophomore discus thrower Al Oerter, who would later go on to win four Olympic gold medals.

February 6, 1956 – Missouri 85, Kansas 78

Missouri, behind future head coach Norm Stewart's 20 points, handed KU its first loss in Allen Fieldhouse in front of 10,000 fans ... it marked the eighth game in the new building.

March 6, 1956 – Kansas State 79, Kansas 68

The Jayhawks suffered their second setback in AFH in the final game of the season, a 79-68 loss to K-State in front of a sellout crowd of 17,000 ... it marked the final game coached at home by Allen and clinched the Big Seven title for the Wildcats ... Allen had reached the mandatory retirement age of 70 and stepped down after 39 seasons and 29 league titles.

March 16, 17, 1956 – NCAA Tournament

Kansas played host to the West Regional as SMU, Houston, Oklahoma City and Kansas State played four games in two days in Allen Fieldhouse ... the regional was won by SMU.

December 3, 1956 – Kansas 87, Northwestern 69

The season opener in 1956 marked the debut of Dick Harp as head coach and of 7-0 sophomore Wilt Chamberlain ... Northwestern had won its opening game by 39 points ... Chamberlain set a KU scoring and rebounding record with 52 points and 31 rebounds ... "The Dipper" went 20 of 29 from the floor and dropped in 12 free throws (20 attempts) ... Chamberlain scored the game's first 11 points before Gene Elstun scored ... Allen didn't see the game ... he was making a speech at a high school in Bushton, Kansas ... attendance at the game was listed as 15,000.

January 2, 1958 – Oklahoma State 52, Kansas 50

Oklahoma State edges the Jayhawks, 52-50, in overtime as Chamberlain misses the game with a glandular infection ... Eddie Sutton leads the Pokes with 12 points in the victory.

February 3, 1958 – Kansas State 79, Kansas 75

Bob Boozer of K-State erupts for 32 points leading the Wildcats to a 79-75 double-overtime win over KU ... the Jayhawks won two of the three meetings with K-State during the 1957-58 season.

February 8, 1958 – Kansas 102, Nebraska 46

Wilt Chamberlain pours in 46 points as KU downs Nebraska by 56 points, a new Fieldhouse record for margin of victory ... Chamberlain's point total represents a new Big Seven scoring record ... The 102 points also set a school single-game record ... Chamberlain's scoring total inflated his season average to 32.2, just behind Seattle's Elgin Baylor and Cincinnati's Oscar Robertson for third nationally.

February 15, 1958 – Kansas 90, Iowa State 61

Wilt Chamberlain pulled down a school-record 36 rebounds in leading the Jayhawks' win over Iowa State ... Nine days later the Cyclones were successful with stall tactics and beat KU, 48-42, in Ames.

March 15, 1958 – NCAA Midwest Regional

Sophomore Oscar Robertson scored an Allen Fieldhouse-record 56 points as Cincinnati defeated Arkansas, 97-62, in the third-place game of the tournament ... Kansas State defeated Oklahoma State, 69-57, in the championship game

December 1, 1958 – Kansas 65, Rice 49

Playing the 1958-59 season opener—and its first game in the post-Chamberlain era—KU defeated Rice in a game that marked the debut of 6-5, 219-pound sophomore Bill Bridges at center ... Bridges scored six points in the victory in front of a crowd of 6,000 fans ... Tom Robitaille of Rice set the Fieldhouse record (which still stands) for most rebounds by a visiting player as he pulled down 23 against the Jayhawks.

February 23, 1958 – Kansas 85, Missouri 81

Bill Bridges scored 19 points and had 22 rebounds in the Jayhawks' win over Missouri ... the game had a bizarre twist late in the contest when KU head coach Dick Harp requested that the officials call a technical on his own fans who were booing the Tigers' Mike Kirsey while he was shooting free throws ... the crowd had ignored Harp's public address plea to stop the booing ... Kirsey hit three free throws to pull MU to within 77-69.

December 14, 1959 – Kentucky 77, Kansas 72

Legendary Kentucky head coach Adolph Rupp, a member of the 1923 KU Helms Foundation National Championship team, brought Kentucky to his home state for the first time and was honored with the presentation of a K blanket by Phog Allen and former teammate A.E. Woestemeyer in a pregame ceremony ... a crowd of 7,500 fans was on hand to watch Kentucky defeat the Jayhawks, 77-72, in overtime despite 33 points from center Wayne Hightower ... earlier in the day, nine new flag poles were installed in front of Allen Fieldhouse to display a banner from each conference school and the American flag prior to home events.

Dick Harp and the KU bench react to action on the court.

The Sixties

A Coaching Change and a Jayhawk Named JoJo

The sixties were marked by turbulence on college campuses. President John F. Kennedy was assassinated, an unpopular war was being fought and race riots brought tension throughout the land. But basketball remained an integral part of the culture in Lawrence, Kansas.

Dick Harp opened the decade with a conference co-championship as Wayne Hightower and Bill Bridges combined to lead the Jayhawks to a share of the 1960 title with Kansas State. But after a 17-8 record the following year, success and attendance started to sag in Allen Fieldhouse and hastened a decline of interest. Harp resigned following the 1963-64 season and was replaced by assistant coach Ted Owens. That year also marked a change in the leadership of the athletic program. Arthur "Dutch" Lonborg, who was a basketball All-American at Kansas in 1919, retired as athletic director. Instrumental in shepherding Allen Fieldhouse through the design

With Riney Lochmann (left) and Jo Jo White at his side, Walt Wesley clips the net celebrating KU's conference title in 1966.

© 2003 Rich Clarkson and Associates

Ted Owens (kneeling) along with assistants Sam Miranda and Bob Frederick during a tense moment on the bench.

and construction process, he would later be inducted to the Naismith Basketball Hall of Fame. Lonborg was replaced by former Jayhawk football standout Wade Stinson.

Owens guided KU to glory once again and ushered in renewed interest in games at Allen Fieldhouse. In just his second season, Kansas captured the 1966 Big Eight title. Basketball in Allen Fieldhouse was affordable entertainment in the mid-1960s. A reserved season chair-back seat was $25, and all other reserved season tickets were $16. The KU faithful saw the arrival of a future star when JoJo White debuted as a Jayhawk during the second semester of the 1965-66 season.

Kansas won 20 or more games in each of the final four seasons during the 1960s. White concluded his career following the first semester of the 1968-69 campaign and Kansas won its 1,000th all-time game. Recruiting brought a new array of future stars—Dave Robisch and Bud Stallworth—to conclude the sixties and offered the hope of additional conference championship banners.

The Jayhawks finished with a 79-30 home-court record under Harp and Owens during the sixties.

There were no major changes to Allen Fieldhouse in the decade. However, an article published in *Kansas Engineer Magazine* in January 1960 provided an early analysis of the building many thought to be "too big" and "too far away from campus." The essence of the facility was captured in these words:

"This Mecca of KU sports might be compared to a shapely woman swathed in the heavy drapery of a bulky gown. Crafted of steel, her vital parts constitute a breathtaking display of beauty and daring; yet, as if ashamed of her charms, she keeps them hidden from view in her masonry skirts. The view she presents to the public offers no indication of the delights in store for those who enter the doors."

North Carolina came to Lawrence in 1960.
Photo provided by KU Sports Information

The analysis noted that the positioning of the building away from other structures and the lack of extensive landscaping made it difficult to discern how large the building actually was. The stately design was consistent with other buildings of an educational institution, but the report did bemoan the fact that the outside appearance was "hardly what we would expect as a setting for thrilling exhibition of athletic prowess. We associate sweeping free-form lines, curves and circles with activity. Unfortunately these symbols of action are missing from the exterior of the building."

The building was also being crowded for space as the athletic programs grew. Stinson, citing "woefully inadequate" facilities, announced February 15, 1968, that work would begin on a two-story structure that would connect to the northwest corner of Allen Fieldhouse. Offices for the athletic administration, football and basketball staffs, a training room, a film library and a weight room were targeted for the new building that would cost approximately $400,000. It would be named the Parrott Athletic Center in honor of an athletic department donor.

Scoreboard Sabotage

I s it possible to win a game, but lose the battle on the scoreboard? Let the record show that such an occurrence actually took place once in Allen Fieldhouse.

It was a late February afternoon in 1965 and the excitement of another intriguing Sunflower State Showdown at Allen Fieldhouse between the Jayhawks and Wildcats was midway through the first half of play.

The building was packed to the rafters, and the KU faithful were in a dizzying swirl of celebration as the Jayhawks jumped out to a sizable advantage over the hated Wildcats. The Allen Fieldhouse scoreboard was a happy sight that had seduced Kansas fans into smiles until the 8:02 mark of the first half, when something happened above the court that altered everyone's expression.

KU's first-year coach, Ted Owens, had just tilted his head upward to take note of the game clock when, to his amazement, a pair of six-by-12-foot banners unfurled on the east and west side of the scoreboard.

The message on each banner read: "Go Cats, Kill Snob Hill Again."

Fans, players, coaches and game officials looked up in jaw-dropping disbelief at the scoreboard sabotage. The banners had been attached to curtain rods and rolled up like window shades with weights attached to make them unfurl. The banners came tumbling down, according to reports, when they were tripped by a wire that had been stretched to the south end zone in the Kansas State section of fans.

Kansas athletics director Wade Stinson later acknowledged that the stunt was worthy of a compliment, but had not spoiled the moment. "It was ingenious and it took a lot of planning and daring," said Stinson. "Fortunately for us, it backfired since we were ahead at the time."

With two sides of the scoreboard completely obscured from view, public address announcer Ed Elbel was forced to announce the score and time with each basket. KU had a commanding lead the remainder of the first half, and with each Jayhawk score, Elbel's booming voice of the score seemed to bring emphasis to the Wildcats' poor performance.

The Jayhawks' Al Lopes played in the game and remembers the moment with a degree of respect for those who made it happen. "I couldn't believe my eyes," said Lopes, now a Lawrence attorney. "It was a pretty impressive stunt. I don't know who did it, but whoever was responsible deserves credit for pulling it off."

The scoreboard was lowered at halftime with the Jayhawks holding a 42-26 advantage, and the banners were removed. KU coasted to an 88-66 victory, ending a three-game losing streak to KSU in Lawrence.

The perpetrators of the crime were never caught or identified. KU officials were scratching their heads for weeks attempting to figure out how anyone could have overcome such obstacles in making the escapade a reality. The scoreboard, which was 60 feet above the court, hung some 30 feet below a padlocked catwalk.

Officials noted that the scoreboard had been lowered Saturday morning to allow workmen to insert the team names on the scoreboard. No one, however, involved with that routine game-day task noticed anything out of the ordinary.

The scoreboard had also been lowered to floor level several times in the days

Photo provided by KU Sports Information

A bad sign for K-State.

prior to Saturday as workers repaired damage on the north side of the scoreboard that had resulted from an off-target discus toss during KU track practice. Again, no one was aware of any unauthorized activity in the vicinity of the board.

There were many theories and a multitude of unconfirmed reports about what happened that day. A popular belief was that a handful of ambitious Kansas State students snuck into the building on Friday evening and stayed throughout the night to rig the banners on the scoreboard.

The Manhattan Mercury received an anonymous phone call a few days following the encounter from someone claiming that he was part of a group of 12 students involved in the scheme. The caller claimed the group had blueprints, 400 feet of cable and an electric triggering device to unlock the banners. The caller did not give his name or provide any additional clues about the incident.

It was an unusual moment in the intense rivalry, and for several years after that game, it brought a whole new meaning to "keeping an eye on the scoreboard" for game officials, coaches and fans.

The Gold Standard

Phog Allen was honored to have his name on the building, but head track coach Bill Easton was just happy to call Allen Fieldhouse home. After training in the cramped quarters underneath the east side of Memorial Stadium, the Jayhawk men's track and field team had as good a facility as any in the nation.

But Kansas wasn't just any track program. Since churning out its first Olympian in 1904, names of Jayhawk athletes have dotted world record honor rolls and have won events on nearly every continent. Ironically, those early teams were coached by Jayhawk basketball coaches James Naismith (1901-06) and W.O. Hamilton (1910-18). The second World War took its toll on college athletic programs, but Kansas track and field returned to premier status with the arrival of head coach Bill Easton in 1948. All told, he won 23 conference indoor and outdoor titles and had six top-five NCAA outdoor finishes, including national championships in 1959 and 1960. He tutored the likes of Wes Santee, Al Oerter, Billy Mills, Bill Nieder and Charlie Tidwell.

"Bill had a great program and Allen Fieldhouse allowed him to make it even stronger," said his successor Bob Timmons.

"Not many had an indoor facility of that size. He could train teams year round." Curtis McClinton, a KU football All-American and a three-time Big Eight Conference indoor hurdle champion, marveled at Easton's ability to maximize the facility. "Coach Easton was amazing in that he used every inch of the building he could, the organization was precise," McClinton said.

In addition to the six-lane, 220-yard track, the dirt surface allowed space for weight throw, jumps and pole vault competitions. The runway for the pole vault was actually an old conveyor belt acquired from the Garvey Grain Elevator in Wichita. On the second floor, white lines were painted around the entire concourse to provide a "second" area to train. Netting was hung on the third floor to provide a practice area for the discus and hay bales were stacked in the corner to allow for javelin throwers to hone their skills.

The first indoor track meet was February 2, 1956, as Kansas defeated Oklahoma 56-48 before a crowd of 2,000. Olympic gold medalist Bill Nieder's shot put of 58' 5 3/8" broke the school record of 50' 1 1/2". Timmons arrived in 1965 and continued the excellence of the Jayhawk track and field program. He coached until 1988, winning 13 indoor and 14 outdoor Big Eight championships, and four NCAA team titles.

Allen Fieldhouse was a magical stop on the track circuit. On February 18, 1967, Jayhawk sprinter Lee Adams set a 60-yard low-hurdle indoor world record at the Kansas Federation Meet, turning in a time

Lee Adams set a world hurdles record in Allen Fieldhouse.

Photo provided by KU Sports Information

of 6.6. Legendary Jayhawk miler Jim Ryun established a world record in the 880-yard run at 1:48.3 in a dual meet versus Oklahoma State, February 23, 1967. The record came as a surprise given the slow track (earthen surface with no banked curves) and Ryun's less than desirable prerace lunch of sauerkraut, hot dogs and onion soup.

"I realized that it isn't the ideal lunch before going out and running a race like this," he said after setting the record. "But that is what was on the menu at the dormitory."

Long after setting the record, Ryun chuckles that his appetite almost got the best of him.

Kansas track flourished with Allen Fieldhouse as its indoor home.

"The coaches and I thought there was a good chance to set the record. We set out to do that. But just before the race, I knew I had the wrong lunch. I didn't feel right. I just went out and ran on adrenaline."

The dirt surface presented challenges for athletes, coaches and administrators alike. At the start of each day, maintenance staffers would drag the surface to level any imperfections. The area would then be watered down to prevent dust from filling the air. It was not a perfect solution, however. Dust would still work its way to all corners of the building and those walking from the track to the hallways would drag dirt with them. That compounded the problems caused by the track team working out at the same time as the men's basketball program.

"There was a lot of commotion going on from all of the different athletes working out," Timmons said. "You had basketball going on, and then you had us running around the track and up and down the stairs, our throwers on the south end and the jumpers on the north end. You had cages and nets on the second and third floors where golfers and baseball players were practicing, too. You even had football players tossing the ball around. My Lord, I don't know how anyone could concentrate."

Contrary to what many others purported, Ryun said the dirt surface was not necessarily a hindrance to the runners. True, there were no banked curves and the turns were tight, but the watered-down surface did create a cushion that was absent on some of the harder wooden surfaces or other outdoor surfaces. The biggest challenge was a "choppy" inside lane that developed later in the meets as a result of the heavy traffic.

Although the basketball court was lined with a curtain, all of the distractions could not be eliminated. Timmons said one of the main sources of contention was a contraption that simulated a starter's gun. It was made of two, two by fours, connected by a hinge. When clapped together, the sound echoed throughout the building much to the consternation of the unsuspecting.

Doug Knop was part of the greatest trio of throwers to compete on the collegiate level. Along with teammates Karl Salb and Steve Wilhelm, the "Pachyderms" (as the 300-pounders were known) went 1-2-3 at the 1969 and 1970 NCAA outdoor track and field championships. Knop's specialties were the 35-pound weight throw and the discus, but those were not necessarily conducive to a multipurpose indoor facility.

Photo provided by Kenneth Spencer Research Library

The dirt track required a daily dose of water.

"I was never going to beat Karl and Steve in the shot, so I picked the 35-pound weight and the discus to focus on," he said. "You can imagine what tossing a big object like the indoor hammer did on the dirt surface. It made the loudest noise and kicked up a ton of dirt. Dust would fly everywhere. I know Ted Owens wasn't too happy every time a cloud of dust rose in the fieldhouse."

Knop also nearly took out the basketball scoreboard as he practiced tossing the discus into netting on the third floor. One of his mighty heaves escaped the net, flew through an entrance in the stands and landed on the empty court. Knop chuckles at the stories that have come out of that event, although he does not believe he actually hit the scoreboard. Suffice it to say, the netting was reinforced and extended shortly thereafter.

Knop does not deny that he and his fellow weight men were prone to hijinx on occasion. Before practice one day, he, Salb and Wilhelm noticed their throwing ring had not been moved into position by the facility staff. A forklift was required to move it about 30 yards. After finding no one to help, Salb decided the three could do the job themselves.

"Karl had some experience in farming, so he said, 'This thing can't be much different than a tractor,'" Knop said. "So he started the thing up. To balance the ring on the lift, Steve and I got on it and Karl started the lift and picked it up a few feet off the ground. Just as he began to move, the maintenance man saw us. He came running after us and gave us an earfull."

In addition to the lack of banked curves and the slow surface of the track, the positioning of support pillars made the inside lane rather treacherous on the turns. Ryun said runners hugged the outside of the first lane to keep from meeting head on with the steel supports.

"There was padding on the pillars because they were so close to the track, plus you really had to lean into the tight turns. There were a few occasions when you would see a runner disappear off the track. Either another runner forced them off the track or they just leaned into the turn too tight. I never saw anyone collide with the pillars, however."

There were also some limitations for the fans who came to watch track meets. The lower-level bleachers were pushed to the walls to allow space for the track, throwing area and jumping pits. That forced fans to sit in the balcony, and thus they were not able to see the competitors on the track directly below them. For the most part, crowds averaged two to three thousand from the mid-1960s to the early 1970s.

"We never filled the place for a track meet, but we had a few crowds that were close," Knop said. "The meets were exciting and the fans really got into it. It could get pretty loud."

Photo provided by Kenneth Spencer Research Library

Netting around the court helped keep balls and players off the dirt track.

While the other athletes using Allen Fieldhouse left the weight men to them-selves, they occasionally found the long and high jump pits worthy diversions. Timmons noted that if an errant ball found its way outside of the curtain, a basketball player or two would take a path that led to the jumping pits. The feeble attempts brought a wry smile to the track athletes, except when a little Tyke took aim. Tyke Peacock played two years for Owens, but he also happened to be a world-class high jumper. During the indoor season, he would juggle basketball and track responsibili-ties.

"Tyke was tremendous," Timmons said. "He was a better jumper than basket-ball player, but he loved basketball so much. I remember he would be in his basketball shoes and with no warm up at all, clear the bar with little effort. He made some of our guys really mad, and Ted, too. We didn't need him getting hurt fooling around."

Peacock's claim to fame while at Kansas came February 27, 1982, when the schedule called for him to play basketball in Allen Fieldhouse versus Iowa State and compete at the Big Eight Conference Indoor Track and Field Championships in Lincoln, Nebraska. It would be a tumultuous day as the Kansas contingent faced not only a tight schedule, but also opposing coaches who sought to keep Peacock from completing the rare double.

Owens was successful in getting the basketball game moved up to 1 p.m. from its scheduled 2 p.m. tipoff time. In place was a plan to have Peacock flown to Lincoln to compete in the league track and field championships. Peacock played 20 minutes, scoring six points in a 63-61 loss to the Cyclones. The game ended at 2:50 p.m. and within 10 minutes he boarded a private plane headed for Lincoln, changing from basketball to track gear in mid-flight. A nervous Timmons was busy lobbying opposing coaches who sought to disqualify his star. A vote that morning ruled Peacock would be ineligible if the high jump began before he arrived. The coaches relented after another highly charged meeting of the minds.

"They didn't want him to compete," Timmons said. "The meetings got pretty intense. But in the end, they did what was right."

Peacock landed at the Lincoln airport at 3:32 p.m. and six minutes later entered the arena. The competition began before Peacock arrived, but Timmons passed for him on the beginning height of 6' 5". Although in the arena, he also passed at the next height, 6' 9". After clearing 6' 11" on his first jump and 7' 1" on his third jump, he set a Big Eight record at 7' 7 3/4" to help Kansas win the team title.

As impressive as Peacock's performance was, it was actually the second time a Kansas student-athlete had completed the feat. On Friday evening, February 28, 1958, Wilt Chamberlain scored 32 points in a 60-59, overtime win over Oklahoma in Allen Fieldhouse. The next afternoon at Kansas City's Municipal Auditorium, Chamberlain won the Conference high jump title clearing 6' 6 3/4".

Allen Fieldhouse remained the home of the Kansas men's and women's track teams until the 1984-85 academic year, when Anschutz Sports Pavilion was built just to the west. The new indoor workout facility featured a track, an artificial football surface, batting cages and nets for the golf teams.

"We were fortunate to have Allen Fieldhouse to train in," Ryun said. "It was an advantage for us. But we also had a lot of fun in there. After a late practice we would often stick a shoe in the door so we could come back early the next morning and play basketball on the elevated court. The coaches didn't like us doing that, but it was great to play in that building."

Sunflower Doubleheader

Despite having one of the nation's largest athletics facilities, Kansas did not host many regular-season tournaments or special events. That was due largely to scheduling issues, which made such competitions nearly impossible. The Big Six/Seven/Eight Holiday Tournament was conducted in Kansas City from 1946-1978 the week between Christmas and New Year's. Later on, Kansas would be an oft-invited participant in some of the more highly regarded tournaments such as the Preseason NIT, the Maui Invitational, the Great Alaska Shootout, etc.

KU was difficult to stop in Allen Fieldhouse. Photo provided by KU Sports Information

However, for an 11-year period (1958-1968), Kansas and Kansas State would host the "Sunflower Doubleheader." On one night, the two Sunflower State schools would play non-league foes in either Manhattan or Lawrence, the next night the venue would change and the opponents would switch. One fan of the event was former Iowa State head coach Johnny Orr, whose first experience in Allen Fieldhouse was as a Wisconsin assistant coach, scouting future opponents.

"That was a great event. You had two good programs hosting two pretty good teams on consecutive nights," Orr said. "I remember I came to Lawrence and somehow got hooked up with St. John's. I met (legendary head coach) Joe Lapchick and (assistant coach) Louie Carnesecca. They were great. I went on to Manhattan with them and then ate the pregame meal with them. That wouldn't happen today. But that just shows you how times have changed. But it (Allen Fieldhouse) was a great facility then and it is a great facility now."

Kansas went 14-8 in the event, including wins in the last nine games of the competition. The Jayhawks were 6-5 in games in Lawrence and 8-3 in games in Manhattan.

Jayhawk Sunflower Doubleheader Results

Year	Opponent (Ranking)	Score
12-19-58 (M)	St. Joseph's	(14) L, 65-67 (OT)
12-20-58 (L)	N.C. State	(4) L, 63-66
12-18-59 (L)	San Francisco	W, 73-42
12-19-59 (M)	Brigham Young	W, 96-64
12-16-60 (M)	Michigan State	W, 93-69
12-17-60 (L)	North Carolina	(5) L, 70-78
12-15-61 (L)	St. John's	L, 59-64
12-16-61 (M)	Marquette	W, 76-62
12-14-62 (M)	Arizona State	L, 62-71
12-15-62 (L)	Cincinnati	(1) L, 49-64
12-13-63 (L)	USC	W, 60-52
12-14-63 (M)	UCLA	L, 54-74
12-11-64 (L)	Penn State	L, 48-50
12-12-64 (M)	Loyola (Ill.)	W, 80-60
12-10-65 (L)	Maryland	W, 71-62
12-11-65 (M)	St. John's	W, 61-55
12-9-66 (M)	Florida State	W, 62-48
12-10-66 (L)	Baylor	W, 66-58
12-15-67 (L)	Cincinnati	W, 67-61
12-16-67 (M)	Texas A&M	W, 78-52
12-13-68 (M)	Creighton	W, 78-65
12-14-68 (L)	Syracuse	W, 71-41

(L - Lawrence; M - Manhattan) (national ranking of opponent)

The View from a Foe

To say that Kansas has enjoyed a home-court advantage in Allen Fieldhouse is stating the obvious. Jayhawk opponents won only 101 of 652 games (.155) played in the facility, so labeling any opponent as successful would be a stretch.

It should come as no surprise that Kansas' longtime rivals Missouri and Kansas State have won more games than any others in the house of Phog. The Tigers are 14-35 in the building, including an 11-20 mark under Norm Stewart, who retired following the 1998-99 season. Kansas State is 17-35 in Allen Fieldhouse, but battled the Jayhawks on nearly an even basis in the first 30 years of the building's existence, winning 14 of 29 games from the 1954-55 season (the year it opened) until the 1982-83 campaign. Since that time, the Jayhawks own a 20-3 advantage in Lawrence.

On a percentage basis (minimum three games), Kentucky is the only foe that has dominated Kansas on its home turf. The Wildcats are 7-3 in Allen Fieldhouse, including a five-game winning streak from 1975-76 to 1983-84. The first two games in Lawrence were won by the Wildcats, as Kansas graduate Adolph Rupp defeated his alma mater 77-72, December 14, 1959, and 79-69, December 4, 1971. Rupp would retire following the 1971-72 season, but his presence loomed in the following years. On December 10, 1977, Kentucky played Kansas at Allen Fieldhouse on Adolph Rupp Night. Fans bowed their heads in a moment of silence for Rupp, who was back in Lexington fighting a losing battle with cancer. Kentucky defeated Kansas, 73-66, but Rupp did not live long enough to hear the final score of the game.

To put it in perspective, Kentucky, Missouri and Kansas State accounted for 38 of 101 opponent victories in Allen Fieldhouse.

From an individual coaching perspective, Kentucky's Joe B. Hall was the most successful Jayhawk opponent. His only loss in six games in Allen Fieldhouse was his first game (71-63, December 3, 1973). Stewart won more games than any other coach (32-42 overall and 11-20 in Allen), but was also a very respectable 4-4 (1954-56) as a player, including a 2-1 mark in Lawrence. The only other coach to have at least a .500 record (minimum six games) was Kansas State's Tex Winter, who was 7-7 from 1953-54 to 1967-68. In fact, Winter won three in a row in 1962-3-4. Among the other coaches to have a modicum of success were Hartman (6-10) and former Oklahoma State coach Henry Iba (6-9).

There was no greater individual antagonist who visited Allen Fieldhouse than Missouri's Stewart. He was a member of the Tiger squad that levied the Jayhawks their first loss in their new facility by an 85-78 count, February 6, 1956 (Kansas won its first seven games in the building).

"I think it took a while for them (Kansas) to recapture what they had in Hoch," Stewart said. "I think anytime you move from one facility where you have been successful to a new building, you lose a little advantage. But it sure didn't take them long to get it back, and of course they have done quite well there since."

Truth be known, the Shelbyville, Missouri, native considered joining fellow Missourian Phog Allen as a Jayhawk. A family friend from Shelbyville, Dr. Harry Tally, lived in Lawrence and suggested Stewart visit Kansas. Recruiting was much less sophisticated in those days; Stewart drove to Lawrence and was shown the campus by Allen and assistant Dick Harp. While he also visited Missouri and SMU, Stewart contends the decision where to go to school was heavily influenced by his high school coach, C.J. Kessler. A close friend of Indiana coach Branch McCracken, Kessler relied on McCracken's advice as to where to steer his star pupil. Stewart indicated McCracken believed he would be more comfortable in his home state. Jayhawk fans would contend that McCracken would do anything to steer Stewart away from Kansas after Allen lured Hoosier Clyde Lovellette to Mt. Oread in the early 1950s.

Stewart claims his relative success in Allen Fieldhouse did not come about from a master plan, at least not in the beginning. Jayhawk fans often rode Stewart for his sideline antics, which often seemed to inspire his team.

"I wish I could say I was smart enough to create distractions that would take the pressure off my team," Stewart said. "Heck, I was just trying to do anything to win. After a while it dawned on me that there were things I could do to put the players a bit at ease."

One such tactic was the frequent retelling of a story that has gained legendary status as a motivational ploy for his teams. It dates back to his playing days when the Tigers were greeted by a locker room full of snow at Allen Fieldhouse. Allegedly, a window in the visiting locker room was left open during a heavy snow on game day. Even Stewart admits he may have taken some liberties with the story through the years.

"I remember running into the locker room after pregame shootaround and there were about four inches of snow on the benches. (Missouri coach) Sparky Stalcup was steaming. It got us a bit riled, too. He gave us quite a pregame talk. But I bet if you took a vote, half of us would say Doc Allen left the windows open and the other half thought Sparky did it on purpose himself."

Despite his status as public enemy No. 1, Stewart and Kansas fans shared a level of mutual respect. When Missouri played Notre Dame in the 1976 NCAA Tournament in Lawrence, Stewart was heartened by the strong support the Kansas faithful provided his team. Years later after he retired, Stewart was invited back by Jayhawk head coach Roy Williams to be honored at halftime of the Kansas-Texas contest, January 27, 2003. He was presented a rocking chair and serenaded by the familiar chant of "Sit Down Norm."

"The atmosphere of Allen was always great for our games," Stewart said. "The fans are loud and knowledgeable. They didn't always like us, but they are respectful of the game."

As an opposing student-athlete, Kim Anderson could appreciate what his head coach did in trying to take the pressure off his team. Anderson, who was also recruited by Kansas, played from 1974-77 and won one of four games in Allen Fieldhouse. He would later go on to become the Tigers' assistant coach for 15 years, serve as the director of basketball operations for the Big 12 Conference for three years and then as head coach for Central Missouri State.

"Kansas had such an advantage at home," Anderson said. "We had to do everything we could not to appear to be intimidated. My most vivid memory is the time Jim Kennedy and I and Donnie Von Moore and Herb Nobles got into a bit of a brawl. We all ended up off the court and out of the tunnel.

"I think the thing that makes Allen Fieldhouse special is that the fans are knowledgeable, especially the students. As a player and a coach, you really are focused on the game and don't get to truly experience the atmosphere. As an administrator for the Big 12 I really gained an appreciation for the environment in Allen. "

Long before the Kansas-Missouri rivalry heated up, the Kansas-Kansas State series had gained the reputation as of one the best, if not the best, in college basketball. The two teams dominated the league in the 1950s, '60s and '70s and both were often found in the national rankings. One person who experienced the rivalry first-hand is current Jayhawk assistant coach Tim Jankovich. As a child, in Kansas City, he remembers attending his first collegiate game as a six-year-old, taking in an NCAA Tournament doubleheader in Allen Fieldhouse. Jankovich grew up as a Jayhawk fan, but his family moved to Manhattan and he eventually became smitten by the purple pride.

He attended Washington State for a year, but returned to Manhattan to play under Jack Hartman from 1980-82. He remembers his coach employing a unique strategy in preparing his team for games at Allen Fieldhouse. It began the day before the game when he talked to his squad about the nature of the rivalry.

"There was never any hate or loud pep talks," Jankovich said. "He would impress upon us how important the game was and how crucial it was to take care of the ball. He believed we could neutralize the crowd by not turning the ball over. To him, the first five minutes of the game would be the most important. It was more about the mental aspect of the game than game-planning.

"On game day, we would usually arrive at the arena and go straight to the locker room. But when we played at Allen, we would come just a bit early and he would tell us to walk around the arena floor in our street clothes. I remember him saying, 'Let them see you.' It was his way of showing that we weren't to be intimidated."

Did it work? Jankovich isn't sure, but he does not remember Hartman plotting such a strategy for any other opponent. As for his first game in Allen, Jankovich found it a bit unsettling. After going through pregame drills, he found his heart racing and his nerves on end. His jaw had tightened and he does not remember having uttered a word for at least 10 minutes. Today, Jankovich finds himself thoroughly enjoying the Allen Fieldhouse atmosphere.

"It was a bit surreal at first to be on the home team bench," he said. "I got chills during the announcement of the starting lineups for the Michigan State game (November 2003). I remember it being loud as a player, but it seemed even louder as a coach. It's hard to imagine that it could be any louder than when I played. The environment is just incredible."

Hartman was also afforded a respectful send-off from Kansas fans and administrators when he retired following the 1986 season. He was presented a golf bag, putter and wedge in his final game at Allen Fieldhouse. Some fans made a large banner that read "We Will Miss You Jack." The Jayhawks prevailed in the game, 84-69, February 23, 1986 to clinch the Big Eight title. But in honor of Hartman's contributions to the game, Kansas head coach Larry Brown ordered his squad not to cut down the nets to celebrate winning the title.

"Those things are very humbling," Hartman said at the time. "I appreciate it very much. When you are on the road and get that kind of respect, it's a very, very nice gesture. I get treated with a lot of respect at Kansas and it is a very healthy rivalry."

Hartman spoke a bit too soon about his retirement. Some 10 years later he was asked to return to bench to coach the last seven games of the 1995-96 season for the Wildcat women's basketball team. He coached one more time in Allen Fieldhouse, dropping a 66-56 decision, February 25, 1996.

Not all coaches drew the ire of Kansas fans. In fact, the close proximity of the seats at Allen Fieldhouse allowed both parties to get an up-close and personal view of each other. It would not be uncommon to hear a coach engage in dialogue with a fan, often pleading his case or sharing a humorous thought. Iowa State's Johnny Orr, Nebraska's Joe Cipriano and Colorado's Sox Walseth brought great personalities to Allen Fieldhouse. Walseth, like Hartman, coached both his school's men's and women's programs in games at Allen Fieldhouse. Orr's sideline antics were legendary, as was his high, shrill voice that revealed one of the quickest wits in the game.

"It was great playing there," Orr said. "The fans were great. They were loud and they knew basketball. I only won there once (63-61, February 27, 1982), but four times they (conference administrators) made me play there on Senior Night. Man, there's no way a guy's going to go in there and win like that. But it was great. The atmosphere was super."

Allen Fieldhouse Moments

1960s

December 3, 1960 – Kansas 86, Northwestern 69

As was the case five years earlier, KU opened the season with Northwestern and a Jayhawk center recorded an impressive rebound total ... Bill Bridges pulled down 30 rebounds (along with 11 points) and Wayne Hightower scored 21 as the Jayhawks downed the Wildcats.

December 17, 1960 – North Carolina 78, Kansas 70

Dean Smith returned to his alma mater as an assistant coach under Frank McGuire at North Carolina and the Tar Heels made it a successful homecoming for the former Jayhawk with a 78-70 win in the Sunflower Classic doubleheader game ... UNC was led in scoring by future NBA coach Doug Moe and York Larese with 21 points each.

March 18, 1961 – NCAA Midwest Regional

Cincinnati downed Kansas State, 69-64, in front of 10,000 fans in Allen Fieldhouse to claim the regional title ... the Bearcats would later win the NCAA National Championship.

December 1, 1961 – Kansas 85, Arkansas 74

Expectations were not high when KU opened the 1961-62 season in front of just 3,500 fans with a win over Arkansas ... the win proved to be the Jayhawks' only home victory of the season as KU set a school record with nine consecutive home court defeats.

February 5, 1962 – Missouri 79, Kansas 66

Missouri head coach Sparky Stalcup made his final visit to Allen Fieldhouse and came away in successful fashion with a 79-66 final advantage.

February 7, 1962 – Kansas State 91, Kansas 72

Kansas State scored the most points ever by a Wildcat team against the Jayhawks as 6-8 center Mike Wroblewski poured in 46 points in a 91-72 KSU victory ... Wroblewski's point total represents the most ever by an opposing player at Allen Fieldhouse.

March 1, 1963 – Kansas 72, Missouri 68

Interest in Jayhawk basketball was declining as KU closed out the season against Missouri in front of just 2,800 fans with a four-point win over the Tigers.

February 8, 1964 – First Wrestling Match

It was Kansas versus Kansas State in the first-ever wrestling match in Allen Fieldhouse.

February 22, 1964 – Kansas State 70, Kansas 46

Kansas State administered the worst defeat ever in Allen Fieldhouse history by an opposing team with a 24-point victory over the Jayhawks.

March 7, 1964 – Kansas 58, Oklahoma State 46

Dick Harp coached his final game in Allen Fieldhouse and guided the Jayhawks to a win over Oklahoma State ... the win boosted KU's final season record to 13-12 ... Harp made his decision to resign public after eight years as head coach on March 26 and was replaced by assistant coach Ted Owens.

December 3, 1964 – Kansas 59, New Mexico 40

Ted Owens, a 35-year-old former player at Oklahoma, made his debut at home as head coach of the Jayhawks and directed KU to a 19-point win over New Mexico ...Owens opened with a win on the road against Arkansas and initiated the year with wins in 10 of his first 13 games.

February 20, 1965 – Kansas 86, Kansas State 66

The Jayhawks were on their way to a decisive win over Kansas State when late in the first half, with the Jayhawks ahead 23-9, two large cloth banners bearing the message "Go Cats, Kill Snob Hill Again" unfurled above the Allen Fieldhouse scoreboard, blocking the score and time on two sides ... despite the hijinx by an unknown source (believed to be KSU students), KU prevailed in the game as the scoreboard was lowered at halftime and the signs removed.

March 6, 1965 – Oklahoma State 64, Kansas 58
The Jayhawks concluded the season with a 64-58 loss to Oklahoma State and ended Owens's first season at the helm with a 17-8 record.

February 12, 1966 – Kansas 59, Oklahoma State 38
Freshman JoJo White, who enrolled at KU at mid-semester, gained eligibility and made his debut by scoring six points in helping KU defeat the Cowboys in an important conference encounter ... White proved to be a key component in helping the Jayhawks to a conference championship that season.

February 26, 1966 – Kansas 110, Nebraska 73
KU hosted Nebraska in a battle between the Jayhawks (ranked sixth) and Joe Cipriano's Huskers (ranked eighth) ... NU had lost to KU in the title game of the Big Eight Holiday Tournament but beat Kansas, 83-75, in Lincoln ... before a crowd of 17,000, KU destroyed Nebraska, 110-73, in a game that assured a tie for the conference title and the Jayhawks celebrated by cutting down the nets after the game.

March 18-19, 1966 – Big Eight Gymnastics Championships
KU hosted the men's and women's gymnastics championships.

March 17, 1967 – Houston 66, Kansas 53
Big Eight Conference champion and third-ranked Kansas served as host of the Midwest Regional in Allen Fieldhouse and was paired against Houston in its first-round game ...

the Cougars put an abrupt and unexpected end to the Jayhawks' title hopes with an upset win ... Houston was led by Don Chaney, 20 points, and Elvin Hayes, 19 points ... the defeat also ended a 21-game home-court winning streak ... KU closed out its season the next night at home with a 70-68 win over No. 2 ranked Louisville.

November 30, 1968 – Kansas 88, St. Louis University 65

A crowd of 12,500 was on hand to witness the season-opener and debut of 6-10 sophomore Dave Robisch in a victory over St. Louis University ... Robisch has an impressive beginning to his college career, scoring 18 points in a starting role.

February 1, 1969 – Kansas 80, Colorado 70

Because he started playing at mid-semester of his sophomore year, guard JoJo White saw his Jayhawk career end before the conclusion of the 1968-69 season ... the standout guard scored 30 points in his final game in a win over Colorado in front of 17,000 cheering fans ... White was honored after the game with the presentation of the game ball ... the win also marked a milestone for Owens as he recorded his 100th career win as head coach.

February 3, 1969 – Kansas 64, Oklahoma State 48

Two nights after White's final game, KU recorded an historic victory with the 1,000th win in school history ... midway through the second half, head coach Ted Owens accidentally ripped the seat out of his trousers and was forced to wear a towel around his waist to cover his posterior in a postgame ceremony in recognition of the milestone win.

December 1, 1969 – Kansas 96, Marshall 80

KU opened the 1969-70 season with a 96-80 win over Marshall as 6-5 sophomore Bud Stallworth made his collegiate debut by scoring 27 points ... Dave Robisch contributed 38 in the win.

The
Seventies
Final Four
Launches Decade

The Jayhawk fortunes during the seventies ebbed and flowed like the Kansas wheat waving in the wind. The program managed six winning seasons but dipped below .500 three times and recorded a 13-13 record midway during the decade (1975-76). The advent of the '70s welcomed one of the great KU teams. The 1970-71 Jayhawk squad went 27-3, won the conference title and advanced to the NCAA Final Four.

"TO ME, WHEN YOU WALK INTO ALLEN FIELDHOUSE YOU KNOW IT'S A BASKETBALL ARENA. IT JUST SMELLS LIKE A BASKETBALL ARENA. IF A BLIND PERSON WALKED INTO ALLEN FIELDHOUSE, HE WOULD KNOW IT WAS A BASKET-BALL ARENA."
—*Bud Stallworth*

The euphoria of the Final Four faded the following season as KU did an about-face with an 11-15 record. Senior Bud Stallworth provided the Jayhawk faithful with a moment of satisfaction when he scored 50 points in the season's final home game to lead the Jayhawks past 14th-ranked Missouri.

Following back-to-back losing seasons, Owens rebuilt his team once again. KU rebounded with a 23-7 mark in 1973-74 (capped with another NCAA Final Four berth) and a 19-8 record the following year. Kansas had another season of glory late in the seventies. The Jayhawks won a conference title and went

Owens was on the bench for KU's 1,000 all-time victory.

24-5 during the 1977-78 season and took No. 2 UCLA to the last minute, losing 83-76 in the first round of the NCAA Tournament.

KU had modest success to close out the decade, but not before compiling a dominant 113-25 home record.

Allen Fieldhouse served as host site for 13 NCAA Tournament games during the decade and helped launch the Indiana State Sycamores and standout Larry Bird toward the NCAA title game in 1979.

The decade also marked the debut of Marian Washington as head coach of the women's team. Washington took control in 1973-74 and directed KU to an 11-8 record in her initial season at the helm. The women's basketball program took a giant step in a positive direction with the arrival of Lynette Woodard late in the 1970s. Woodard ended her career as the all-time leading scorer in women's basketball history and certified herself as a legend in women's basketball.

Washington also served as the women's athletic director from 1973-79. Clyde Walker replaced Stinson as the men's athletic director in 1973 and managed operations until 1977. Bob Marcum, an assistant athletic director at Iowa State, took over the reins of the athletic department following Walker and led it until 1981.

It was also during this decade that the original scoreboard, considered to be state of the art when installed, was replaced in time for the Oklahoma game February 7, 1976. The 14' by 12' structure came in at a cost of nearly $140,000, plus another $6,000 for elec-

Marian Washington took over women's basketball at KU in 1973.

Photo provided by Jeff Jacobsen

trical work. To accommodate the new scoreboard, the roof was reinforced and a hoist was installed to support the 8,000-pound unit.
McDonalds, Phillips Oil Co., Mitchell-Stephens Agency and University
State Bank split the cost and controlled the advertising for 10 years. It
was designed and installed by American Sign and Indicator of Spokane,
Washington. Two auxiliary scoreboards were added at each end of the
court.

The Court as His Canvas

Michelangelo had the Sistine Chapel. D.W. Acker has James
Naismith Court in Allen Fieldhouse.

Acker, the graphic artist for the University of Kansas athletic
department, has been integrally involved in the design, painting and/or
upkeep of the basketball court in Allen Fieldhouse since 1977. He has also
been somewhat of a historian in charting the evolution of the playing surfaces since that time.

"Truth be told," Acker said. "A court design is a group effort.
Everyone has input on lettering, graphics, color and placement. Everyone
contributes—fans, coaches, other universities, companies, staff and
friends. You build and compile files of information, ideas, concepts, opin-
ions and facts, some good, some not so good."

A new court was necessary when Allen Fieldhouse first opened in
1955, as the flooring at Hoch Auditorium was inlaid permanently and
could not be transported. Built by Welch Planing Mill of Midvale, Utah, for
a cost of $15,732, the new floor had the identical design of that used in

Hoch. The center circle was crimson outlined in blue. A blue, block "K" spanned the inner-jump circle. The free throw lanes and apron were crimson in color. What differed about the court in Allen, however, was that it was elevated 28 inches, sitting on risers that rested on dirt. A system of cables kept the floor level. The court was taken up in the spring after the basketball season and laid down in the fall for practices. That process caused considerable wear and tear.

That court remained in use into the 1970s. A process to replace it began on August 13, 1971, when the athletic board appointed a special committee to explore potential upgrades for the facility. At the time, athletic director Wade Stinson said he was "hopeful we can come up with a plan that would enable us to cover the entire dirt floor and do away with the wooden court."

Stinson was joined in the lobbying by head football coach Don Fambrough, who noted the raised court severely limited the area his team could use when weather forced it inside. Head track coach Bob Timmons also supported the change because his squad was still running on a dirt surface. Not only was there greater risk of injury for runners, but there was also considerable effort and expense in getting it ready for practices and meets.

Before the 1974-75 season, a new synthetic surface known as tartan was "poured" in the area that had been dirt. The basketball court was a smooth surface, while the rest of the area including the running track was slightly cushioned with a pebble-like finish. Monsanto Co., completed the project at a cost of $75,995. The design of the court was a bit more detailed, with a full-color Jayhawk spanning the entire 12-foot diameter center court circle replacing the block "K" at the inner-jump circle. The free throw lanes and the apron surrounding the court were painted blue. The words "Kansas" and "Jayhawks" were located on the north and south endzone aprons, respectively.

Photo provided by Kenneth Spencer Research Library

KU's basketball legacy—and logo—were enlarged in Allen Fieldhouse.

Some of the old wooden court was cut up into 4' x 4' squares that were sold for $25 and 4' x 8' squares that sold for $50. Proceeds went to the Williams Educational Fund to support student-athlete scholarships. A significant portion of the court was "forgotten" in storage in the depths of Memorial Stadium. It was later divvied up to those who would come and pick it up.

The center court circle was moved to the east lobby of Allen Fieldhouse in 1977 and still resides there today. It was the first component of the creation of the KU Hall of Fame. Trophy cases were installed and portraits by renowned Kansas artist Ted Watts were added.

Synthetic courts became the rage nationally but did not last long because of the toll they took in the form of knee and ankle injuries. A maple wood court returned

Photo provided by Kenneth Spencer Research Library

A synthetic surface served as the court from 1974 through 1979.

for the 1979-80 season. It was put together in three-and-a-half-foot by seven-foot sections and sat on the old tartan surface, giving it a slight elevation of approximately five inches. The design retained the full-color Jayhawk at center court, and four large Jayhawks were added to each corner on the apron. The free throw lanes and the apron were painted blue.

Prior to the 1985-86 season, the cushioned synthetic surface that ringed the court was removed to the point of the fourth lane of the track. A smooth tartan undersurface was poured to provide a multi-court arrangement for summer camps and coaching stations. The floor was also refinished that year, with head coach Larry

Brown adding the tradition of putting the outline of the state at center court. It was something his coach at North Carolina, Kansas alumnus Dean Smith, instituted in Chapel Hill. The state was colored in blue with a red "KU" located in the jump circle and a Jayhawk positioned where Lawrence is located.

This court remained in use with some minor changes in the type style and positioning of the words until the 1991-92 campaign. That year, Hart Floors of Doniphan, Nebraska, provided a new floor at a cost of $125,000. The old floor was cut up and auctioned off for $150,000 which was earmarked for the new court and basketball goal supports. When they heard the court was going to be auctioned, former Jayhawk coach Larry Brown and assistant R.C. Buford purchased sections to give to every letterwinner who had played at Kansas under Brown. The surface not only covered the court, but the synthetic area that had been added in 1985. It was 17,000 square feet and allowed for a greater area to practice. Unlike its wooden predecessors, this court was inlaid and permanent in nature. It sits on a foam base to provide spring.

Head coach Roy Williams had the state of Kansas at center court painted yellow with a star placed where Lawrence is located. The star would later be replaced by a Jayhawk. The text "Allen Fieldhouse" was located in the state outline. Acker remembers a seemingly innocent decision caused significant consternation for some fans.

"We got quite a few letters," Acker remembers. "The fans didn't like us using the yellow in the map of the state. They thought it too Missouri for Allen Fieldhouse."

The "offending" color finally gave way in 1997-98 to the color scheme and design of the rectangular Kansas "game day flag" that adorns the top of Fraser Hall on campus. It had a white panel sandwiched between two blue panels. A red "K" was centered on the white panel. That year Kansas also named the court in honor of Dr.

James Naismith, inventor of the sport and the first coach of the Jayhawks. The text "James Naismith Court" adorned each baseline apron.

With the arrival of Bill Self for the 2003-04 season came a new court design featuring a large Jayhawk, measuring 26 1/2 feet from the top of the head to the bottom of the foot. Lettering identifying "Allen Fieldhouse" and "University of Kansas" were also moved. The Big 12 Conference logo was placed near both free throw lanes. Acker noted there was again strong feedback to the design.

"Kansas fans are passionate about their basketball," Acker said. "The big Jayhawk was quite a change and we heard about it—both good and bad. But you get that any time you change. I think it has grown on people." According to Acker, basketball courts must be maintained annually and periodically. They need to be surface screened, sealed, repainted and refinished. In his mind, the court represents more than a place to play basketball. It is a form of art that requires "pride, passion and a whole lotta sweat."

KU brought back a wood floor prior to the 1979-80 season. Photo provided by KU Sports Information

Running Allen Fieldhouse Kept Temple Busy

Floyd Temple wore many hats during his 40 years in the athletics department at the University of Kansas. A baseball and football standout during his playing days as a Jayhawk, Temple retired from KU in 1991 and now spends many of his days on the golf course.

He's best known for his 28 years as head baseball coach at KU, a job he was hired to do in 1954. But he also served on the staff of three football

The center jump originated in the state boundaries during the Larry Brown era.

Photo provided by Jeff Jacobsen

coaches at KU and spent many years overseeing the day-to-day operation of Allen Fieldhouse.

Only one other coach—Phog Allen—served KU athletics for more than 40 years.

Temple remembers the days when the lower bleachers of Allen Fieldhouse were also used for baseball and football.

"There were stationary bleacher sections at the lower level, and workers would fork-lift them out for basketball season in Allen Fieldhouse. When basketball was over they moved them to the baseball field. Once baseball was over, they would come out with their tractors and move them to Memorial Stadium. Then after football, they would go back to basketball."

Temple was named assistant athletics director for facilities in 1981 after retiring as head baseball coach and served as a liaison in scheduling the building. His experience as a baseball coach helped prepare him for the challenge.

The massive Jayhawk dominated the court when it was added in 2003.

"In the early years when we had basketball, baseball and track all practicing at the same time, we had our share of challenges to make it all work," noted Temple. "I can remember working with the baseball team and hitting fungos to the team. One time, I hit one that bounced through the netting on the third floor down to the court where Dick Harp was running basketball practice.

"I looked down to the court and smiled at Coach Harp," recalled Temple. "I said, 'Sorry, Coach. I guess we need to get that hole fixed in the net.' You had to just laugh at it all."

Whether it was baseballs bouncing on the basketball court, a sprinter on the track team nearly colliding with a staff member coming out of an office door, or ROTC cadets conditioning while the football team attempted to conduct indoor workouts, Allen Fieldhouse was used to solve about everyone's facility need.

But keeping the building clean, as Temple recalls, was a nightmare for the building's custodial staff.

"Probably the worst thing was the dirt surface when the building first opened," recalled Temple. "I can remember that it had to be watered down twice a day and that clay dust would settle on the basketball court. We had to sweep it constantly.

"And if you had an office in Allen Fieldhouse, you normally arrived at work and found several inches of that dust on your desk top."

Temple has witnessed his share of unusual moments or events in the history of the building. One of his favorite incidents came during the holiday season and involved a jolly old fellow with a white beard and a red suit.

"We decided one year that we were going to do something to observe Christmas," Temple said. "I came up with the suggestion that Santa could come down out of the scoreboard at halftime.

"So we found a Santa Claus and on game day, before we opened the building, we lowered the board, loaded him inside and hoisted it back up to its normal location," said Temple. "He had to be up there four or five hours before it was time to lower it and have him climb out.

"We gave him plenty of food and water," noted Temple. "We teased the crowd over the public address system that he would be arriving. Finally, halftime came and we lowered the scoreboard. I felt sorry for the poor fellow having to sit in that cage all that time. But it was well received and he passed out a lot of candy."

Temple was in charge of the building when the concept of student camping first started in the early 1980s. He remembers the student groups being

Former head coach Dick Harp was a frequent visitor to practice sessions.

cooperative and easy to police. But it did take one violation of the rules to set the tone.

"The campers had a system and they policed themselves," said Temple. "We worked with them and provided the access. One of the major rules was staying in the designated area, which was the north corridor of the building.

"One night pretty late I called my assistant, Darren Cook, and we decided to check in on the campers and make sure they were not getting into trouble. We arrived late in the evening and found a pickup basketball game in progress among the campers. As a result, we kicked them all out and suspended camping. I locked the doors.

"They got the message and we never had any other problems."

Bud Stallworth: Unusual Beginning, but Great Ending to His Career

Isaac "Bud" Stallworth originally arrived at the University of Kansas to blow a horn, not shoot a basketball. As it turned out, it was his ability to make music on a basketball court that brought him acclaim as one of the all-time great Jayhawks to play in Allen Fieldhouse.

A tall trumpet player who envisioned himself as the next Louis Armstrong, Stallworth traveled from his hometown of Hartselle, Alabama, the summer between his junior and senior years in high school to attend the Midwestern Music and Arts Camp on the KU campus.

"My parents, being educators, didn't think that bouncing that ball offered a very promising career," said Stallworth in an interview for the book *Max and the Jayhawks.* "So I wound up at the music camp."

Stallworth was an unknown to the Kansas coaching staff. Head coach Ted Owens and his assistants had no idea a talented prep prospect from Alabama was visiting campus during the summer of 1968.

While attending the music camp, Stallworth learned from a friend of a regular noon basketball game in Robinson Gymnasium. The pick-up game coincided with his break from practicing the trumpet and allowed him to test his skills in the basketball competition.

"I didn't have time to meet all of the players," said Stallworth. "I just went and played.

"I got back one afternoon from one of my rehearsals and the counselor came up to me and said, 'Bud, do you know who Ted Owens is? He's been calling up here to find you. He's the head basketball coach at KU.' I had never heard of Coach Owens, but I decided I'd better call."

As it turned out, Stallworth had unknowingly been auditioning in front of KU players such as JoJo White, Rich Bradshaw, Vernon Vanoy and Bob Wilson. The skinny six-five Stallworth made a good impression, and word of his skills soon reached the KU basketball office.

"I spoke with Coach Owens on the phone and gave him a little bit of information about me," said Stallworth. "I also told him that I shouldn't be playing basketball at the camp because my father didn't want me to get hit in the mouth."

The Jayhawk staff followed Stallworth's progress his senior season and offered him a scholarship.

"After KU had shown interest, I started hearing from some schools like Vanderbilt, Alabama, and Auburn. In the back of my mind, I guess I knew that KU would be the place for me," added Stallworth. "Sam Miranda (KU assistant coach) once said I was the easiest recruit they ever had. I showed up for my recruiting visit in a blazer with a Jayhawk on it."

Stallworth was inserted into the Kansas starting lineup and averaged 12.7 points as a sophomore.

The following season, Stallworth was a key player on one of the great Kansas teams of all time. Combining with Dave Robisch, Roger Brown, Pierre Russell and Aubrey Nash, Stallworth helped the Jayhawks to a 27-3 record in 1970-71, a conference championship and a spot in the NCAA Final Four. He averaged 16.9 points that season to rank second on the squad behind Robisch.

Graduation claimed Robisch, Brown and Russell, weakening the Jayhawks in Stallworth's senior season. The team won just 11 games in his final year on the KU roster, but Stallworth never lost his rhythmic shooting stroke. He made his final appearance at Allen Fieldhouse a memorable one.

Kansas hosted Missouri in the year-end clash of rivals. The Tigers were ranked 14th nationally, and head coach Norm Stewart stirred Stallworth's competitive spirit when he suggested that MU's John Brown was more deserving for conference player of the year honors.

"It was a game where I wanted to leave my little piece of history," said Stallworth. "There had been a quote from Norm Stewart in the paper saying that Brown was the best player in the league and that he should be player of the year. Norm said I had nice statistics, but Brown deserved the award. I guess that bothered me.

"I was sitting in my apartment that morning, not really feeling well. My mom had come to Lawrence, and it would be the first time she would see me play in Allen Fieldhouse. My roommate was Aubrey Nash, and I told him this was an important day. He said, 'Bud, you just get open, and I'll get you the ball.' "

The game also featured a reunion of Kansas' 1952 national championship team. Many of those players were on hand to see one of the most impressive performances in Allen Fieldhouse history.

Stewart and the Tigers were well aware they had to stop Stallworth to have success that day. A sign unfurled before the game, playing off a popular beer commercial. Perhaps a good omen, it read: "When you say Bud Stallworth, you've said it all."

Stallworth also wanted to send a message back to the Allen Fieldhouse crowd before the game got underway. He had a Frisbee signed by everyone on the team that he hurled into the crowd as he was introduced.

"I later found out that the Frisbee became part of a divorce settlement," said Stallworth.

Bud Stallworth was mobbed after scoring a Fieldhouse-record 50 points.

Photo provided by Jeff Jacobsen

Stewart started the game with a small, quick guard trying to stop Stallworth. When that strategy failed, he assigned a bigger, heavier player. Nothing seemed to work on the Jayhawk sharpshooter.

"It helped starting out with a smaller player," recalled Stallworth. "I was taller than he was and just as quick. I loved shooting the basketball, and once I got in the zone, it didn't matter who was on me. All I had to do was run to a spot, and Aubrey got me the ball. I hit a few jump shots and felt the flow of the game. I couldn't have written a better script for myself."

Stallworth connected on 19 of 38 shots and scored 50 points. His point total was a record for a Big Eight Conference game and the second-highest single-game output in Kansas history. Only Wilt Chamberlain's 52-point game against Northwestern in 1957 was bigger.

Stallworth's outstanding play led Kansas to a 93-80 victory that day. Stallworth finished the season with a 25.3 points per game average and was named Player of the Year in the conference.

"I still love to shoot the basketball and like playing those noontime pick-up games in Allen Fieldhouse," said Stallworth. "It has always been my favorite place to play basketball."

Allen Fieldhouse Moments

1970s

December 1, 1970 – Kansas 69, Long Beach State 52

KU hosted Long Beach State and head coach Jerry Tarkanian in its season opener ... Kansas dominated the game early as Long Beach set a new standard for futility, falling behind 32-4 and trailed 32-8 at halftime ... a bomb threat had been called into the building, but officials didn't disrupt the game ...the victory turned out to be one of the Jayhawks' most impressive of their Final Four season ... Long Beach finished 16th in the final college basketball poll.

February 26, 1972 – Kansas 93, Missouri 80

Bud Stallworth played his final game in Allen Fieldhouse and made it one to remember as he torched Missouri for 50 points ... Stallworth's point total is second only to Chamberlain's 52 for a KU player in Allen Fieldhouse ... the game marked the first time Stallworth's mom had been in the stands to see her son play a college game at KU ... the game also marked the 20-year reunion of the 1952 national championship KU team.

December 1, 1973 – Kansas 103, Murray State 71

Kansas opened the season with a win at home against Murray State as freshman center Norm Cook set a freshman career debut record with 21 points.

February 2, 1974 – Basketball/Gymnastics Doubleheader

The Jayhawks hosted Northern Iowa in gymnastics competition following a women's basketball game that tipped off at 11 a.m.

November 30, 1974 – Kansas 65, Northeast Missouri State 55
KU opened the season at Allen Fieldhouse with a win over Northeast Missouri State
... it marked the first game since the death of Phog Allen (September 16).

November 27, 1976 – Kansas 104, Montana State 47
With Ken Koenigs scoring 18 points and four other Jayhawks in double-figures, the
Jayhawks opened the season by setting an Allen Fieldhouse record for largest victo-
ry margin (57 points) in a 104-47 win over Montana State.

November 28, 1977 – Kansas 121, Central Missouri State 65
The Jayhawks initiated the 1977-78 season with an impressive 121-65 victory over
Central Missouri State as freshman guard Darnell Valentine made his first appearance in a Jayhawk uniform and scored 11 points in the victory ... the 56-point margin
victory (at the time) tied as the second-largest in Allen Fieldhouse history behind the
57-point win a year earlier against Montana State.

January 28, 1978 – Woodard Establishes New Rebounding Record
Lynette Woodard pulled down a school-record 33 rebounds in leading KU to a 76-73
victory over Kansas State.

February 2, 1979 – Woodard Sets Fieldhouse Scoring Mark
Lynette Woodard exploded for 44 points in setting a new women's basketball scoring
mark in Allen Fieldhouse as the Jayhawks downed Iowa State, 101-64 ... eight days
later, Woodard set the all-time single-game scoring mark in KU history as she poured
in 49 points in leading KU to a 105-54 win over Southwest Missouri State.

March 11, 1979 – NCAA Midwest Regional
Larry Bird, playing with a broken thumb on his left hand, scored 22 points and
grabbed 13 rebounds, in leading the Sycamores to a 86-69 win over Virginia Tech in
the regional finals in front of 15,110 fans.

The
Eighties
A Climate of Change:
Ted, Larry and Roy

A new athletics director—Monte Johnson—ushered in a decade of significant change to the landscape of Kansas basketball. Following back-to-back losing seasons, Johnson determined a new direction was needed in the leadership of the program. After the 1982-83 season, he replaced Owens with Larry Brown, just the sixth head coach in school history.

"WE COULDN'T PAY LARRY VERY MUCH IN THAT FIRST YEAR. I TOLD HIM WE WOULD CREATE AN ENVIRONMENT FOR HIM TO MAKE AS MUCH MONEY AS HE HAS EVER MADE IN HIS LIFE."
—Monte Johnson on the hiring of Larry Brown

Brown stayed on the Jayhawk bench for five seasons, and was responsible for a revival of national acclaim for the Kansas program. Johnson was the man behind the scenes during a time of considerable change in the athletic department. Arriving in 1982, he was the first Kansas alum in the position since Wade Stinson (1964-72). Johnson created a feeling of stability after Bob Marcum served only three years (1978-81) and Jim Lessig but six months after that. Johnson also initiated several upgrades to Allen Fieldhouse and the addition of Anschutz Sports Pavilion.

The Jayhawks were 71-5 in Allen Fieldhouse during the Brown era, going undefeated at home during three of his five seasons as head coach. KU went to the Final

Danny Manning and Larry Brown celebrate another victory.

Four twice under Brown (1986, 1988), and claimed the NCAA championship at the end of the 1987-88 season.

Four of the Brown years encompassed the KU career of Danny Manning, who left as the all-time leading scorer and rebounder in school history (2,951 points/1,187 rebounds) and certainly one of the most talented players ever to wear a Kansas uniform. Brown returned to the NBA following the national championship season.

Another Kansas alum, Dr. Bob Frederick, also occupied the athletic directors' office during this most successful decade. A former walk-on basketball player and assistant coach, he replaced Johnson in 1987. Frederick followed the advice of former Jayhawk head coach Dick Harp and consulted another Kansas grad—North Carolina head coach Dean Smith—to locate a replacement for Brown. Harp urged him to take a chance on unknown Tar Heel assistant coach Roy Williams, and with the endorsement of Smith, Frederick had his man.

The 37-year-old Williams, a coach of great ambition and drive, was tapped by Frederick to advance the KU program that had been hit with NCAA sanctions for recruiting violations committed under the previous coaching regime.

It didn't take the dynamic young coach long to restore pride and dignity to KU basketball. The Jayhawks went 19-12 in Williams' first season (1988-89) and went 30-5 the next (1989-90).

With Williams on the bench, Kansas closed out the decade in memorable fashion with a 150-95 win over Kentucky at Allen Fieldhouse. It marked the most points ever scored in a game by a Kansas team.

Under the direction of three head coaches, KU finished 111-22 in Allen Fieldhouse during the decade of the eighties. Between 1984 and 1988, Kansas won 55 consecutive games at home.

The movement of the media to the east side court level from the lower rows of the upper west balcony, and the addition of chair-back seating to that area further reduced capacity of the facility to 15,200 entering the 1980-81 season. On December 10, 1983, a less obvious, but nonetheless important, facility upgrade resulted in the dedication of a newly remodeled Charlie Black Locker room. Black was a four-time All-American from 1942-43— 1946-47. The Morgan family of Lawrence and Kansas City funded the $135,000 project.

Darnell Valentine ended his Allen Fieldhouse career in 1981.

Photo provided by KU Sports Information

Another extensive renovation prior to the 1985-86 season called for a new playing surface and other enhancements. The changes were facilitated by the completion of Anschutz Sports Pavilion just to the west of Allen Fieldhouse. The indoor multipurpose facility left only men's and women's basketball and volleyball as the tenants of Allen Fieldhouse. Anschutz was dedicated October 27, 1984, the same day the Kansas football team upset No. 2 Oklahoma, 28-11 at Memorial Stadium. A total of 60 donors, who gave $3.5 million, made the indoor training facility possible. Adjacent to that building was the $415,000 Shaffer-Holland Strength Center. The Anschutz, Shaffer and Holland families were originally from Russell, Kansas, located in the west central part of the state.

The cushioned synthetic surface that ringed the court was removed to the point of the fourth lane of the track. A smooth tartan undersurface was poured to provide a multi-court arrangement for summer camps and coaching stations. This allowed for the installation of new retractable seats on each side of the court. They were elevated five inches to allow fans an unrestricted view from the media and team benches. Four rows of seats were added just above each of the four entrances of the court, and a 25th row was added at the top of the arena.

In all, 600 seats were added by Dant Corp. of Louisville, Kentucky, bringing the capacity to 15,800. The new seats also allowed for a reconfiguration of traffic flows that provided wider, continuous aisles from the very bottom to the top of the arena. The movement of the other sports to Anschutz also allowed for permanent concession stands to be positioned on the lower level for the first time. The final element of the renovation was the addition of a new sound system and scoreboard, bringing the project to $250,000.

"The current seating is the same that has been there since the fieldhouse opened in 1955, other than minor changes in the north and south sections," athletics director Monte Johnson said. "We were getting to the point that something had to be done.

"There will be a little bit better aesthetics in the arena area. The seating will be more colorful, and it will surround the court more for a better playing atmosphere."

The program's success created significant demand for every seat that was added during the decade. The arrival of Brown and NCAA tournament berths in his first two seasons resulted in a season ticket-sellout situation in 1985-86. Every season has since been sold out.

Despite pressures on other campuses to limit student seating and offer it to the general public, Kansas students could not complain about their standing. Historically, records indicate that students had approximately half of the seats in Allen

Permanent bleachers were part of a major overhaul in 1985.

Fieldhouse. In 1983, the athletic department and the Student Sports Council negoti-

ated a 7,000-seat lower limit and a $41 "all sports ticket" that got students into all

home football and basketball games that season.

A Memorable Senior Day for Danny and the Miracles

Just as the Rock Chalk Chant is recognized as the signature moment of a home game, Senior Day represents the true emblem of closure for those players who run through the Allen Fieldhouse tunnel to a standing ovation one final time.

Brown offers advice to Manning from the bench. Photo provided by KU Sports Information

No KU game during the basketball season is more memorable than the closing chapter of a senior's playing career beneath the hallowed blue rafters of Allen Fieldhouse.

Senior Night is the Allen Fieldhouse graduation exercise that has evolved into an annual Lawrence love fest. It became a point of emphasis during the Larry Brown and Roy Williams eras of coaching at Allen Fieldhouse.

While that final home game has produced its share of poignant moments, it's doubtful more emotions were ever ignited than during the tribute to the 1988 class of Danny Manning, Chris Piper and Archie Marshall.

Kansas entered the 1987-88 regular season with ambition and high hopes, only to see it fall short of expectations. The Jayhawks sported a disappointing 19-10 record as they prepared to host Oklahoma State on Senior Night.

With the season seemingly a lost cause, the spotlight was on the seniors, and in particular Manning. Fans flocked to Lawrence to see the 6-10 All-American play one last time in Allen Fieldhouse.

At a press conference prior to the game, however, Manning deflected the attention to another senior. He thought that Archie Marshall, the 6-5 forward who was in the early stages of rehabilitation of a left knee that had been ripped apart in the finals of a holiday tournament in New York in late December, should start the game.

"We can put Archie out there," quipped Manning. "We'd get the tip, then stop the game. I don't think Archie would do it, but it would be nice."

Danny and the Miracles returned for a reunion in 2003.

Photo provided by Jeff Jacobsen

Manning's suggestion did not go unnoticed by Larry Brown.

"I'd love to see him introduced as a starter, but his knee is pretty darn bad. But Danny's sentiment is the way everyone feels," said Brown. "I doubt we'll even get him to dress. He came by practice and couldn't bring himself to watch. He wants to play so bad."

The building was filled with moist eyes during pregame ceremonies as the three seniors were introduced for one final time in Allen Fieldhouse. Fans launched hundreds of roses on the floor as each player was presented with a color portrait and embraced by members of his family.

KU basketball band director Ron McCurdy had his musicians outfitted in tuxedos for the event and McCurdy directed in a stunning white tuxedo. The band played "Oh, Danny Boy" in tribute to Manning's career at Kansas.

The game followed the script of most Senior Day contests. The emotional crowd helped lift the Jayhawks to an insurmountable advantage in the final stages of the game. Manning gave one final, memorable performance with 31 points, 10 rebounds,

Archie Marshall was an inspiration when both healthy and injured.

Photo provided by KU Sports Information

six assists and one blocked shot. Piper scored 10 points and pulled down seven rebounds.

But easily the most enduring moment of the day came with just 1:33 left on the scoreboard clock.

KU was in-bounding the ball just in front of the Jayhawk sideline when Brown, allowing a wide grin to explode on his face, signaled down to the end of his bench for Marshall to take off his warmups and enter the game.

The tragedy of Marshall's season had been well documented and his sudden and unexpected appearance in the game brought a massive explosion of emotion unlike anything longtime observers had ever witnessed in Allen Fieldhouse.

With 15,800 fans' thunderous applause and roaring encouragement, Marshall limped into the game wearing a heavy knee brace. He positioned himself just in front of the KU bench.

Oklahoma State coach Leonard Hamilton, understanding the moment for Marshall and realizing the game was lost, signaled for his defender to back away from Archie. An interested observer on the OSU bench assisting Hamilton was Bill Self, who joined Larry Brown's staff at KU the following season.

The ball was passed into Manning who immediately flipped the ball to his injured teammate. Marshall caught the pass, hesitated for a moment, then lofted a 40-foot three-point attempt that clanged off the rim. Clint Normore grabbed the missed shot and was fouled. Moments later, Marshall took a few steps back to the bench, acknowledged the standing ovation, and took his seat.

The moment brought tears to the eyes of many in the crowd as well as the KU coaching staff on the bench.

"It was the seniors' last home game," Marshall said after the game. "I wanted to be a part of it. The way the fans reacted is something I will remember the rest of my life."

Brown called it one of the special moments of his coaching career. "All senior days are special, but obviously this situation was a little different. We'll have 600,000 people saying they were here for this one," Brown said.

The Kansas coach later explained that he had approached Marshall one day earlier with the notion of making an appearance in the game.

"He was not going to shoot in the original plan," said Brown. "We were going to throw him the ball and call timeout. But he was open, so we figured, 'Why not shoot it?'"

"Danny was phenomenal," noted Brown when asked about Manning's effort after the game. "When kids think back to what they'll remember, it'll be the crowd. I know that's what I will remember as a coach. I hope the people realize what an opportunity they've had to see Danny play four years."

Marshall's unexpected appearance may have served as a good omen for something else unexpected by the KU faithful.

It was a magic moment that taxed the hearts of all Kansas fans, but it was not the final one of that season. Inspired, perhaps, by Marshall and the seniors in their final game, Kansas went on an improbable joyride and surprised the college basketball world by winning the NCAA championship several weeks later in Kansas City.

As a testament to their final achievement, the team picked up the nickname "Danny and the Miracles" after its surprising national championship performance.

Fittingly, Archie Marshall was just one of the Miracles of the 1987-88 season.

Holy Peach Baskets, Kansas!

Doug Beene has been the official scorekeeper for Kansas men's games since the 1963-64 season. Wearing an official's striped shirt and seated at mid-court between

Photo provided by Jeff Jacobsen

the two opposing team benches, Beene is an obscure figure in Kansas basketball history.

But Beene's pencil-pushing skills have recorded the drama of nearly every point scored in Allen Fieldhouse over the past 40-plus years. None of those games, however, has taxed the lead in his writing instrument more than the 1989 contest in Allen Fieldhouse when Kentucky and its first-year head coach Rick Pitino arrived in town.

"The NCAA official scorebook only allows for the recording of 136 team points," said Beene. "I had to manufacture the rest of it in the book."

Make no mistake about it, this was not a vintage Kentucky basketball team. Pitino left the professional ranks to take over a program that had been rocked by an NCAA investigation.

At best, Kentucky was in the embryonic stages of redevelopment. The Wildcats arrived in Lawrence with a 3-1 record, but had just eight players on scholarship and no one on the roster taller than 6-7. Pitino, as a result, attempted to turn his team's obvious vulnerability into a strength.

The Wildcats attacked first and foremost as three-point shooters under the gospel of Pitino's teachings and became known later in the season as "Pitino's Bombinos." Clear evidence of their long-range firepower came in a preceding game against Tennessee Tech, when UK launched a staggering NCAA-record 41 three-point field goal attempts.

Pitino coached what he called the "mother-in-law defense" on the other end of the court. "It's based on the principles of total pressure and harassment," said Pitino in an interview prior to his journey into Lawrence.

But even in their wounded condition, Kentucky was still Kentucky. It was a program, after all, that had won 16 of the previous 18 meetings between the two schools and ranked No. 1 all time in college basketball wins. Kansas players and their fans would not be swayed into feelings of sympathy for the boys from the Bluegrass and its upstart new head coach.

Kansas entered the afternoon in search of the school's 350th all-time win in Allen Fieldhouse. Williams had coaxed a consistent effort from his team during the preseason schedule; the Jayhawks were 8-0 and ranked second nationally.

Another capacity crowd jammed into Allen Fieldhouse for the contest—which was not televised live—and they were treated to two hours of racehorse basketball unlike anything James Naismith, Phog Allen or even Kentucky's legendary coach and KU graduate Adolph Rupp could ever imagine.

A headline over the game story in the following day's *Lawrence Journal-World* told its readers where this game ranked among the memorable moments in Kansas basketball history.

The large, bold type read: "Holy Peach Baskets, Kansas!" What better attention-grabber could be written in reporting a game that brought writer's cramp to the official scorekeeper and sore necks to the fans in attendance?

The final score—Kansas 150, Kentucky 95.

Primarily on the strength of long-range three-point shooting, Kentucky bolted to an early 18-11 lead, connecting on nine of its first 11 field goal attempts. But its early success masked the talent disparity between the two teams, and the game's momentum quickly switched uniforms.

Kentucky's up-tempo, high-pressure defense played directly into the signature running game Roy Williams preached from the home bench. Like an unpredictable twister on a Kansas prairie, the Jayhawks ran up and down the court, scoring on uncontested dunks, lay-ups and three-point field goals. A frustrated Pitino picked up the first of his two technical fouls at the five-minute mark of the first half, when he tossed a blue towel on the court in protest of a call by referee Ed Hightower.

Much to the delight of the home crowd, KU reached half of a hundred early in the game. A Kevin Pritchard basket and free throw lifted KU to a 50-37 lead at the 7:14 mark of the first half.

When the dust had settled at halftime, Kansas led by the remarkable score of 80-61.

"I didn't think we could score 80 points in a half against St. Mary's of the Western Plains. I didn't think we could do it against a high school team," Pritchard would later acknowledge.

The Kentucky meltdown continued in the second half as Kansas outscored the overwhelmed Wildcats 70-34.

"It was like Custer's last stand, only there was no surprise," said Pitino. "Kansas was beating people on the road by an average of 26 points."

Mark Randall (left) and Kevin Pritchard helped KU to a 30-5 record in 1989-90.

Photo provided by KU Sports Information

The two teams combined for an NCAA-record 57 three-point field goals attempts, including 40 by Kentucky. Guard Terry Brown, one of seven Jayhawks scoring in double figures, led KU with 31 points. Kansas also had school-record 36 assists and 52 field goals in the contest.

Pritchard easily recalls the high-scoring encounter, but a moment late in the game unnoticed by many fans, is a story he enjoys telling when giving an example about the competitive spirit of his head coach.

"Coach Williams noticed that Kentucky's players were obviously exhausted and Pitino was out of timeouts. He caught the eye of Pitino and offered to call a time-out and allow his players to catch their breath.

"Well, Pitino waved back to Coach Williams in a very negative fashion. Coach had already taken most of the starters out, and I was seated on the bench. He came back after Pitino's insult with fire in his eyes and waved us back into the game. And he didn't tell us to take it easy. He basically told us to put the pedal to the metal and send a message."

Postgame questions, primarily from Kentucky area media, about Williams's running up the score were put to rest by both head coaches. Pitino refused to bite at the suggestion while Williams expressed his feelings of empathy for Kentucky and its players.

"I sat there. I'm human. I love what our guys are doing, but I feel compassion for the other guy and his players," offered Williams.

No one, however, ever uttered pity or sympathy for Beene on that memorable day.

TIES

The 55-Game Homecourt Streak Ends, but Brown Is Upbeat

Beyond savoring bragging rights and defining state supremacy, much was at stake when Kansas State made its annual trek to Lawrence in late January of 1988.

For the beleaguered Jayhawks, a win would have immense impact in the team's attempt to salvage a disappointing season. Kansas entered the contest with an 11-6 record and 1-2 Big Eight mark after losing back-to-back games at Notre Dame and Nebraska.

In addition, KU boasted college basketball's longest home-court winning streak at 55 games. The Jayhawks had not lost a game in Allen Fieldhouse since the memorable 92-82 overtime loss to Oklahoma in 1984. KU's senior duo of Danny Manning and Chris Piper had never experienced a losing game on their home court.

The Wildcats basketball fortunes were polar opposite from their neighbors to the east. Kansas State came to Lawrence leading the league following consecutive wins over Oklahoma, Colorado and Oklahoma State. KSU also had the added incentive of breaking a 10-game losing streak to its in-state rival.

A sub-plot for the game was the duel between a pair of All-Americans—the Jayhawks' Manning and 6-5 Mitch Richmond of the Wildcats. KU head coach Larry Brown was also tinkering with his starting lineup. For the first time, Brown moved sophomore Kevin Pritchard into the point guard position.

With a full house of frenzied Jayhawk fans roaring their approval, KU showed signs of dominance as it darted to a 22-12 advantage with just under eight minutes remaining in the first half. But the Wildcats fought back to tie the game at 29-29. A 10-foot jumper by Manning with 26 seconds left put KU up 31-29 at halftime.

The game see-sawed back and forth in the second half with neither team gaining momentum until Wildcat guard Steve Henson drained a three-pointer with six minutes left to put K-State up 52-49. KSU then outscored the Jayhawks 12-5 to increase their lead to 62-54. Forced to foul, KU could get no closer than five, 64-59, with 51 seconds left in the game. The Wildcats converted eight free throw attempts down the stretch to seal the victory.

Larry Brown was 71-5 during his five seasons in Allen Fieldhouse.

Photo provided by KU Sports Information

Richmond won the individual battle of the All-Americans, scoring 35 points and pulling down 12 rebounds to Manning's totals of 21 and eight.

The winning streak ended and KU fans watched the visitors celebrate for the first time in four years. The loss dropped KU's record to 11-7, leaving some athletic officials wondering if there would be an NCAA postseason in their future. Privately, athletics director Bob Frederick was already staring squarely at the possibility of printing NIT tickets as the team's only postseason option.

But head coach Larry Brown, to the surprise of many, saw a silver lining behind the dark cloud of defeat.

"We've beaten some great teams in this building and a great team beat us tonight," said Brown indicating a comfort level with his team's performance. "I'm encouraged with the way we played."

Brown also indicated the loss was a turning point in his relationship with the players. "For the first time all season I didn't have to yell at them about effort and how they were playing."

Although he hit just three of 21 field goal attempts in the game, Pritchard ran the team in impressive fashion. He dished out eight assists, and KU was guilty of just nine turnovers in the contest.

A few days later, Kansas lost again at home, 73-65, this time to seventh-ranked Oklahoma. Later in the year, highly regarded Duke—behind 21 points from guard Quin Snyder—handed KU its third Allen Fieldhouse defeat of the 1987-88 season.

The three home-court defeats dealt KU by Kansas State, Duke and Oklahoma would later serve as a testament to the team's magic spell.

Those losses were avenged in significant fashion as the Jayhawks' final three victims en route to the national championship were, in order, the Wildcats, Blue Devils and Sooners.

The Campers

They represent the center of a storm that ignites the earsplitting bedlam of each game in Allen Fieldhouse.

Frenzied and crazed, they are the most dedicated and colorful of those who witness basketball from November until March in Allen Fieldhouse.

For the sake of identity, they are KU students who—for more than two decades—have arrived many hours, most often days ahead, for the privilege of first choice in the prime student seating areas. In many respects, they are the energy that makes a Kansas basketball encounter an event to behold.

"Outside of the players in uniform, they are easily the most beloved students on campus in the hearts of anyone who serves as head coach at Kansas," said former athletics director Dr. Bob Frederick. "Just ask Larry Brown, Roy Williams and Bill Self."

Operating under group aliases such as SuperFans, Phog Fanatics, Bleacher Bums or Roy's Boys, they are true difference-makers in separating the game-day atmosphere in Allen Fieldhouse from other college gymnasiums around the country.

After long periods of time taking up residence on the hard floors of the north corridor of Allen Fieldhouse, they are unleashed through student entrances when the building opens on game day for the mad rush to seats behind the bench, the lower end zone sections and pockets of bleacher planks in the high reaches of the building.

Most arrive early, often days ahead of a scheduled game. The bigger the game, the earlier the campers arrive.

They come with books to study, newspapers to read, a deck of cards or, at times, a television monitor and video games.

When not studying, playing games or engrossed in conversation, the campers pass time attempting to coax comfort from the corridors of a building that was never designed as a nighttime sanctuary for relaxation.

Camping in Allen Fieldhouse.

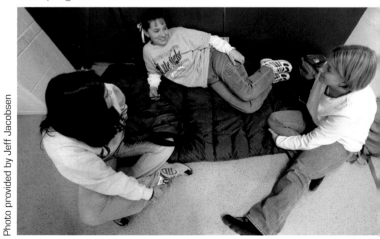

Photo provided by Jeff Jacobsen

Some campers bring pillows and blankets, while others lay prone on lawn chairs or air mattresses. Occasionally, creative students have been known to haul a vintage overstuffed chair to the designated area for the foremost in luxury camping. Those lacking in resources just rough it on the hard, cold, concrete floor.

Their bodies blend into the area like furniture during basketball season. Foot traffic for those who have business reasons to hike through the north corridor of Allen Fieldhouse means stepping over and around the mass of bodies.

Photo provided by Jeff Jacobsen

"There were times when it gave the appearance of a crowded homeless shelter," noted one long time athletic department employee. "You came in the morning for work and saw all of those kids asleep on the floor and you felt guilty if you made noise."

The self-imposed laws of camping start with a sheet of notebook paper taped to the door for a chronological sign-up of group names as they arrive on the scene. Campers have their own rules and serve as their own police. Random roll calls by camp leadership maintain order and preserve each group spot on the sign-up sheet.

Guidelines for camping call for a 6 a.m. arrival and a 10 p.m. departure. Each group represents a maximum of 30 students who take turns at the campsite.

The first groups to arrive are the first ones permitted into the arena when the building opens for game day. The prize of camping is the best in student seating.

Traditionally, Brown, Williams and Self have treated hungry campers with doughnuts in the morning and the occasional pizza at night. Williams, once a year, per-

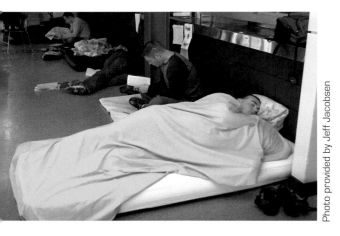

Photo provided by Jeff Jacobsen

sonally gave a guided tour to the campers through the KU locker room and coaches offices.

Since the start of the Brown coaching era in the early 1980s, student camping has been an important part of the ritual of Kansas basketball.

"It was a party," recalls Curtis Marsh, who was among the very first group of students involved in arriving early for games.

"That's why we enjoyed it, and that's why we put up with it, actually."

Camping for Kansas basketball can be traced to occasional games in the mid-1970s during the Ted Owens era. When Larry Brown brought renewed excitement to Allen Fieldhouse during the early 1980s, the custom of camping gained in length and popularity.

Students turn Allen Fieldhouse into a makeshift bedroom while camping for a prime seat.

Photo provided by Jeff Jacobsen

"There were three groups in the beginning. I was involved with one, Todd Gilmore another and Mark Hershman had his crew," recalled Mike Gentemann, who never missed a game in Allen Fieldhouse between 1984 and 1988.

"We pretty much invented camping out at Allen Fieldhouse. I remember in the pre-Danny Manning days a person could arrive by 4 p.m. for a 7 p.m. game and still sit behind the bench. In '84-85 that all changed and we started getting there at 7 a.m. for a 7 p.m. game or the night before for weekend games.

"As I recall," Gentemann added, "the Oklahoma home game in January during the 84-85 season was the first ever camp out en masse and started a tradition that has grown to what it is today."

Marsh remembers the late nights outside Allen Fieldhouse, when students pitched tents and laid claim to limited patches of green real estate outside the north doors.

Photo provided by Jeff Jacobsen

"We were restricted to be outside overnight," said Marsh. "At a certain point, obviously with kids staying all night long there was a concern for people getting frost bite and hypothermia. The athletics department was kind enough to roll out extension cords for us because they simply wanted us to be warm.

"I don't remember any occasion of someone becoming seriously ill, but certainly there was a chance of that. As a result, extension cords just appeared for our electric blankets and our electric heaters."

"But you can't expect the students to stop there," Marsh continued, "so you had Nintendos and televisions and stereos. But that created problems because we

Photo provided by Jeff Jacobsen

Roy Williams was a sweet sight when he brought doughnuts for campers.

were killing the power source in the building and someone from the department had to flip the circuit breakers pretty much every day we stayed."

Marsh and his camping partners turned the wait for entry into Allen Fieldhouse into a festive, party-like atmosphere.

"There was a point when the players lived in Jayhawker Towers and they would often come down and join us," said Marsh. "There were times we would bring stuff to barbecue. We tried to make a party out of it so people wouldn't mind staying 24 hours a day."

The camping rules were changed in the mid-1990s as athletic department officials grew concerned about issues related to electricity use and the possibility of fire. The practice of staying all night was discontinued and replaced with the 16-hour schedule.

"We took away the fire issues and reduced security concerns," said former KU assistant athletics director Floyd Temple, who kept a watchful eye over camping during his years in charge of athletics department facilities. "Hopefully, we put the students back in their normal living environment and didn't interfere with sleep that might impact class attendance,"

Darren Cook, who replaced Temple as director of facilities, remembers that the issue of changing camping procedures went to the desks of athletics director Bob Frederick and head basketball coach Roy Williams.

"We consulted with the campers first and let them vote on it," said Cook. "They had no problems making the adjustment. We consulted Bob and Coach Williams and they agreed that the change made sense.

"It was for safety reasons and academic reasons," added Cook. "It just had gotten too big and too difficult to control."

Gentemann and his friends relied heavily on the cooperation of Temple to make the early days of camping a success.

"In the beginning, the first camp-outs consisted of maybe 50 people and grew from there," recalled Gentemann. "I remember Floyd Temple taking pity on us and allowing us to sleep in the vestibule so we didn't freeze to death, and after Floyd got to know us even better, we actually got to start sleeping in a gated area just inside the building."

"Larry Brown started a little tradition of bringing Pyramid Pizzas at night and coffee with Joe's Donuts in the morning, but Floyd was the one who took care of us. He always made sure we had time to store our gear prior to game time before he opened the other doors."

Marsh and his friends helped form the SuperFan group that initiated many of the student traditions that continue to be prevalent in the stands at home games.

"We felt there were responsibilities that came with sitting behind the basket," said Marsh. "It was an interesting challenge, because if you have an opponent trying to shoot free throws you want one thing to be done in unison to distract the shooter and not a weird menagerie of things going on."

Marsh and his band of friends initiated actions in the lower-level seats that were imitated by students above them in an effort to distract the free throw shooter. The students, at that time, also started the custom of waving arms, jingling of keys, the "whoosh" yell on made free throws and the fan toss during time-outs.

Marsh was one of seven students who formed the launch power of Captain Jayhawk from 1988 through 1993.

Captain Jayhawk was an alias name for Joe Zielinski, and his character first came to life in Allen Fieldhouse at the Kansas-Duke game in 1988.

"We thought the 'Hey Cheer' would be a great song to throw people up in the air," said Marsh. "So, we sacrificed a basketball while we were waiting for the Duke game and put it on this guy's (Alex Logan) head. He was actually the original Captain Jayhawk, not Joe."

Zielinski later gained attention, not for his Captain Jayhawk routine, but for his attempt to make an impromptu change on an Allen Fieldhouse scoreboard.

"Joe tore his ACL while playing a pickup basketball game, which obviously hindered our ability to toss him into the air," said Marsh. "He was on temporary hiatus from being Captain Jayhawk and sitting in the section that is immediately above the entry way with the scoreboard and where the players come on the court.

"It was the unfortunate game against Long Beach State," recalled Marsh. "We were getting upset and Joe made the not-so-intelligent decision to lean over and take the "Home" placard and the "Guest" placard and switched them to make it look like we were winning.

"He got caught and was subsequently kicked out of the Fieldhouse for the rest of the season. We appealed the decision and Joe apologized, but the decision stood. We lost

Photo provided by KU Sports Information

Oklahoma's Wayman Tisdale fights off a significant distraction while shooting free throws.

Captain Jayhawk for the rest of the season."

Marsh, Gentemann, Gilmore and Hershman were among the pioneers who established the Kansas camping traditions. They all take pride in the fact that many of those traditions continue to be carried on by a new generation of campers at Allen Fieldhouse.

Beware of the Phog

Fans have carted an array of homemade signs and banners across the threshold of Allen Fieldhouse throughout its illustrious history. Some with simple statements, others elaborate in their design.

Paper and cardboard messages offering an assortment of messages generally have a brief life in the world of basketball gymnasiums. Treasures proudly displayed for a matter of hours, they normally become someone's trash problem soon after a game.

One special sign did avoid the Allen Fieldhouse trash heap and may have set a world record for banner longevity.

It has endured as a lasting fixture on the vast walls of the Sunflower State's cathedral of basketball, spreading out of the upper darkness of the building like a unique Kansas rainbow.

Its originators were a pair of fifth-year architectural students known affectionately as "Gumby" and "The Mauu." Devoted Kansas basketball fans, they first collaborated on the manufacturing of a banner while seated in a professional practice class one February afternoon.

"Gumby" is Todd Gilmore, who envisioned the nine-word message: "Pay heed all who enter: Beware of The Phog."

"The Mauu's" given name is Mike Gentemann, and it was his distinctive lettering skills that provided the banner with its unique style and personality.

"We weren't face painters, TV camera show offs or big sign wavers," noted Gentemann, who, like his partner in banner design, has carved a successful career as an architect.

Basketballs were not the only thing launched during a game in Allen Fieldhouse.

"Gumby and I had done one other banner together in 1985 for the Kentucky game and I had done a banner—'On the Sixth Day God Created Manning'—for a school-sponsored contest in 1984 that took first place and the prize was a keg of beer."

Both were regulars at Jayhawk home games, brothers in a union of team devotion but seated in separate sections of the building.

Gentemann and his crew of friends were dedicated beyond reproach during the years of Larry Brown and Danny Manning. They occupied the same bleacher seats in the same order—three rows behind the KU bench—for every home game between 1985-88.

Gilmore, equal to Gentemann in his zest for Jayhawk basketball, had his own posse of ardent KU fans to anchor the student section in the north end zone four rows up during the same period of time.

Photo provided by Jeff Jacobsen

With their career as Jayhawk students winding down, the upcoming Duke game represented one of the last visits to Allen Fieldhouse for Gilmore and Gentemann. It represented one of the last opportunities for the two passionate fans to stoke the Allen Fieldhouse inferno of emotion.

Gilmore had been contemplating the production of a banner message for several days as he and other Kansas fans awaited the much anticipated arrival of Duke for an unusual late-season nonconference game in Allen Fieldhouse.

With the basketball game overriding his thoughts in class, Gilmore scribbled the nine words on a notepad and shared his vision with Gentemann who was seated nearby.

A special partnership in the business of banner-making evolved with Gilmore as author and Gentemann agreeing to be illustrator.

Fueled by pizza and beer, the two inspired architecture majors gathered a supporting cast of basketball fanatics and spent the majority of one evening with paint brushes in a hallway of Marvin Hall. Collectively, they created a regal piece of art that has since become a staple of the Allen Fieldhouse landscape.

"Beware of the Phog" first appeared on the south wall between the signature windows of Allen Fieldhouse in late February of 1988 at the Kansas–Duke basketball game. The nine-word message has been on display on the limestone walls of the structure for every game since its debut.

To put its uniqueness in perspective, the 35-foot-long, six-feet-high banner was painted on a canvas of 10 pilfered dormitory shower curtains and was originally held together by straight pins used to make foam core models in architecture classes.

"All of the materials, except the shower curtains, were things we scrounged from our studio supplies," recalled Gentemann.   "It wouldn't have been like us to go out and purchase anything special.

"Gumby deserves the credit," said Gentemann. "I would say that his idea padded the pockets of many a t-shirt vendor over the years and it is still cool to see close ups of the banner on ESPN games or hear the announcers refer to Allen Fieldhouse as 'The Phog.' "

It was during Gilmore and Gentemann's watch as student fans that Allen Fieldhouse traditions such as camping, the "whoosh" yell on made free throws and the tossing of a student in the air at timeouts evolved.

Gilmore was among the first to camp overnight inside the building for games. He had a deep appreciation for the basketball tradition at KU, but felt Allen Fieldhouse needed its own special branding in the form of a nickname.

"The 'Pay heed' thing kind of came out of nowhere," said Gilmore. "The 'Beware of the Phog' was a play on the ads for a John Carpenter movie called 'The Fog' and in the ads, they used that line. I just changed the spelling.

"It really goes back to thinking it was cool for stadiums to really have an identity. New Mexico had 'The Pit' and Clemson had 'Death Valley.' I thought Allen Fieldhouse should have something like that. I never dreamed it would take off like it did."

Hoping to amplify an image already steeped in tradition, Gilmore and Gentemann brought together their respective friends to bond for an evening of beer and banner making.

"We bought some beer, recruited some help and then took over the hallway in Marvin Hall (Architecture building) to get the job done," said Gentemann. "I'd say we had eight people working on it off and on. Marvin Hall was the only place long enough to lay everything out. I don't know that we ever intended it to be as large or long as it turned out, we just fit it to the length of material available.

"Regarding the origins of the shower curtains, hopefully the statute of limitations has run out on this, so I'll tell the story," added Gentemann.

"We assigned jobs to our various accomplices. Some pinned the sheets, some painted, but the most crucial was the material.

"We sent our friend, we'll call him 'Kippen,' on a scavenger hunt and he promptly returned with more material than we had hoped. Let's just say that the residents of McCollum Hall woke up the next day to find their showers had no curtains. I don't know that they were clean, but they were sturdy, dry and the eyelets made them custom-made for hanging."

Once the paint had been applied, all that remained was waiting and hoping the shower curtain canvas would be dry in time for the game.

The Beware of the Phog banner first appeared in 1988 and was painted on shower curtains.

Photo provided by Jeff Jacobsen

"We put it in our design studio for the night to dry and we went home," noted Gilmore. "It took a long time for the paint to dry, so there was no time to have it sewn together before the game. We were worried how it would hold up, but luckily it didn't come apart. That would have been a disaster."

Gilmore and Gentemann were among the early camper arrivals at Allen Fieldhouse the night prior to the Duke game. They carried with them the large shower curtain banner and paid a visit to Floyd Temple, in charge of game-day management of Allen Fieldhouse.

"I wanted to help them get that banner hung because I was a big fan of Doc Allen," said Temple. "As I remember, they had some problems getting it hung from the rafters and needed some assistance."

With the paint still fresh on the banner, Gilmore, Gentemann and friends selected the north wall of Allen Fieldhouse and had strung a 100-foot rope through the top of the shower curtains. The plan called for the banner to be tied between the catwalks in the upper reaches of the roof area, but building policy prevented students from reaching that height.

"We got around the problem by tying a shoe—which belonged to a friend named Brad Oliver—to the end of the rope and throwing it over the catwalk and then tying it down by the last row of seats," said Gilmore. "On the second toss the shoe came loose and landed right on top of the catwalk."

Although it required the sacrifice of Oliver's shoe (a KU maintenance worker retrieved it after the game), the banner was now on display.

"After we tied it down, we realized that the middle was too heavy and sagged so badly you couldn't read it," recalled Gilmore. "We were at a loss what to do when

Floyd (Temple) pointed out a rope hanging down in just the right place, which even had a clip on the end of it. It held the middle up perfectly."

The contingent of banner makers, including one wearing a single shoe, completed the task. Duke coach Mike Krzyzewski and his Blue Devils were the first visitors to Allen Fieldhouse to be exposed the warning: "Beware of the Phog."

Among those dressed in a Duke uniform for the 1988 game was a young guard named Quin Snyder, who, later in his coaching career, would have to face the banner again as head coach at Missouri.

"The first time we put it up, I remember noticing how it blew around a little because of the air supply ducts at the top of the seats," recalled Gilmore. "It kind of made it come alive. It was like Phog Allen was there moving it around himself."

Duke won the game, 74-70, in overtime. The loss was later avenged as the Jayhawks defeated the Blue Devils in the semifinals of the national championship, 66-59, before beating Oklahoma two nights later for the NCAA Championship.

The banner was removed following the Duke game. But Phog Allen's granddaughter and Lawrence resident—Judy Morris—was interested in seeing it return to the north wall on a permanent basis. Her lobbying efforts with Temple and the KU athletic department leadership scored points.

Temple was already a fan of the banner as were other athletic department administrators. Its message, they concluded, fit perfectly with the aura of Allen Fieldhouse.

Gilmore got word that Temple wanted the banner as a fixture in the building. He quickly went to friend and architectural classmate Donna Griffin to undertake the massive job of sewing the shower curtain pieces together. With the help this time of athletic department staff members, the banner was returned to its original location where it remained until the summer of 1999.

Kansas won the NCAA championship that season, bringing another significant banner to Allen Fieldhouse. Manning took his immense skills to the NBA and Brown also departed Allen Fieldhouse to coach once again in professional basketball.

Gilmore and Gentemann received their sheepskins that spring and left their seats in Allen Fieldhouse for a new generation of basketball fanatics and banner makers.

They exited Lawrence with the satisfaction of knowing one of their first designs is easily one of their most memorable.

"It's almost beyond words and it's been long enough now that it's even a bit surreal," said Gilmore. "I still get a big kick out of seeing it on TV and hearing people talk about it."

Gentemann, who joins Gilmore and his other KU alumni friends for a yearly reunion to "drink beer and talk about Kansas basketball," credits his partner in the project for the banners' meaningful life and place in Allen Fieldhouse history.

"To toot his horn, it's a legacy Gumby left on an elite program steeped in tradition," said Gentemann. "It's still rewarding to tell alumni I meet about my part in the creation of the banner—though they probably think I'm lying."

The original "Beware of the Phog" banner greeted visitors to Allen Fieldhouse through the 1998-99 season. Years of hanging on the wall in the ancient building, however, took its toll on the shower curtain material.

"We noticed that it was decaying badly, almost to the point of coming apart at the seams," noted former Allen Fieldhouse director of facilities Darren Cook. "It just couldn't hold up any longer. "We decided that we wanted to preserve it for future display in our athletic hall of fame. To leave it hanging would risk it falling apart completely."

The athletic department carefully removed the banner in the summer of 1999, but had a replica made in January 2000 for display on the north wall of the building.

The original banner is now folded and stored in Allen Fieldhouse, awaiting the time it will once again stir emotions as an artifact in the athletic hall of fame.

The banner's message does ring true for opposing teams. Heading into the 2004-05 season, Kansas basketball teams were 215-19 at home with the words—Pay heed all who enter: Beware of the Phog—hanging overhead.

"The Day After"

Normally, when Allen Fieldhouse is shown on television, it is the site of exciting basketball and wildly cheering fans. The band is playing, people are cheering on their Jayhawks and the floor is full of healthy people.

However, the one time the building was used in a feature-length movie as a backdrop, it was the scene of sadness, despair and lost hope—much more serious than most opponents feel when they leave the court in Allen Fieldhouse.

In the movie, Allen Fieldhouse and the city of Lawrence became obliterated, causing actor John Lithgow to utter the words, "This is Lawrence, Kansas. Is anybody out there? Anybody at all?"

Of course, that was all part of the ABC made-for-TV movie *The Day After,* which aired in November 1983 and was filmed almost entirely in Lawrence. This movie brought actors such as Lithgow, Jason Robards, Steve Guttenberg and Amy Madigan to the Midwest. What trip to Lawrence, though is complete without a visit to Allen Fieldhouse? The producers thought the same, and so the historic basketball arena played a prominent role as an infirmary in the aftermath of the nuclear explosion, in one of the more moving scenes of the movie.

A page from the *Jayhawker* Yearbook.
Photo provided by Kenneth Spencer Research Library

Approximately 1,200 KU students were up before dawn the morning of September 7, 1982, to make the trek to Allen Fieldhouse and serve as extras in the movie. The students had been encouraged not to bathe for as long as the people with whom they lived could stand it prior to that Saturday morning to add to the "authenticity" of their acting parts as extras.

According to the 1983 *Jayhawker* Yearbook, the fieldhouse scene made one of the more poignant statements of the movie: "Caked in mud and grease, dressed in rags, and bathed in blood, students filled Allen Fieldhouse, September 7. These students were nuclear fallout victims and had come to the fieldhouse, turned into a make-shift hospital. In perhaps the most fantastic single scene in the picture, Steve Guttenberg weaved his way through the ragged, dying crowd, looking for a girl he had met. As one took in the miserable mess, the filthy bodies, and the feelings of despair you could almost hear the silent prayers of many that a holocaust like this would never become a reality."

Jon Niccum of the *Lawrence Journal-World,* wrote in his 20th anniversary article of the filming *The Day After* about the number of extras needed for the movie, "Among the more memorable of these assemblies was for a sequence near the finale where hundreds of ailing victims crammed into Allen Fieldhouse, which was the only place left on campus big enough to accommodate so many wounded."

Lawrence attorney Charles Whitman said in Niccom's anniversary article in November 2003, "I persist in the conviction that part of the reason this film struck such a nerve is that Kansas is an icon. It may be an icon everywhere. It partly has to do with *The Wizard of Oz*. It partly has to do with the idea that that's where your mother lives. Everybody's grandma lives in Kansas. The idea that nuclear war could happen here was just too much for people to deal with."

The movie, which was originally scheduled to be four hours in length and shown over two nights, was edited and aired as a one-night, two-hour movie November 20, 1983. According to television ratings, it was watched by half of the adult population—nearly 100 million—that night. That was the largest viewing audience for a made-for-TV-movie up to that point in time.

It provoked numerous discussions both locally and nationally as hotlines were set up for people to

An unusual sight on the Allen Fieldhouse court.

Photo provided by Lawrence *Journal-World*

call. ABC distributed viewers' guides prior to the showing as a way to help people deal with the subject matter. Ted Koppel of ABC's *Nightline* fame hosted a live panel discussion following the movie that night, consisting of comments from, among others, Dr. Carl Sagan, Henry Kissinger, Robert McNamara, William F. Buckley and George Schultz.

The production was nominated for 12 Emmys and won two. It pumped more than $1 million into the Lawrence economy during the filming with all of the crew in town. It also made a lasting impact on the nation in dealing with the possibility of a nuclear attack.

In contrast to the grimness of the movie, the atmosphere inside Allen Fieldhouse returned to form a little more than two months later, when the Jayhawks opened the home portion of their 1982-83 schedule with a 91-74 win over U.S. International.

The Fieldhouse was turned into an infirmary for the movie *The Day After.*

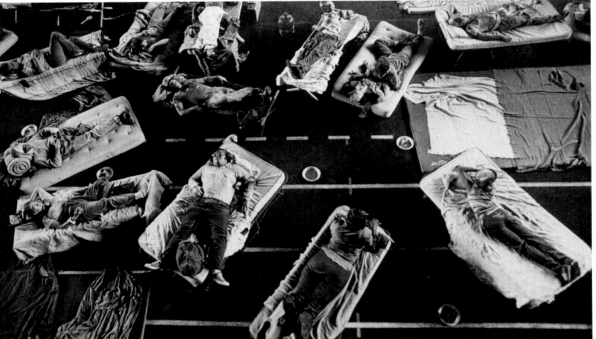

Photo provided by Lawrence *Journal-World*

TIES

Home Also for Volleyball, Wrestling, Gymnastics, High School Championships and More

While Allen Fieldhouse is best known as a college basketball venue, there has been a wide variety of other athletic competitions in the 50-year history of the building. It first opened as a basketball and track complex, but numerous other events have been conducted over time.

The wrestling program at Kansas, which started with 27 student-athletes mostly from the varsity football team, began putting its mats down on the fieldhouse floor in 1963-64, its inaugural season. The wrestlers would practice in one of the gyms in old Robinson Gymnasium, the predecessor to Hoch Auditorium as the home of the Jayhawk basketball team. KU's grapplers hosted their first competition February 8, 1964, when rival Kansas State came to town for a dual meet. The Wildcats prevailed 26-6.

The men's gymnastics program for the most part conducted its practices and competitions in old Robinson Gymnasium. However, KU played host to the Big Eight Conference Championship in Allen Fieldhouse, March 18-19, 1966.

"In 1966, that (conference championship) was a big thing for us," said former coach Bob Lockwood. "The sport was new. We had a facility being built that would become new Robinson, so there was a lot of excitement over that; the Big Eight had recognized gymnastics as a sport, so it was a big deal. We had the support of a lot of other people to put this meet on. And we had a real successful meet as a team on top of everything."

KU finished second in the first Big Eight Championship meet, and Kent Dobbins placed first in the all-around competition. The Jayhawks again hosted the league meet the following March.

The first women's sport to compete in competition on the court in Allen Fieldhouse was basketball, beginning with the 1973-74 season, followed by the volleyball team in 1976. KU's first volleyball match was contested against rival Missouri, October 19, 1976. For the next four years, Kansas played the majority of its contests in Allen. The team played in Robinson Gymnasium, though, when conflicts arose with the start of basketball season. Beginning in 1980, all home events were contested in Allen Fieldhouse until the construction of the Horesji Family Athletic Complex in 1998.

"It was definitely a challenge in those first years we played in Allen Fieldhouse," explained Lockwood, who took over the volleyball coaching reins with the 1979 season. "It was very difficult because we didn't practice in the fieldhouse; we practiced in one of the gyms in Robinson. The air currents are different in the fieldhouse from the ones in Robinson. But it was nice to be able to utilize all of the extra room around the court. Allen Fieldhouse was definitely a step up for us. It was a prestige thing to say you played in the fieldhouse."

KU played host to its first high school state boys basketball tournament competition in 1964 (Class AA championships). Wyandotte High School defeated Shawnee Mission North for the state championship behind future Jayhawk George Yarnevich's 50-point, 19-rebound performance March 14, 1964. The Boys' Class AA championship returned to Allen Fieldhouse in March 1965, 1966, 1967 and 1968. With larger high school enrollments and more class divisions, KU hosted the Class 5A state championship in 1969.

In 1970, the Kansas State High School Activities Association began a rotation for the larger-class schools with the state tournaments among Allen Fieldhouse, Ahearn Fieldhouse at Kansas State University and Henry Levitt Arena at Wichita State University. Kansas hosted the 5A class championship in 1971 and 4A class championship in 1972. The Class 4A championship returned in 1975 with Salina Central winning the title.

With the rotation and scheduling conflicts with Kansas' NCAA Regional Tournament games, it was 1984 before KU was able to host the championships again. In March 1984, KU hosted both the boys' and girls' state 6A championships with both teams from Lawrence High School playing for the championship. The Lawrence boys, led by future Jayhawk All-American Danny Manning, lost by a single point, 50-49, to a Wyandotte High School team that featured future Kansas football standout Willie Vaughn and future Oklahoma basketball star William Davis. The Lawrence girls defeated Derby High School 49-48 for the championship title. KU hosted the 6A state championship through March 1987.

Two sports with little notoriety debuted in Allen Fieldhouse in the 1960s. It was the scene of a Pershing Rifles Drill Meet February 26, 1966, which became a doubleheader when the men's basketball team played later that night. The fieldhouse floor was the site for a Judo Exhibition May 2, 1966. Neither sport made a return appearance to the facility.

The Harlem Globetrotters, the first professional team to play a game in Allen Fieldhouse, appeared February 10, 1987. The Globetrotters, who would later feature the first female on the team—Kansas graduate Lynette Woodard—defeated the Washington Generals in that game.

The Los Angeles Clippers and New Jersey Nets played an exhibition game October 20, 1988, in the first NBA game in Allen Fieldhouse. It was set up to be a homecoming for Danny Manning, who was the No. 1 pick in the NBA draft that year. However, Manning and the Clippers had not come to contract terms and thus he did not play. Michael Jordan and the Chicago Bulls came to town October 11, 1997, to play against the Seattle Supersonics. Former Jayhawk head coach Larry Brown returned to Allen Fieldhouse October 18, 2001, as his Philadelphia 76ers met the Utah Jazz in another NBA exhibition game. Brown sat on the visiting team bench and the Sixers lost by a 95-70 count before 10,100 fans. Prior to the game Jayhawk head coach Roy Williams presented Brown a KU letterjacket. It was also a homecoming for former Jayhawk Greg Ostertag, who played for the Jazz.

Other elite athletes who have displayed their athletic ability in the fieldhouse include those participating on the 1987 Junior World Basketball Team. That team included future collegiate standouts Kevin Pritchard (KU), Larry Johnson (UNLV), Robert Brickey (Duke), and was coached by Larry Brown in an exhibition game July 15, 1987, against former KU players, including Darnell Valentine, Cedric Hunter, Mark Turgeon, Greg Dreiling, Ron Kellogg and Carl Henry.

The AAU National Junior Olympics hosted the 22nd annual event in Lawrence in August 1988, and opened their ceremonies at Allen Fieldhouse. The opening ceremonies for the Sunflower State Games were first staged at Allen Fieldhouse July 26-28, 1990. The Games basketball competition also took place inside the Fieldhouse. The U.S. Volleyball Association had a tour stop at Allen Fieldhouse April 29-30, 1989, for its national tournament.

The University of Kansas added women's rowing as a varsity sport in 1996. The team recorded a "first" for Allen Fieldhouse when it hosted an indoor regatta February 12, 2000. The invitational drew teams from all over the Midwest to the fieldhouse floor to race on the ergometer machines.

Among the numerous other events of the amateur variety in Allen Fieldhouse are basketball game fund-raisers, barnstorming games put on by graduating basketball seniors and former players, and camps and clinics for every sport sponsored at KU.

Allen Fieldhouse Moments

1980s

March 12, 1980 – First Women's Postseason Tournament Game
Kansas hosted Cheyney State in the AIAW Sectional game ... It marked the first-ever women's postseason tournament game in Allen Fieldhouse ... With Lynette Woodard leading the way, KU won the game, 75-66.

January 7, 1981 – Lynette Woodard Sets AIAW Career Scoring Mark
The Kansas women's basketball team hosted 13th-ranked Stephen F. Austin, but it was senior All-American Lynette Woodard who grabbed the spotlight ... Woodard's medium-range jumper at the 18:37 mark of the first half gave her 3,206 points to move her past former Tennessee standout Cindy Brogdon (1979) into first place on the all-time AIAW scoring list ... play was stopped and Woodard was greeted with a bouquet of flowers and a surprise visit by her parents ... KU went on to post an 80-59 victory in the game behind Woodard's 24 points.

January 17, 1982 – Finals of the Preseason Big Eight Women's Tournament
Before a KU women's basketball record crowd of 3,750, the fifth-ranked Jayhawks won the preseason conference tournament, 85-60, over 15th-ranked Kansas State as Lynette Woodard scored 36 points and pulled down 17 rebounds ... Woodard was named MVP of the tournament.

January 21, 1981 – Kansas 63, Missouri 55
Allen Fieldhouse was packed to the rafters for the annual showdown with Missouri and head coach Norm Stewart ... standout MU center Steve Stiponovich in late December claimed he had been shot in the upper left arm by an intruder in his apartment ... he later admitted that he had made up the story ... KU students unfurled bull's-eye targets and some brought cap pistols and during the playing of the National Anthem there were volleys fired when the lyrics got around to "... the bombs bursting in air."

December 12, 1981 – Kentucky 77, Kansas 74

The Jayhawks opened the season with a 74-67 loss to North Carolina in Charlotte, N.C., but came back to beat Arizona State, Texas Southern, Michigan State and Arizona in four consecutive home games at Allen Fieldhouse ... Kansas had a 17-game home-court winning streak broken, however, when No. 2-ranked Kentucky took a 77-74 overtime victory.

January 16, 1982 – Kansas 77, Oklahoma State 72

Kansas opened the home portion of its conference season hosting Oklahoma State and edged the Cowboys, 77-72 ... OSU made the game close, in part, thanks to 14 points off the bench from guard Bill Self, who was playing his first game against a school he would later serve as head coach.

February 26, 1983 – Kansas State 70, Kansas 63

A jam-packed Allen Fieldhouse crowd of 15,200 was disappointed as Kansas dropped a 70-63 decision to rival K-State in the 200th meeting of the schools ... the win marked the Wildcats' fifth straight in the rivalry.

November 14, 1983 – *The Day After*

Allen Fieldhouse was used as an on-location site for production for the made-for-television movie *The Day After.*

December 3, 1983 – Kansas 75, Morehead State 57

After opening the season with two road games, new head coach Larry Brown walked into Allen Fieldhouse for the first time as head coach and orchestrated a win over Morehead State ... Kelly Knight led the way with 19 points.

February 22, 1984 – Oklahoma 92, Kansas 82

Playing before a home crowd of 14,400 against the Oklahoma Sooners and head coach Billy Tubbs, the Jayhawks dropped a nail-biting 92-82 overtime decision and lost important ground in the conference race ... the game went into overtime as KU's Calvin Thompson sank a 40-foot jumper at the end of regulation ... OU, getting 31 points from Tim McCalister and 28 from Wayman Tisdale, outscored KU 18-8 in overtime ... the crowd booed the Sooners as they celebrated the victory on the floor, calling timeout with just eight seconds remaining in the game and later cutting down the Allen Fieldhouse nets ... in his postgame comments, Larry Brown noted: "The world is round." ... Seventeen days later, KU would get revenge in a 79-78 win over the Sooners in the finals of the conference post-season tournament.

February 9, 1985 – Kansas 75, Memphis State 71
KU hosted No. 3-ranked Memphis State and head coach Dana Kirk in a sold-out Allen Fieldhouse for a memorable encounter ... Ron Kellogg had 30 points to lead the way, marking his fourth straight Saturday of 30 or more points in a Kansas game ... Danny Manning was held to just five points in 21 minutes of action.

September, 1985 – New Lower Level Bleachers
The 30-year-old original wooden lower-level bleachers in Allen Fieldhouse were replaced with permanent metal seating just prior to the start of the 1985 season at a cost of $250,000 ... New retractable bleachers were added on the east and west sides of the building, and permanent bleachers were constructed in the north and south ends ... The changes in the building were made available, in part, following the completion of the Anschutz Sports Pavilion, which takes over housing of indoor track.

October 14, 1985 – Late Night With Larry Brown
The inaugural Late Night event in basketball history was staged in Allen Fieldhouse and attracted an estimated crowd of 6,000 fans ... the primary attraction was a 40-minute scrimmage with KU students—picked from an essay and poster contest—serving as team coaches ... Danny Manning was the leading scorer with 18 points.

December 14, 1985 – Kansas 83, Kentucky 66
It was a season of great expectations as Larry Brown, in his third year on the KU bench, led the Jayhawks to a 7-1 start as Kentucky rolled into town ... the Wildcats owned a nine-game winning streak over Kansas dating back to the 1974 season ... UK was under the direction of first-year head coach Eddie Sutton and the Cats arrived with a sparkling 5-0 mark ... the game, however, was never close as KU hit 61.5 percent of its field goal attempts in an impressive victory over Kentucky ... Danny Manning was the top point producer with 22 points.

January 25, 1986 – Kansas 71, Louisville 69

A national television audience saw one of the great games of the college season as the two future Final Four teams went back and forth for 40 minutes ... KU's seven-foot center, Greg Dreiling, picked up two fouls in the first 19 seconds of the game and spent the remainder of the first half on the bench and the Cardinals held a five-point advantage at halftime ... Dreiling opened play in the second stanza with three consecutive dunks ... he ended the game with 18 points in leading KU to a 71-69 victory ... the win tied a school record as the 28th consecutive home-court victory.

February 11, 1986 – Kansas 100, Missouri 66

Danny Manning scored 27 points in leading KU to a 100-66 win over Missouri at Allen Fieldhouse ... the 36-point victory margin marked the most ever by a KU team over the Tigers in Lawrence.

October 14, 1986 – Second Annual Late Night With Larry Brown

A crowd of 12,000 fans was treated to an appearance by David Lettermen foil Larry "Bud" Melman at the first basketball practice of the season.

November 29, 1986 – Kansas 86, UT Martin 69

The Jayhawks opened the year with a 86-69 victory over UT Martin, winning for the 34th consecutive time in Allen Fieldhouse as Danny Manning contributed 26 points and 15 rebounds ... Kevin Pritchard made his first appearance in a Jayhawk uniform and converted the first three-point field goal in Allen Fieldhouse.

February 8, 1987 – Kansas 70, Notre Dame 60

Notre Dame, fresh from an upset win over No. 1-ranked North Carolina, arrived in Lawrence looking for another upset victory ... Danny Manning scored 40 points and KU prevailed 70-60 ... KU entered the game minus starting point guard Cedric Hunter, who was out with an ankle sprain ... Mark Turgeon moved into the starting lineup and held Irish standout David Rivers to just 13 points.

February 10, 1987 – Harlem Globetrotters vs. Washington Generals

The Globetrotters continued their win streak by defeating the Washington Generals.

December 1, 1987 – Kansas 94, Pomona-Pitzer 38

Kansas broke a Big Eight Conference record for consecutive home-court victories, winning its 49th straight game, with a victory over Pomona-Pitzer ... KU shot a school-record 76 percent in the victory and limited the Sagehens to just 13 second-half points ... Pomona-Pitzer was coached by future NBA head coach Gregg Popovich, who had spent the previous season on sabbatical working on Larry Brown's staff.

January 30, 1988 – Kansas State 72, Kansas 61

Mitch Richmond's 35-point performance sparked a Kansas State rally as the Wildcats came from 10 points down to beat KU, 72-61, and end the Allen Fieldhouse record 55-game home-court winning streak in front of a full-house crowd of 15,800.

February 22, 1988 – Duke 74, Kansas 70

Sixth-ranked Duke erased a six-point Kansas overtime lead to defeat the Jayhawks, 74-70, in front of a full house and a national television audience ... Danny Manning led KU with 31 points, while Duke was led by Qunn Snyder with 21 points ... a group of KU students unveiled a large banner made from shower curtains that read: "Pay heed all who enter: Beware of the Phog."

March 5, 1988 – Kansas 75, Oklahoma State 57

Seniors Danny Manning, Chris Piper and Archie Marshall, along with manager Bill Pope, were honored in pregame ceremonies prior to their swan song at Allen Fieldhouse as the Jayhawks rolled against Oklahoma State behind 31 points from Manning ... Marshall, who had suffered a season-ending knee injury earlier in the year, was inserted into the lineup against the Cowboys at the 1:33 mark in the second half for one brief, final appearance and attempted, but missed, a three-point shot in one of the most emotional moments in Allen Fieldhouse history.

March 16, 1988 – Women Host First NCAA Tournament Game

KU downed Middle Tennessee State, 81-75, while playing host to its first ever NCAA Tournament game in Allen Fieldhouse ... Lisa Baker led the way with 28 points while Lisa Braddy contributed eight assists.

April 8, 1988 – Larry Brown Press Conference

In one of the most memorable press conferences in Allen Fieldhouse history, head coach Larry Brown walked into Allen Fieldhouse at 3 p.m. on the Tuesday after guiding KU to the NCAA title, and announced to the media and some 200 interested fans that he would remain as head coach at Kansas and not take a position as head coach at UCLA.

October 14, 1988 – Late Night With Roy Williams

The first Late Night event for Roy Williams was successful, as 10,000 fans were on hand to welcome the new head coach to Allen Fieldhouse ... among the highlights of the night was Alonzo Jamison breaking the backboard support during scrimmage warm-ups.

December 1, 1988 – Kansas 98, Seattle 65

The Roy Williams era in Allen Fieldhouse started on a successful note as KU downed Seattle ... Mark Randall led the Jayhawks with 31 points in front of 13,500 fans.

January 3, 1989 – Kansas 115, Brown 45

With seven players scoring in double figures, Kansas rolled past Brown, 115-45, as Milt Newton led the scoring parade with 23 points ... the 70-point scoring margin was the highest in school history.

January 7, 1989 – Kansas 127, Iowa State 82

The Jayhawks set a school record for most points scored in a conference game in humbling Iowa State before a packed house in Allen Fieldhouse ... nine different Jayhawks scored in double figures—also a school record—and KU set a new school standard by scoring 71 points in the second half in Roy Williams' conference coaching debut ... some 80 former Jayhawk players were also in attendance for a special lettermen's reunion.

February 25, 1989 – Kansas 111, Colorado 83

KU became just the third college basketball program in history to record 1,400 all-time wins when it downed Colorado ... the Jayhawks connected on an amazing 86.7

percent of their second-half field goal attempts ... Kansas hit an impressive 70.4per-cent (38-54) of their field goal attempts for the game.

October 14, 1989 – Late Night With Roy Williams
For the first time, organizers charged a $5 admission fee for Late Night to offset expenses for two bands that performed on a massive sound stage.

December 9, 1989 – Kansas 150, Kentucky 95
It was a record-breaking day for Kansas as the Jayhawks rolled past Kentucky, 150-95, in KU's highest scoring game in history ... KU led at the half, 80-61, over the Wildcats, who were under the direction of first-year head coach Rick Pitino ... Terry Brown led KU with 31 points, including seven-of-10 from three-point land, while play-ing just 19 minutes ... the win was KU's 350th in Allen Fieldhouse.

The Nineties
One of the Nation's Elite Programs

How dominating were Kansas teams during the decade of the 1990s? Under the steady leadership of Roy Williams, Kansas won or shared seven conference championships during the 10-year span, went to the NCAA Tournament each of those seasons and was ranked in the top 10 nationally in seven of the final Associated Press polls. The Jayhawks won 25 or more games eight times during the nineties.

> "THE FIRST NIGHT WALKING IN THERE ONTO THE FIELDHOUSE COURT, WALKING THROUGH THE TUNNEL, I GOT COLD CHILLS. AND 10 YEARS LATER I STILL GET COLD CHILLS EVERY NIGHT THAT I WALK OUT THERE.
> —*Roy Williams on the eve of KU's 100 years of basketball celebration*

Kansas set an Allen Fieldhouse record for consecutive home-court victories, winning 62 straight games between 1993 and 1998.

Williams orchestrated KU to 138 wins in the school's 148 games in Allen Fieldhouse during the decade, including five undefeated seasons at home.

It was a decade in which Kansas paid tribute to its great players and great teams of past years. The jerseys of Paul Endacott (1992), Charles T. Black (1992), Charles B. Black (1992), Clyde Lovellette (1992), B.H. Born (1992), Wilt Chamberlain (1998), Lynette Woodard (1992) and Danny

Roy Williams tossed a KU t-shirt in the stands to signal his appearance in Allen Fieldhouse.

Manning (1992) were officially retired and displayed from the rafters of Allen Fieldhouse.

Various milestones were reached during the decade. Cumulative Allen Fieldhouse attendance topped the five-million mark, coming in its 37th season in a 77-64 win over Oklahoma State, March 2, 1992. On December 20, 1993, the Jayhawks celebrated the 500th game in the building with a 101-60 win over Furman. A fixture in the building, the Longines clock that had adorned the south wall above the last row of seats, was moved to the west wall. The move was made to make way for the newly retired jerseys. KU celebrated its 40th anniversary in Allen Fieldhouse, defeating Oklahoma State, 78-62, March 5, 1995, to clinch the Big Eight Conference title. To recognize the event, a large replica of a birthday cake with four large candles and the number 40 printed on it was wheeled out on the court at halftime. The 16,300 fans in attendance sang "Happy Birthday," led by several member of the Allen family and former Jayhawk letterwinners.

The Longines clock is an Allen Fieldhouse fixture.

Photo provided by Kenneth Spencer Research Library

A statue of Phog Allen, located in front of Allen Field-house, was unveiled and dedicated at the start of the 1997-98 season and the Fieldhouse court was named in honor of Dr. James Naismith, the inventor of the game and KU's first head coach. Kansas defeated Santa Clara, 99-73, November 14, 1997 the night of the dedication. Also, former All-American Ray Evans had his jersey retired and hung in the Fieldhouse rafters that season.

Wilt Chamberlain returned in 1998 for the official retirement of his jersey and gave a moving halftime speech while wearing his KU letter-man's jacket. More than 270 former players returned during the 1997-

98 season to celebrate the 100th anniversary of Kansas basketball and the school paid tribute to its 10 Final Four teams. A bit of chicanery almost caused the celebration to be a bit less festive. In early December of 1997, Kansas officials noted that the retired jerseys of Manning and Woodard, plus three 100-Year Anniversary banners were heisted from the rafters. On January 23, 1998, a shipment from Champaign, Illinois, received by the

Photo provided by Jeff Jacobsen

A new tribute to Phog Allen came in 1998.

Kansas athletic department contained the missing jerseys and banners. Authorities speculated the heist had been part of a fraternity prank.

The nineties also served as an important decade in the women's basketball program. Marian Washington directed the Jayhawks to three conference championships and eight NCAA tournament appearances.

Several facility upgrades were instituted in the 1990s, beginning with the addition of the building's fourth scoreboard in January 1991. One year later, a new basketball court was installed for the start of the 1991-92 campaign. The wood surface covered not only the court, but also the synthetic area that had been added in 1985. It was 17,000 square feet and allowed for a greater area to practice. Unlike its other wooden predecessors, this court was inlaid and permanent in nature. It sits on a foam base to provide spring for the players.

In the fall of 1994, a $1.9 million project to bring the facility into compliance with the fire code included the installation of a sprinkler system and the creation of stairs and ramps. An additional 541 seats were added, bringing capacity to the present 16,300. In 1996-97, the coaches' and team locker rooms were enlarged and renovated at a cost of $230,000. The Stewart Horejsi family of Salina, Kansas, provided funding for that portion of the project.

The last major renovations to Allen Fieldhouse were completed prior to the 1998-99 season when $4 million was invested in new and larger restrooms, concession stands and an elevator on the south end of the building. The remaining portion of the tartan track was removed and replaced with a solid surface.

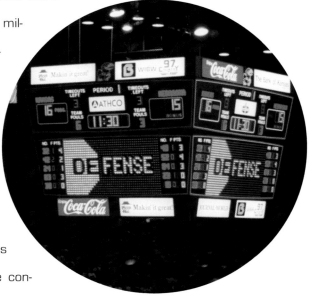

Photo provided by Jeff Jacobsen

The athletic complex at Kansas continued to grow in the 1990s. The need for additional offices, locker room space, updated training facilities and an academic support center resulted in the construction of the $8.5 million Wagnon Student Athlete Center. Completed in 1993, it integrated the Parrott Athletic Complex structure. Named in honor of the Wagnon family from Wichita, the building connected Allen Fieldhouse to Anschutz Sports Pavilion. On December 9, 1998, the Horejsi Family Athletics Center was completed just to the south of the Wagnon Student Center. The 16,500-square-foot facility became the home of the Jayhawk volleyball squad and serves as an additional practice venue for the basketball teams.

The decade of the '90s also saw policies and procedures enacted for Allen Fieldhouse that had been nonexistent in its previous 35 years. On May 11, 1990, Kansas athletic department officials announced a ban on smoking in the building beginning with the 1990-91 season. Although limited advertising previously existed in the building, significant signage was added to various regions of the Fieldhouse for the start of the 1992-93 season. Athletics director Bob Frederick and KUAC's marketing partner, Creative Sports, met initial opposition from members of the Kansas University Athletic Board.

"When Bob Frederick introduced me to the group, one of the board members raised a concern about over-commercialization," then-Creative Sports general manager Ralph McBarron said. "He said, 'We think of Allen Fieldhouse as a church, and it is concerning to see our church being commercialized.'

"I told him, 'I am a church goer myself, and if you notice, they pass around a plate during every service for the attendees to contribute money. Churches need money, and so do athletic departments.'"

Finances were weighing heavily on the minds of Kansas officials as the decade came to a close. The entrance into the Big 12 Conference, the need to expand/upgrade facilities and less than expected football attendance led to the difficult decision to drop the sports of men's tennis and swimming. It also led to the first serious discussions by Frederick and his staff to implement a basketball seating policy that was based on athletic department donations. It was a concept that was gaining popularity in collegiate athletics but was put on hold at Kansas for the time being.

Celebrating 100 Years of Kansas Basketball

They were all there under the big crimson roof, a collection of former Jayhawks representing seven decades of Kansas basketball and gathered on the court named in honor of the coach who got it all started.

Clyde Lovellette and Danny Manning stood on James Naismith Court in front of a packed house beneath the two NCAA championship banners they helped bring to Lawrence.

John McClendon, Ralph Miller, Dick Harp, Ted Owens, Dean Smith, Larry Brown and Roy Williams shared the floor and a representation of more college basketball wins than anyone could imagine.

Ted O'Leary, Bub Shaffer and Fred Pralle, all standouts on Jayhawk teams in the 1930s, shared center stage with current team members such as Paul Pierce and Raef LaFrentz.

It was an assembly of greats and not-so-greats returning home as heroes once again to share in the drama of an anniversary celebration.

From Bob Allen, son of the building's namesake, the roster of Jayhawk legends included Wayne Hightower, Bill Hougland, Bud Stallworth, Walt Wesley, Tom Kivisto, Ron Kellogg, Kevin Pritchard, Mark Randall and Rex Walters.

It was two days of non-stop smiles for those watching and those returning.

A collection of nearly 300 former players, coaches and managers came back just to stand on the court in Allen Fieldhouse and feel the honor of being a Jayhawk one more time.

Allen Fieldhouse had been the site of many events over five decades, but never a birthday party and certainly not one of this magnitude.

The 1997-98 season brought justification to a birthday event in the venerable old building. It marked a century of intercollegiate basketball at the University of Kansas and athletic officials staged a year-long celebration to acknowledge the anniversary.

Bob Allen (right) and chancellor Robert Hemenway unveil the Phog Allen statue.

It started with the unveiling of a nine-foot statue of Phog Allen in front of the building and the naming of the court in honor of Naismith, inventor of the game and the school's first head coach.

The celebration continued with the triumphant midseason return of legendary Wilt Chamberlain for the official retirement of his Kansas jersey, and concluded in February with a Legends Game and Reunion Weekend, when players and coaches returned to stand side by side and hear the "Rock, Chalk, Jayhawk" chant again.

"The 100 years of Kansas basketball might be the richest in the country," noted KU athletic director Bob Frederick, "when you include the inventor of basketball, James Naismith; the father of basketball coaching, Forrest C. (Phog) Allen; and all the great players, teams and coaches during that period."

To help celebrate the season-long milestone, KU produced a special video and a 100-year logo, which combined an iron hoop and a peach basket. Rich Clarkson, nationally recognized sports photographer and KU alum, published a book chronicling 100 years of Kansas basketball.

The culminating weekend of the anniversary celebration included a Legends Game of basketball alumni, played before a full house in Allen Fieldhouse on Saturday, and the return of former players and coaches for a halftime ceremony during the nationally televised Kansas-Missouri game on Sunday .

"If there's a list, it ain't a long one," observed Roy Williams when asked about what other college programs could attract a sellout for an alumni game.

"Indiana might have a shot, Kentucky might have a shot. North Carolina might have a shot. At the same time, I'm not sure any of them would get it done."

Williams was among the spectators who watched that Saturday night as the aging Jayhawks suited up and put their basketball skills on display once again.

When Blaine Hollinger (1953-57) worked a two-on-one fast break with Ron Loneski (1955-59) for the game's first field goal, Allen Fieldhouse roared its encouragement as if it were a real game.

"Sixteen thousand people came out there today to watch a bunch of old guys run up and down the court," observed former Jayhawk center Paul Mokeski (1975-79), the game's leading scorer with 10 points. "That tells you a lot about what this means to those people."

The 57 players who suited up for the event included Hutch Walker, a member of the 1942 Jayhawk team and Steve Ransom, who finished his career the previous season.

The game had its share of highlights. Milt Newton (1984-89) dunked off a pass from Kevin Pritchard, and Booty Neal (1977-81) hit a pair of three pointers and the crowd chanted "BOOTY." Mokeski led his team to a 68-67, win and the two squads combined to shoot 76 three-point field goal attempts.

The following afternoon, Kansas hosted rival Missouri for the culmination of the anniversary celebration. Representatives of KU's 10 Final Four teams were introduced and escorted onto the court as a team during time-outs.

At halftime, broadcaster Max Falkenstien read the name of each returning Jayhawk as he strolled out on the court. At the end of the introduction, the floor was packed, and the reunion honorees were treated to a standing ovation.

"It was a great feeling to be with all of those guys," noted Jerry Waugh (1948-51). "Everyone bonded together. It was like we were all together as one Kansas team."

The legends of KU basketball are honored on the south wall of Allen Fieldhouse.

Photo provided by Jeff Jacobsen

The Big Dipper Returns to Allen Fieldhouse

Allen Fieldhouse is college basketball's theater of the hardwood, where one spectacle after another has delighted and entertained faithful fans for the past 50 years.

A giant of a man from Philadelphia named Wilton Chamberlain orchestrated two of the most memorable moments staged behind the limestone walls of the building named in honor of the coach who brought him to Lawrence.

The first moment coincided with his collegiate debut and the last marked his final appearance in Allen Fieldhouse.

Chamberlain arrived at Kansas as a basketball prodigy and amazed everyone in his first varsity game as a Jayhawk. He returned more than 40 years later in the twilight of his all-too-short life. But in his final appearance in Allen Fieldhouse, it was his words, not his ability to score, rebound or block shots, that defined his passion and commitment to KU.

Chamberlain was on the cusp of greatness when he made his varsity debut as a Jayhawk in 1955.

The towering seven-foot sophomore quickly certified himself worthy of legendary status, as he obliterated school records with a 52-point, 31-rebound performance against Northwestern in his first game in Allen Fieldhouse. Chamberlain's initial outing also marked Dick Harp's debut as head coach of the Jayhawks.

In 1998 the Big Dipper returned to the site where he launched his college career. Chamberlain journeyed back to the University of Kansas to help celebrate the 100th anniversary of basketball at KU and to witness the official retirement of his No. 13 game jersey. And when he strolled on the court under the Allen Fieldhouse roof for the final time, the 61-year-old Chamberlain captivated his Jayhawk audience in a manner as spectacular as his initial performance as a player.

"He couldn't have been a more gracious person," noted Bob Frederick, then KU's athletics director. "Everything he did seemed golden at the time—even wearing his old letter jacket and staying long enough so everyone could get his autograph."

Wearing his well-preserved crimson Jayhawk letterman's jacket and a blue KU baseball cap, Chamberlain was welcomed on the court at halftime by Frederick, his assistant coach Jerry Waugh, longtime KU radio voice Max Falkenstien and chancellor Robert Hemenway.

Chamberlain sent a clear signal to everyone in attendance during a dramatic halftime ceremony that he was, indeed, proud to be a member of the Kansas basketball family.

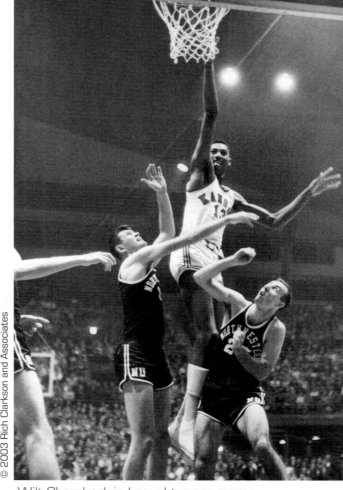

© 2003 Rich Clarkson and Associates

Wilt Chamberlain brought many memorable moments to Allen Fieldhouse.

"I've learned in life that you have to take the bitter with the sweet. And how sweet this is!" said Chamberlain at halftime of the KU–Kansas State game. "I'm a Jayhawk and proud to be a part of the tradition here."

It was his final words, however, that rocked the old building once again and helped close a chapter on a period of time when some Jayhawk fans wondered about his true feelings regarding his college career.

"Rock, Chalk, Jayhawk," said Chamberlain in a voice that echoed through the building and ignited a thunderous applause. Wilt died October 12, 1999, less than two years after his final and most memorable appearance in Allen Fieldhouse.

Chamberlain was coaxed back to his college campus, thanks in part, to the efforts of former teammates Bob Billings and Monte Johnson, longtime friend Joan Edwards and Kansas basketball coach Roy Williams.

Johnson later learned that his former teammate endured an assortment of health challenges to make the trip possible.

"Bob (Billings) and I spent Friday, Saturday and Sunday with him," recalled Johnson. "We met him at a hotel in Kansas City and I remember seeing him get off the elevator. In my mind, he looked as if he could still play the game. We later found out that Wilt was terribly sick. His sister, Barbara, later told us he had no business making the trip because of his health.

Chamberlain signed autographs for over two hours when he returned to Lawrence in 1998.

Photo provided by KU Sports Information

"But he was so committed. He was so sick with heart problems and bothered with his hip problems. He was almost deathly ill."

Many longtime followers of Jayhawk basketball were uncertain of what to expect when Chamberlain agreed to return to campus. It marked the first time he had been in Lawrence since the 1970s, and efforts to get him back sooner had not been successful.

It turns out, after all, that Chamberlain had stayed away largely because he had blamed himself for Kansas' heartbreaking, triple-overtime loss to North Carolina in the 1957 NCAA championship game.

"A little over 40 years ago," he told the Allen Fieldhouse crowd, "I lost the toughest battle in sports in losing to the North Carolina Tar Heels.

"But when I come back here today and realize not a simple loss of a game, but how many people have shown such appreciation and warmth, I'm humbled and deeply honored."

The heartfelt roar of the crowd told Wilt that Kansas fans' love for him far outweighed their disappointment in the result of that 1957 game.

In an afternoon press conference the day before, the two-time All-American had put to rest rumors that he had avoided KU because of bad feelings toward his school.

"A lot of people thought there was something missing between me and the University of Kansas in a negative way," said Chamberlain to a packed room of media types and fans. "But it was a great building block for me. It helped prepare me for life. I'm negligent in not being here sooner."

Johnson recalled that Chamberlain was busy from the moment he arrived and was anxious and eager to accommodate every request.

"He spent well over an hour at the press conference and afterwards offered to spend time talking to people one on one," said Johnson. "Coach Williams wanted him to come by the locker room before practice and say a few words to the team.

After talking to the media, I took him in the locker room and just sat back and watched.

"I have never seen a collection of great athletes such as we had at that time so awestruck by someone's presence.

"Roy was wonderful with Wilt," added Johnson. "He treated Wilt like he was as big a celebrity as KU has ever had. I always felt like that was one of the reasons Wilt was so touched by the entire weekend."

Johnson recalled that as a testament to his Jayhawk heritage, Chamberlain wore his lettermen's jacket for the halftime ceremony.

"On Friday night, Bob hosted an event for Wilt at Alvamar Country Club and he came over to my house to change clothes," said Johnson. "He brought in his suitcase and I remember seeing him open it. Right on top of everything was his letter jacket. How many people would think to come back like that and bring their letter jacket? His sister told us it was one of his prized possessions."

Kansas won the basketball game against Kansas State, 69-62, and, coincidently, forward Paul Pierce scored 11 points to tie Chamberlain for 12th on the all-time scoring list at Kansas. Of course, Chamberlain hit that point total in just 48 games, while Pierce was playing his 93rd. The victory was also the Jayhawks' 55th consecutive in Allen Fieldhouse, which tied the school record.

Afterwards, a table and folding chair were positioned on the Allen Fieldhouse court and Chamberlain patiently signed autographs for over two hours, accommodating any Jayhawk fan who wanted the opportunity to meet him and get his signature.

"He told Bob and me just before he left that it was one of the—if not the most—meaningful days of his life," recalled Johnson. "And if you think about all of the meaningful days he had in his life, that is quite a statement."

In 2003 Chamberlain's true feelings for KU were exemplified by a $650,000 gift from his estate that will aid Jayhawk student-athletes for many years to come.

Chamberlain's
Halftime Speech

"**A** little over 40 years ago, I lost the toughest battle in sports in losing to the North Carolina Tar Heels by one point in triple overtime (national championship game). It was a devastating thing to me because I let the University of Kansas down and my teammates down.

"But when I come back here today and realize not a simple loss of a game, but how many people have shown such appreciation and warmth, I'm humbled and deeply honored.

"I've learned in life that you have to take the bitter with the sweet and how sweet this is, right here! I'm a Jayhawk and I know now why there is so much tradition here and why so many wonderful things have come from here, and I am now very much a part of it by being there (pointing to his jersey hanging from the rafters) and very proud of it.

"Rock, Chalk, Jayhawk."

Photo provided by KU Sports Information

The Phog — In Audio, Video and Print

Tipoff is a little more than 30 minutes away and Jay Kutlow is racing the clock.

As the producer for *ESPN's Big Monday* basketball games, he is making sure the final commercial reel is ready to air. At the same time, he knows the Kansas Jayhawks will be racing out of the locker room to begin pregame drills at any moment. He tells his crew to take a break as he rips off his headset, hops from his chair and races out of the production truck parked just outside the west entrance of Allen Fieldhouse. He navigates through the crowd and positions himself near the game's announcers.

"Anyone who has played basketball in college knows the lay up line is where the excitement begins," Kutlow says. "The team runs out of the locker room and onto the court in a single file line while the fans go crazy and the band begins to play. As a player, that is when you begin to get pumped up. Kansas is the only place that I made it a point to make sure I was out on the court for the lay up line. I wanted to feel that same excitement when I worked a game."

Kutlow played collegiately at Columbia and produced games for ESPN in Allen Fieldhouse for 10 years, from the 1993-94 to the 2002-03 seasons. While he says the biggest fear a producer has is the lack of excitement in the arena, such has never been a problem in Allen Fieldhouse. In fact, Kutlow says the energy level gets too high at times.

"When you are in the production truck, you are watching a wall of TV monitors, talking on your headset to a dozen people and trying to keep track of the game, all at the same time. Even when the game is relatively low key, it can be stressful. But at Kansas, the action gets so intense and the crowd so loud, it becomes almost chaos in the truck. We never worry about having a bad game from the standpoint of having great pictures and a great atmosphere."

Lawrence Journal-World sports editor Chuck Woodling finally did something about the noise in Allen Fieldhouse—he began wearing earplugs. He first covered games as a senior journalism major at Missouri in 1968-69 and has been chronicling the action there ever since. But it wasn't until a few years ago that he began to combat the noise.

"I was talking with a speech, language and hearing professor and he told me that the noise in Allen Fieldhouse is equivalent to a 747 taking off," Woodling said. "That was good enough reason for me to try earplugs. There are times when the noise reaches the level of a sonic boom and everything seems to stand still."

To know Allen Fieldhouse is one thing, to experience it is another. Fred White was a broadcaster in tiny Hastings, Nebraska, when WIBW radio

Allen holds court with *Lawrence Journal-World* reporter Bill Mayer.

© 2003 Rich Clarksonand Associates

and television in Topeka came calling. One of his first assignments was to broadcast on television the game between No. 3 Louisville and No. 4 Kansas in Allen Fieldhouse, December 6, 1967. It was a matchup featuring the Cardinals' Wes Unseld and the Jayhawks' JoJo White. It would be the first of many games White would broadcast in Allen Fieldhouse, as he became a fixture on the Big Eight/Big 12 telecasts. He also did games in several other conferences, giving him a perspective on Allen Fieldhouse.

"It is the best place going," White says. "The intimacy creates a special atmosphere. I think in the Midwest we tend not to boast. Everyone back East told me how great how all those places were. I may be a bit biased, but they aren't Allen Fieldhouse."

Kansas City Star reporter Blair Kerkhoff covered Kansas from the 1989-90 to 1996-97 seasons, and has written two books focusing on elements of the Jayhawk basketball program. He grew up in ACC country and was skeptical that Allen Fieldhouse could match the arenas to which he was accustomed.

"I think most people tend to put Duke at the top, especially over the last 20 years," Kerkhoff said. "But I think Allen Fieldhouse is better. It is twice as big as Cameron Indoor Stadium and twice as loud. The one thing that sets Allen Fieldhouse apart is the sight of people milling around an hour before the game. People are roaming the halls, looking at the trophies and the paintings of the Hall of Fame. It's really something to see a father pointing out a Wilt Chamberlain or Paul Pierce to a son or daughter, explaining why they were so good. It's basketball's equivalent of tailgating."

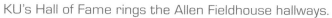

KU's Hall of Fame rings the Allen Fieldhouse hallways.

Photo provided by Kenneth Spencer Research Library

Jayhawk play-by-play voice Bob Davis, whose grandfather Edwin Davis worked on Allen Fieldhouse during its construction, says it is the reaction of the first timer of which he takes special notice.

"I remember glancing over at Bill Self during a point in the Michigan State game when KU was making a run," Davis said. "I saw this little smile and his eyes just told me how much fun he was having and what being in Allen Fieldhouse meant to him. He had been there before, but this time he was the *head* coach.

"I think the other thing that I take note of is when I talk to my counterparts who are making their first visit. You can tell by their expressions and the tone of their voices that they are a bit in awe."

Sometimes the media becomes part of the story, as was the case when Dick Vitale visited Allen Fieldhouse, January 27, 2003. The Jayhawks were entertaining No. 3 Texas, looking a third straight loss squarely in the eyes. But a furious rally, keyed by a 24-point, 23-rebound effort by Nick Collison, gave Kansas a 90-87 overtime win. Collison would not be around for the finish, as he fouled out with just over a minute remaining. It would elicit a standing ovation from Vitale, only the second he has given since joining ESPN in 1979 (David Robinson earned the other while at Navy).

"I did a game involving Kansas early in my career when Darnell Valentine was the star," Vitale said. "I obviously was very impressed with Allen Fieldhouse, and needless to say it still ranks as one of the premier venues in all of college basketball. What makes it so special is the great tradition of Jayhawk basketball and the fact that the fans are so close to the action. Allen Fieldhouse is to college basketball what Wrigley Field (Chicago Cubs) is to Major League Baseball.

"It is a delight for me to enter Allen Fieldhouse and I still get goose bumps when the fans break out into their 'Rock, Chalk, Jayhawk' chant. Some of my greatest moments at Allen Fieldhouse included watching Danny Manning work his magic under

Photo provided by Jeff Jacobsen

"Allen Fieldhouse is Awesome Baby, with a capital A." – Dick Vitale

coach Larry Brown, and also certainly watching the development of Nick Collison and Kirk Hinrich. One thing that has always been so special is that Allen Fieldhouse is always filled to capacity with jubilant fans and basketball hysteria. To put it in Vitalese, 'Allen Fieldhouse is Awesome Baby with a capital A.'"

When Allen Fieldhouse first opened its doors, the raised court prevented the media from working courtside. Approximately 150 media seats were located at mid-court on the west side of the arena on the bottom rows of the upper balcony. According to an article in the October 25, 1980 *Lawrence Journal-World*, the athletic department announced plans to add 204 theater-style seats where the media worked. This would complement the 1,100 wooden chair-back seats on the east side of the upper balcony installed at the time of the original construction. The media would be displaced and moved to the east side floor level beginning with the 1980-81 season. The new seats would be available to ticketholders for an annual donation of $500. The sports informa-tion office was also relocated to the old physiology laboratory on the second floor in the northwest corner of the building.

Though closer to the action, many in the media preferred the higher vantage point.

Kansas' Longest Winning Streaks

G	Began	Ended	Court	Team To End Streak
62	2/26/93	12/8/98	Allen Fieldhouse	Iowa, 85-81
55	3/3/84	1/30/88	Allen Fieldhouse	Kansas State, 72-61
33	3/7/51	1/4/55	Hoch Auditorium	Missouri, 76-65
28	12/1/69	12/4/71	Allen Fieldhouse	Kentucky, 79-69
26	1/15/38	3/7/41	Hoch Auditorium	Oklahoma, 45-37
25	2/10/01	1/25/03	Allen Fieldhouse	Arizona, 91-74
24	2/17/90	1/11/92	Allen Fieldhouse	Louisville, 85-78
21#	12/1/65	3/17/67	Allen Fieldhouse	Houston, 66-63
20	2/6/22	1/14/25	Robinson Gymnasium	Kansas State, 40-28
17	12/6/80	12/12/81	Allen Fieldhouse	Kentucky, 77-74 (OT)
17	12/8/44	1/7/47	Hoch Auditorium	Missouri, 39-34
16	1/7/14	2/10/15	Robinson Gymnasium	Kansas State, 21-18
16	12/15/32	12/14/34	Hoch Auditorium	Kansas State, 39-35 (OT)

NCAA Tournament

Late Night in Allen Fieldhouse

Other than the excitement of March Madness, the most anticipated event for the rabid Kansas basketball fan is the start of practice drills in mid-October.

A public viewing of the first drills, beginning at midnight on the first day of practice legislated by the NCAA, has become another staple of the Jayhawk basketball tradition. At Kansas, most consider the event to have started in 1985, when Larry Brown introduced "Late Night with Larry," but it actually has its roots on Mt. Oread in the mid-1950s. The first publicly attended event to kick off practice drew 14,000 to begin the 1955-56 season. As is the case today, skits called "follies," which were student-faculty productions, were performed prior to the scrimmage.

Photo provided by Jeff Jacobsen

In the 1950s, freshmen were ineligible for official competition. Head coach Phog Allen would begin drills each year with the freshman team scrimmaging against the varsity. In 1955, Allen would find the answer to the question he had uttered to a member of the media when asked if Wilt Chamberlain would attend Kansas. Said Allen at the time, "I certainly hope the young man decides to come out for the basketball team." Did he ever.

The campus was abuzz over the much-heralded freshman prior to the start of the 1955-56 season. The "kickoff" to the season scrimmage was played on the Friday night of Homecoming weekend.

A preseason dance followed by a postseason appearance at the Big Dance.

The 1956 *Jayhawker Yearbook* had this to say about one of the first "Late Nights" in the heralded KU era: "But even overshadowing the glamour of the Jayhawkers' triumph on the gridiron was the performance of another group of young men going through their paces on a hardwood court before 14,000 awed fans in Allen Fieldhouse. This was, of course, the performance of Coach 'Phog' Allen's varsity basketballers in a preseason preview game against Coach Dick Harp's freshman cagers. Always a traditional feature of the homecoming weekend, this game had been catapulted into national interest last spring when a seven-foot phenomenon from Philadelphia named Wilton Chamberlain announced that he would grace the halls of Mt. Oread for the next four years. Billed as the most sought-after, publicized high school player in U.S. history, Wilt, 'The Stilt,' selected KU over one hundred other schools."

Bill Witt, one of the student writers on the staff of the 1956 *Jayhawker* continued, "It is unlikely that ever again will there be a magnetic attraction to draw in 14,000 people for a freshman-varsity basketball game. However, this Homecoming there was; and the near capacity crowd that filled the fieldhouse saw what they were looking for: real promise that KU was again to be in the limelight as a national basketball power."

Wilt didn't disappoint that night, scoring 42 points in leading the freshmen to victory over

Wilt brought fans to the first Late Night.

© 2003 Rich Clarkson and Associates

the varsity, the one and only time in KU history the freshmen won. The scrimmages continued, but the Kansas fans did not turn out in droves again until the mid-1980s. By then, the NCAA had regulated the start day and time for every Division I basketball-playing school, 12:01 a.m., October 15.

The craze called "Midnight Madness" to start the college season began in 1970. Maryland coach Lefty Driesell is credited with starting the preseason event that year. According to the *Lawrence Journal-World's* 1999 Late Night edition, "October 15, 1970—Driesell opened the University of Maryland men's basketball practice at the earliest time teams could work out in accordance with NCAA rules. Terrapin students loved the midnight workout and several coaches on the East Coast followed suit the following year."

A memorable Late Night moment.

Photo provided by Jeff Jacobsen

It didn't matter on what day of the week October 15 fell, there were going to be basketball fans everywhere going to work or school the following day on just a few hours' sleep after watching their team officially kick off the start of a new season. The NCAA solved that problem in 1990 by changing the start date to the Friday closest to October 15. It has evolved to now being the "Saturday nearest October 15," according the latest *NCAA Manual.* This makes the event more "kid-friendly" by having it on a weekend so young ones can stay up past their normal bedtime, and parents don't have to worry as much about getting up early the next morning for work. This also helped schools plan for an all-encompassing fall weekend for alumni to see other fall sports such as football, volleyball, soccer or field hockey.

Brown liked the idea that some of the schools on the east coast had tried. He thought it would be a fun way to include the students and fans in the first practice and get them excited about the season. Seating for the first midnight practice would be limited to the upper balcony as the lower-level seats were being renovated. An announced crowd of 6,000 was on hand.

"It was fabulous," Brown said. "I was thrilled with the students. They made it all worthwhile, and I know our kids enjoyed it."

In 1986, Kansas welcomed Larry "Bud" Melman from the *Late Night with David Letterman* show, and 12,000 fans. Assistant coach Mark Freidinger played the main role in a skit that almost went awry.

"The routine had me set up to lose a bet," Freidinger said. "As a result, I had to drink a concoction of creamed corn, cheese whiz, tabasco sauce and ice tea that was poured out of a Jack Daniels' bottle. They put it all in a blender and then I chugged it. The only problem is the creamed corn and cheese whiz didn't go down too easy. I about gagged on it. A lot of people remember me for that skit, but I'd rather be known for the fact that we went undefeated at home the two years I was there."

A foreshadowing of things to come highlighted the 1987 Late Night as the theme "Goin' To Kansas City" set the backdrop. The Final Four was to be played at Kemper Arena, just a short trip down I-70. Author John Feinstein, who was working on a project chronicling the 1987-88 college basketball season, was on hand for the festivities. Said Feinstein at the time to the *Journal-World,* "I couldn't think of a better place to start a book about an entire season than 12:01 in Lawrence, Kansas."

What Brown created, Williams perfected. Playing off the fact that he was succeeding another Dean Smith disciple, the event became known as "Later with Roy Williams." (Note: It eventually switched back to the "Late Night" moniker.) It also became an important recruiting tool, as some of the nation's top-rated prep stars trekked to Lawrence to witness the new phenomenon.

"I'd been in there (Allen Fieldhouse), but never with a crowd, " Williams said. "I remember walking in and the reception I got from the student body. It really surprised me and made me feel very good. They sort of adopted this dumb guy from North Carolina right off the bat. It's still one of my favorite moments.

"When I go on the road and let the kids read the articles about how we packed the gymnasium for our first practice," he exclaimed, "so many times they'll say, 'You have 16,300 for a practice?'"

Despite the warm ovation for Williams as he was introduced as head coach, the mood turned tense for the 10,000 in attendance, when sophomore Alonzo Jamison's thunderous dunk attempt brought down the goal standard and the backboard support fell on his head. A dazed Jamison suffered only a bruise and scalp lacerations, allowing a relieved Williams to enjoy the rest of the evening.

The event continued to grow with various tweaks throughout the years. In 1991, 15,800 came early to enjoy a Kansas volleyball game preceding Late Night. In 1992, local television broadcast the event. Four high-profile honorary coaches were invited for the Red-Blue scrimmage, including Kansas City Royal Hall of Famer George Brett, PGA Tour Hall of Famer Tom Watson, Kansas City Royal centerfielder Brian McRae and Kansas City Chief All-Pro Deron Cherry.

Late Night went national in 1995 as ESPN2 cablecast parts of the Late Night proceedings with announcer Digger Phelps in attendance. This evening was also highlighted by the appearance of football coach Glen Mason—whose team was fresh off a victory that afternoon and en route to a 10-2 season and Aloha Bowl appearance. He enthusiastically introduced the evening: "Live from Allen Fieldhouse, it's Late Night With Roy Williams!" Fans were turned away from the jam-packed Allen Fieldhouse that year.

In 1996, Californian Scot Pollard made a big splash on the KU campus with his arrival and became the first KU men's basketball player to scrimmage while wearing bright red nail polish on each nail. Oh yes, and he also scored 14 points, grabbed seven rebounds and blocked four shots in the scrimmage. In 1998, he stole the show by proposing marriage to his girlfriend, Mindy, in front of 16,300 of his closest friends.

Self was on hand for the 1985 event as a graduate assistant coach at Kansas, but even he was a bit awed by what he experienced almost 20 years later. As his predecessor did, Self tweaked the name, calling it "Late Night in the Phog."

"They opened the doors at eight o'clock," Self said, "and less than an hour later the place was full and they had to close the doors. It was an awesome night. The fans were just great. It is a bit humbling to get that kind of reception."

Self also paid homage to a select group of individuals who had made a large impact on his personal and professional career. He invited back the 1988 NCAA National Championship team, including head coach Larry Brown, to be honored by Jayhawk fans.

Former Chiefs star Deron Cherry and Royals legend George Brett served as honorary coaches during Late Night.

Photo provided by Scott Indermaur

Perhaps no one person has had as much an influence on Self as Brown. It also gave Brown a chance to reiterate his feelings for Kansas.

"I spent five of the greatest years of my life in this building," Brown said to an adoring crowd. "There is no better place to coach. There is no better place to go to school. There is no better place to play. It's because of you people here. I've never had a chance to properly thank you all from the bottom of my heart. I am so proud to have sat on that bench. God bless you all...and go KU."

It could be said that the Late Night activities added a bit of soul to Allen Fieldhouse. It is only fitting, therefore, that in the 50th anniversary of the building, the 20th anniversary of Late Night is also celebrated.

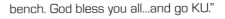
Bill Self enjoys "The Phog."

Photo provided by Jeff Jacobsen

Self was all smiles in his first Allen Fieldhouse game.

Allen Fieldhouse Moments

1990s

February 13, 1990 – Missouri 77, Kansas 71
Kansas saw its 14-game home-court win streak end as the top-ranked Jayhawks were upset by No. 2 Missouri, 77-71.

December 1, 1990 – Kansas 108, Marquette 71
Four days after undergoing surgery to repair anterior compartment syndrome in his lower right leg, Mark Randall returned to score 11 points in helping KU to a win over Marquette in the home season opener ... it had been reported that the surgery would have kept Randall out of action for two weeks ... Alonzo Jamison tied a school record with eight steals and KU broke the school team mark with 22 steals.

January 5, 1991 – Kansas 105, North Carolina State 94
Terry Brown broke a school record and tied a conference mark by hitting 11 three-point field goals en route to a career-high 42 points as Kansas beat North Carolina State, 105-94.

January 16, 1991 – Kansas 73, Miami (Fla.) 60
On the day Operation Desert Storm began in the Persian Gulf, Kansas outlasted Miami (Florida), 73-60, as Terry Brown, who had a sister stationed in the Gulf, led the Jayhawk with 26 points ... KU also unveiled a new Allen Fieldhouse scoreboard.

March 24, 1991 – NCAA Tournament Pep Rally
Just a few minutes past midnight—following KU's dramatic come-from-behind win over Arkansas that earned the team a spot in the Final Four—the Jayhawks rolled into Allen Fieldhouse; a frenzied crowd of 15,000 welcome the team back home. Senior Adonis Jordan uttered his famous line: "Down by 12, win by 12."

November 6, 1991 – Jersey Retirement

The KU athletics department announced—as part of the centennial cele-bration of college basketball—that the jerseys of the following players would be retired and displayed in the south end of Allen Fieldhouse: Paul Endacott, Charles T. Black, Charles B. Black, Clyde Lovellette, B.H. Born, Wilt Chamberlain, Lynette Woodard and Danny Manning.

November 23, 1991 – Kansas 122, Maryland-Baltimore County 58

Richard Scott scored 22 points in leading the Jayhawks to a 122-58 win over Maryland-Baltimore County in the season opener at Allen Fieldhouse ... its final advantage represented the largest margin of victory for the Jayhawks in a season opener.

January 11, 1992 – Louisville 85, Kansas 78

Louisville came into Allen Fieldhouse and ended KU's 24-game home-court winning streak with a 85-78 victory.

March 3, 1992 – Kansas 77, Oklahoma State 64

KU clinched a share of the Big Eight title with a win over Oklahoma State ... the game also saw the five millionth fan come through the turnstiles of Allen Fieldhouse.

December 1, 1992 - Kansas 76, Georgia 65

Danny Manning returns to have his No. 25 jersey retired. Never one to succumb to hyperbole, Manning says the best part of the evening was sit-ting in the student section. "It is always something I had wanted to do," he said.

March 8, 1992 – Kansas 97, Missouri 89

Missouri's Anthony Peeler was unstoppable, scoring 43 points against the Jayhawks, but KU prevailed with a 97-89 victory over rival Missouri ... the victory provided KU players and coaches an opportunity to cut down the nets and break out the conference championship t-shirts and hats as the league title had been clinched earlier in the week ... KU ended the season with another sellout in Allen Fieldhouse and established a new home attendance mark, averaging 15,682 for 13 home dates.

March 3, 1993 – Kansas 94, Nebraska 83
Kansas defeated Nebraska, 94-83, capturing its third consecutive Big Eight Conference title ... the Senior Night victory, honoring Rex Walters, Adonis Jordan, Blake Weichbrodt and Eric Pauley, gave KU its 41st conference championship.

November 19, 1993 – Kansas 73, California 56
The arrival of California and standout guard Jason Kidd in a rematch of the 1993 NCAA Sweet 16 battle brought a full house to Allen Fieldhouse for the second round of the preseason NIT ... Richard Scott scored 20 points in the Jayhawk victory ... Kidd scored 22 points but was guilty of seven turnovers.

Danny Manning returned to Lawrence for the official retirement of his jersey in 1992.

Photo provided by KU Sports Information

December 22, 1993 – Kansas 86, Indiana 83
Freshman Jacque Vaughn swished a dramatic three-pointer in overtime with just 0.2 seconds showing on the clock to provide the final margin in a KU victory over Bob Knight and the Hoosiers ... the Jayhawks were six for six from the floor in overtime ... Damon Bailey, who hit 15 of 17 free throws, scored 36 points to lead Indiana ... Vaughn ended the game with 13 points.

January 9, 1994 – Women's Attendance Record
Coach Marian Washington's Jayhawk women's team upset No. 4-ranked Colorado, 59-57, in front of 13,352 Allen Fieldhouse fans—the highest attendance figure in Big Eight women's basketball history at that time.

January 17, 1994 – Kansas State 68, Kansas 64
KU hosted Kansas State on the same day it emerged ranked No. 1 nationally in the college basketball poll, and the Wildcats handed the Jayhawks just their second loss in 17 games in a 68-64 upset victory.

January 26, 1994 – Kansas 62, Oklahoma State 61
In another dramatic finish for KU, Steve Woodberry fired in a three-pointer with just 1.5 seconds remaining to lift KU to a come-from-behind 62-61 win over Oklahoma State ... the win marked Roy Williams' 150th career victory ... Woodberry scored 17 to lead the Jayhawks.

February 26. 1994 – Kansas 106, Colorado 62
Kansas broke a 37-year school record for single-game rebounds with 72 (breaking the 1957 record of 68 vs. Missouri) in a 106-62 win over Colorado ... KU outrebounded the Buffs, 72-29.

December 7, 1994 – Kansas 69, Florida 63
In a battle between the fifth-ranked Jayhawks and sixth-ranked Florida Gators, guard Jerod Haase scored 23 points and center Greg Ostertag tied a Kansas single-game best with eight block shots, leading the Jayhawks to a 69-63 victory.

January 23, 1995 – Kansas 84, Nebraska 67
Guard Jerod Haase converted seven of 12 three-point attempts and scored a career-high 25 points as KU defeated Nebraska for the 13th consecutive time at Allen Fieldhouse.

February 4, 1995 – Kansas 91, Iowa State 71
Center Greg Ostertag established a new conference record for career blocked shots, swatting away his 229th in a 91-71 win over Iowa State ... Ostertag ended the game with five blocked shots.

March 5, 1995 – Kansas 78, Oklahoma State 62
KU won its 42nd league title with a victory over Oklahoma State ... the encounter will be remembered as the only game in which OSU standout center Bryant Reeves was held scoreless ... Cowboy guard Randy Rutherford connected on 11 three-point field goals and scored 45 points ... KU finished the season unbeaten in Allen Fieldhouse for the 10th time in the 40-year history of the building.

December 1, 1995 – Kansas 85, UCLA 70
Kansas established a school record by erasing a 15-point halftime deficit, outscoring the Bruins by 30 points in the second half in the dramatic victory over the defending NCAA champions ... UCLA led 41-22 after 17 minutes of the first half ... the comeback was the largest halftime deficit overcome in school history.

December 30, 1996 – Kansas 90, Washburn 65
Jacque Vaughn returned to the lineup after sitting out 10 games due to a wrist injury as Kansas romped past Washburn ... the senior point guard came off the bench to score eight points and dish out five assists ... Raef LaFrentz scored the 1,000th point of his career.

February 12, 1997 – Kansas 104, Oklahoma State 72
KU won its 41st consecutive game—the longest active streak in Division I—with a victory over Oklahoma State ... film director Spike Lee spoke to the team following the game.

February 22, 1997 – Kansas 78, Kansas State 58
In the final home game for six seniors, Kansas claimed a 78-58 victory over Kansas State and the first-ever Big 12 Conference title ... Roy Williams, keeping with tradition, attempted to start all six seniors and Raef LaFrentz before walk-ons Joel Branstrom and Steve Ransom left the court before tip-off ... Scot Pollard drained the first and only three-pointer of his career ... the jersey of one of KU's greatest athletes, Ray Evans, was retired during halftime ceremonies.

November 14, 1997 – Kansas 99, Santa Clara 73
Kansas initiated its 100th year of basketball celebration by naming the Allen Fieldhouse court in honor of Dr. James Naismith ... the Jayhawks downed Santa Clara to open the season.

November 19, 1997 – Kansas 75, Western Kentucky 62
Kansas downed Western Kentucky in the first round of the preseason NIT as head coach Roy Williams picked up his 250th career win ... Raef LaFrentz had nine rebounds to pass Wilt Chamberlain for third place on KU's career rebounds list.

December 13, 1997 – Kansas 103, Middle Tennessee 68
A statue of Phog Allen, located in front of Allen Fieldhouse, was unveiled and dedicated by the athletics department prior to a victory over Middle Tennessee State ... Billy Thomas broke Terry Brown's school record with his 201st three-point field goal in the win and KU registered its 51st consecutive home-court victory.

January 17, 1998 – Kansas 69, Kansas State 62
Amidst the backdrop of legendary Jayhawk Wilt Chamberlain's return to Lawrence, KU defeated Kansas State in front of 16,300 fans at Allen Fieldhouse behind Ryan Robertson's 15 points and six assists ... Chamberlain was honored at halftime of the game by having his jersey officially retired; he appeared on court wearing his KU lettermen's jacket ... the win was KU's 55th consecutive at home.

February 7, 1998 – Alumni Game
The 100-year basketball reunion weekend kicked off with an alumni game in front of a packed house at Allen Fieldhouse ... among those former players participating in the game were Walt Wesley, Bud Stallworth, Ron Kellog, John Douglas, Rick Calloway, Jerod Haase, Tom Kivisto, Ron Loneski, Paul Mokeski, Milt Newton and Kevin Pritchard.

February 8, 1998 – Kansas 80, Missouri 70
With 270 former Jayhawk players and coaches on hand for the 100th-year reunion of Kansas basketball, Kansas posted its 30th straight conference home-court win with a 80-70 win over Missouri ... the former Jayhawks were honored at halftime and members of KU's 10 Final Four teams were introduced at each timeout.

February 21, 1998 – Kansas 71, Iowa State 54
KU clinched its second Big 12 Conference title with a victory over Iowa State as Paul Pierce scored 19 points.

February 23, 1998 – Kansas 83, Oklahoma 70
Three Kansas seniors—Raef LaFrentz, C.B. McGrath and Billy Thomas—said their goodbyes as KU scored an 83-70 victory over Oklahoma and recorded its 60th straight homecourt win ... it also was the 58th straight at home for the seniors, who never lost a game in Allen Fieldhouse in four seasons.

December 8, 1998 – Iowa 85, Kansas 81
KU lost for the first time in Allen Fieldhouse since February 20, 1994 vs. Missouri (81-74) as Iowa scored a win over 10th-ranked Kansas ... the Hawkeye victory broke a string of 62 consecutive home-court victories.

January 2, 1999 – Kansas 95, Texas A&M 57
The Jayhawks celebrated the new year with a win over Texas A&M ... Eric Chenowith had a career-high 25 points and 17 rebounds as KU won its 32nd straight home conference game.

February 10, 1999 – Nebraska 64, Kansas 59
Nebraska's 64-59 victory represented its first win over Kansas in Lawrence since 1983.

February 22, 1999 – Kansas 67, Oklahoma State 66
Ryan Robertson's free throw in the last seconds of overtime provided the final margin in a 67-66 win over Oklahoma State ... Eric Chenowith tied a career high with 25 points.

December 16, 1999 – Kansas 80, Ohio State 67
The No. 6-ranked Jayhawks defeated No. 12 Ohio State, 80-67, behind 17 points from Columbus, Ohio native Kenny Gregory.

December 22, 1999 – Kansas 82, Princeton 67
KU defeated Princeton in front of a full house in the last game of the century in Allen Fieldhouse.

A New Millennium

Roy Departs and Bill Self Gets His Dream Job

KU opened a new decade and century in much the same fashion it ended the nineties. With players such as Drew Gooden, Nick Collison and Kirk Hinrich, KU continued to rank as one of college basketball's elite programs.

Kansas won conference championships in 2001 and again in 2002 with records of 33-4 in each season. In addition, KU showed its strength at tournament time, going to back-to-back Final Fours (2002 and 2003). The Jayhawks went to the title game in 2003, before losing to Syracuse, 81-78.

KU finished 41-2 at home under Williams during the first three seasons of the new millennium.

Williams resigned as head coach at Kansas at the conclusion of the 2002-03 season to return to his alma mater, North Carolina, as head coach. In his 15 seasons on the KU bench, Williams directed Kansas to a 201-17 record in Allen Fieldhouse including six undefeated seasons at home. In the

> "I GOT GOOSE BUMPS THE FIRST TIME I CAME OUT OF THE LOCKER ROOM AND WALKED THROUGH THE TUNNEL TO ALL THOSE FANS."
> —Bill Self at Late Night in the Phog

Kirk Hinrich was a catalyst in leading KU to back-to-back Final Four appearances.

spring of 2001, Frederick stepped down as athletic director. He was replaced by Al Bohl, whose term lasted just two years (2001-03).

Former Jayhawks Tus Ackerman, Nick Collison, Howard Engleman, Drew Gooden, Gale Gordon, Raef LaFrentz, Al Peterson, Paul Pierce, Fred Pralle, Jacque Vaughn and JoJo White; and women's basketball All-Americans Angela Aycock and Tamecka Dixon had their jerseys retired and were put on display above the Fieldhouse court.

Bill Self, a former Kansas graduate assistant under Larry Brown, became the eighth head coach in KU basketball history when he was appointed to the position on April 21, 2003. Self, who coached previously at Oral Roberts, Tulsa and Illinois, made his debut in successful fashion, guiding the Jayhawks to a 24-9 mark (13-1 at home) and a spot in the Elite Eight of the NCAA Tournament.

An era in women's basketball came to an end during the 2003-04 season when Marian Washington stepped down after 31 years as head coach. In June 2004, she was inducted into the Women's College Basketball Hall of Fame. Virginia Tech's Bonnie Henrickson replaced Washington and become only the fifth head coach in the program's history.

Also, Kansas great Lynette Woodard became the 15th former Jayhawk to be named to the Naismith Basketball Hall of Fame.

The summer of 2003 marked the opening of the $8 million, 42,000-square-foot, state-of-the-art Anderson Family Strength and Conditioning Center, built adjacent to the west side of Anschutz Sports Pavilion. The Dana Anderson family provided the seed money for the facility.

Washington coached 31 years.

Photo provided by Jeff Jacobsen

Photo provided by Jeff Jacobsen

Lynette Woodard replaced
Washington on the bench.

In addition, Hemenway tapped Lew Perkins to succeed Bohl as athletics director. In February 2004, Perkins announced that donors had committed $12 million, earmarked for renovations to Allen Fieldhouse and the creation of a Hall of Athletics that will be constructed on the east side of the facility. In the first phase of improvments, restrooms on the north side of the building will recieve an expansion and remodeling. Other enhancements considered included replacing the building's windows, repairing the roof, cleaning the exterior of the building, painting and replacing the heating and ventilation system.

Warren Corman, an architect for the Kansas Board of Regents and part of a team that helped design Allen Fieldhouse, is also on the design team for the new addition. "It's going to look great."

Seating became a topic of public discussion early in the decade. Months before he resigned, Frederick dusted off a proposal he first developed in the late 1990s to assign seats in Allen Fieldhouse based on donations. In late May 2001, just weeks after Frederick's departure, Kansas Chancellor Robert Hemenway said any plan would be evaluated by the new athletic director and the Kansas University Athletic Corporation Board. Although Bohl came aboard later that summer, the plan was not implemented during his tenure.

In October 2002, Kansas officials modified the student/general admission seating policy. General admission tickets in the south endzone balcony were now being assigned so that every seat would be accounted for and attendance would be maximized. Students were also allowed to redeem a coupon on a first-come, first-

Photo provided by Jeff Jacobsen

Allen Fieldhouse heats up when Missouri comes to town.

served basis and pay an additional $5 or $10 for a reserved seat. It allowed students who could not stand in line for hours to still get a ticket.

Perkins began his duties July 7, and by late August confirmed that he planned to have a priority points system in place for the 2004-05 season.

Using the input of a 40-member committee representing all constituents, Perkins and his staff developed a plan that would assign seats based on a point system. Points would be accumulated through a variety of means, including donations, previous season ticket purchase for all Jayhawk athletics teams, employment at the university, membership in the alumni and endowment associations, etc. Seats would be assigned annually, based on one's point total.

In late May 2004, athletic department officials began contacting season ticketholders with their point totals and a chart indicating how the system would have worked had it been in effect the previous year. The concept was quite simple: Individuals with the most points received the best seats. A variety of meetings were conducted across the state of Kansas to enable fans to discuss the new system with KU athletics

officials.

While new to Kansas, similar seating policies have been enacted throughout the

country for many years as a means to raise money for athletic programs.

A signature moment in Allen Fieldhouse.

Photo provided by Jeff Jacobsen

A Perspective: The Essence of Allen Fieldhouse

It was 1981 when Darnell Valentine last appeared in uniform as a Jayhawk on the famed Allen Fieldhouse basketball court. Yet, the impact of a playing career in the historic building remains his constant companion.

"The feeling never escapes you," said Valentine. "Now, when I watch Kansas games on television, I feel it all over again.

"It was our home. It was the barn where they kept the horses. Allen Fieldhouse is about incredible energy and spirit where the fans would not let you quit and not let you lose."

Jerod Haase (1994-97) left flesh and blood on the court as a high-energy performer known for his dives after loose balls. Now an assistant coach at North Carolina, Haase has a lasting appreciation for his basketball home in college.

"I remember walking from Jayhawk Towers before a big game and seeing thousands of students lined up around the building in freezing temperatures," said Haase. "I remember the energy the fans brought to the game.

"They were able to encourage and sense a run before it actually happened. But most of all I remember appreciating every minute I logged in that building, not just now, but as it was happening."

For countless players and generations of Jayhawk fans who have journeyed to Allen Fieldhouse over the last five decades, the massive limestone building on Naismith Drive represents an emblem of a basketball culture.

To understand the remarkable joyride the storied building has provided, it is necessary to go beyond the games to identify those instances that form the essence of the building and the energy of the game-day atmosphere.

Allen Fieldhouse is not a structure that impresses you with its architectural magnitude or rich furnishings. It seduces visitors more with its rustic charm and lack of modern frills.

It starts beneath the roof in the blue rafters and surrounding walls where an impressive array of banners, which honor great teams and great players, portray a basketball heritage. They serve as a tribute and preserve a legacy that hovers above the heads of a new generation of Kansas players and visitors to the building.

Draped high on the north wall is the stern message for visitors who wear uniforms representing the opposition: "Pay Heed All Who Enter: Beware of The Phog!" It has blended into the fabric of what helps make the atmosphere of a game so impressive.

For coaches from conference rivals, the "Beware" banner sometimes triggers nightmares.

"When I see that sign on that end of the building, I think of Paul Pierce elevating to another level and hitting 28-foot jumpers on us," said Oklahoma coach Kelvin Sampson. "And me telling him, 'We can't guard you from 15 feet, so I know we can't guard you from 28.'

"You can tell it's a special place. When you combine tradition, great coaches, players and fans, you get one of the special places to play in America."

Photo provided by Jeff Jacobsen

Jayhawk basketball in Allen Fieldhouse is about game-day rituals that evolved into a treasure chest of memories.

Longtime traditions such as the alma mater and the "Rock, Chalk, Jayhawk" chant, the rhythmic "whoosh" shout by fans on made free throws, or the custom of passing Baby Jay up and over rows and rows of fans in the north end of the student section are all signature moments of a Kansas game in Allen Fieldhouse.

KU fans will claim copyright ownership of a unified response that erupts with the fifth foul on an opposing player. It comes packaged in crimson and blue and hovers throughout the building as the Jayhawk band plays the "Wheaties" song while 16,000-plus fans spread their arms upward and "wave the wheat."

The drama of competition, an assortment of memorable players, and the orchestration of great coaches, is ever changing and well documented over the many seasons of Kansas basketball.

But the staples of consistency in Allen Fieldhouse are those simple, yet unique moments that give the building, which has aged like fine wine, its true dignity and character.

Hinrich and Collison say goodbye during Senior Day.

Photo provided by Jeff Jacobsen

"It is impossible for me to put into words what it meant to me to play my college games in Allen Fieldhouse," said Kevin Pritchard (1987-90), a key player on the Jayhawks' 1988 national championship team. "It really doesn't sink in until you are away from it. I get goose bumps every time I come back for a game.

"I had my defining moment as a player on that court. It was a backdoor pass from Mark Randall against Kansas State

The massive limestone building on Naismith Drive represents an emblem of a basketball culture.

and I dunked. For the rest of my life I will remember that as my greatest moment as a player. And one of the reasons I feel that way is because it happened in Allen Fieldhouse."

Kansas fans from the '70s and '80s recall the halftime broom race when two athletic department custodians were assigned to sweep debris from the court. One had a broom with a red mop and the other had a blue mop.

Like racecar drivers, they would start side by side at the baseline and push the brooms up and down the court. The sweeping act evolved into an unofficial race and another form of entertainment with some students yelling for the blue broom and others cheering for the red. The broom pushers were never shy about enjoying the spirit of the race and contributing to the fun.

For that faithful contingent of devotees who gather to pay homage and witness the sights and sounds of KU basketball, it is the assortment of routine moments or points of interest displayed in the vintage building that have become the standards we remember, but often take for granted.

Starting with the traditional Late Night event in October and ending with Senior Day in late February, a Kansas basketball season is a series of defining moments.

Photo provided by Jeff Jacobsen

Allen Fieldhouse offers a smorgasbord of identifying structural designs and displays that help form its identity. From the trademark windows located high on the south wall to the painted planks of wood that provide 18-inch blocks of valuable real estate seating sought by countless Jayhawk fans, the Fieldhouse offers its own unique charm and personality.

High above the rows of bleacher seats is a Longines Clock mounted on a wall at the base of the rafters. The clock has been ticking as long as games have been played in the time-honored site.

Early in its existence, the basketball court rested on 28-inch risers and was surrounded by river-bottom dirt. The building, in fact, bore the name Fieldhouse because of the combination of a hardwood court and dirt floor that gave flexibility in an enclosed building.

"Going from Hoch Auditorium to Allen Fieldhouse was just a tremendous thing," recalled Maurice King (1954-57), who played in the first game in 1955.

"Basketball just took off in Lawrence, and you have to credit the Fieldhouse for helping make that happen."

There are moments or traditional sights that hold special meaning in the spirit of a Kansas game. Others are considered trivial and lost in the blur of the action.

Not much escapes the attention of the KU student section. Along the stacks of papers and books on press row tables that border the court, for many years, was a red phone that was used to retrieve scores and dispatch updates on KU games to media outlets. Its bright red reflective color may have reminded some of a phone that sat on the desk in the Oval Office of the White House.

When a phone call came during a game, its ring activated a loud chorus of alert students yelling, "Phone." It was a quintessential Allen Fieldhouse moment.

The trademarks of a basketball game in Allen Fieldhouse are ripe with emotion, deep pride, tradition and excitement.

The 1952 National Championship team returned for its 50th anniversary.

Photo provided by Jeff Jacobsen

Photo provided by Jeff Jacobsen

It would not be a stretch to say KU has a significant home-court advantage.

Those feelings appear in the faces of students camped on the hard concrete floors in the north corridor of the building, lined up to secure prime seating for the next game—which is often still a week away.

Emotions explode in the flood of excited students rushing to their seats when the doors of the building open. After days of camping for choice seats, they dart past the ushers, who have the impossible challenge of trying to herd the stampede and maintain order.

When opponents come out for pregame warmup, the early fan arrivals settle into their self-given assignment of spinning intimidation from their seats at courtside.

The voices of Kansas basketball, like the building, have remained fairly consistent and identifiable with Jayhawk fans.

Bob Davis and Max Falkenstien, telling the story on radio, don't play or coach, but their impact on the traditions of Kansas basketball carries a special meaning. Fans see different faces each year on the team bench, but Bob and Max represent the connective tissue that binds the KU citizenry from generation to generation.

The depth of feeling in the ancient building extends to the loyalty and near worship mentality that manifests itself in Kansas fans from the moment the first player appears from the locker room.

A testament to their awe is displayed in the human tunnel, deep with admiring Jayhawk faithful, which funnels players from the locker room to the court for pregame warmup, and builds again at the conclusion of a game to form the walls of a return path for players and coaches.

For many seasons, the voice of Allen Fieldhouse was public address announcer Howard Hill. He ignited the emotion by starting each home game introducing the Jayhawk lineup with the line: "Welcome to the University of Kansas and to Allen Fieldhouse...the home of the Jayhawks!"

A quiet moment in the KU locker room.

For years those words set off a frenzied celebration that was accented when students shower themselves and others at courtside with newspaper shreds.

The spirited environment of competition has spawned traditions originated by creative Jayhawk fans.

Captain Jayhawk literally rose to fame out of the student section during the late 1980s and early 1990s. Wearing a homemade cape and a cut-out basketball over his head with two holes for the eyes, Captain Jayhawk was tossed up in the air by five students in the student section while the band played the "Hey!" song at time-outs.

The popular "Candy Lady" paraded in front of the student section in the 1990s tossing tasty treats to out-stretched hands prior to tip-off.

And no tribute in college basketball matches the emotion of Senior Day, as Jayhawk players conclude their careers under a pregame "flower shower" and the KU band performs in formal wear.

Admiration for the time-honored structure also flows from outside the family of Kansas basketball. Oklahoma State coach Eddie Sutton, who has experienced the atmosphere of Allen Fieldhouse as a player and coach of three teams, is among many visitors who sing its praises.

"Allen Fieldhouse is one of the most difficult places for a visiting team to go into," said Sutton.

"I had the opportunity to play in Allen Fieldhouse. I've had teams in there for the NCAA (Tournament). I've taken teams from Kentucky, Arkansas and OSU in there. I

Head coach Roy Williams offers instruction during a time-out.

Photo provided by Jeff Jacobsen

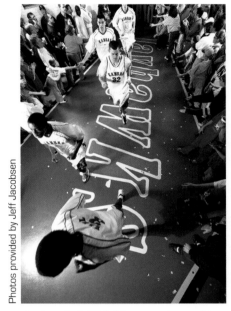

Photos provided by Jeff Jacobsen

Jayhawk faithful form a tunnel to welcome players on the court.

would have to rate it as one of the most difficult places for a team to win. First of all, Kansas always has good teams, and secondly, the crowd plays the part of the sixth man as well as any arena in America."

Sutton is not alone in his respect for the building that has been unkind to many college coaches. Louisville head coach Rick Pitino, during his first season at Kentucky, sat helpless on the visitors bench and endured the torture of a 150-95 loss to the Jayhawks in 1989.

"It's one of the three most imposing home court advantages that I've ever walked into as a basketball coach," said Pitino.

"It offers a great combination of students and devoted fans. You don't often get both. You see crazy students with laid-back fans at other places, but they have both. It's one of the true strongholds in college basketball for a home-court advantage."

An old coach inspired it, an office of state architects envisioned it and a collection of men in hard hats poured years of sweat and blood in making it rise from the earth.

But it has been the pure love and devotion of a group of players and fans that have fueled the personality of Allen Fieldhouse and separated it as one of college basketball's great venues of competition.

Students make Allen Fieldhouse an intimidating venue.

Photo provided by Jeff Jacobsen

No Better View

Game officials are impartial observers, but that doesn't mean they aren't aware of the historic surroundings when they work a game in Allen Fieldhouse.

"There is no better place," official Stanley Reynolds said. "I try to get there early just to walk around to see the memorabilia and soak in the atmosphere. I am a basketball junkie, so when I see the trophies, the paintings and the banners with the names of Lovellette, Chamberlain and Manning—I get goosebumps."

Reynolds first began officiating games in Allen Fieldhouse during the 1979-80 season. A native of Denver, Colorado, and a collegiate player at Northern Colorado, he was keenly aware of the aura surrounding the Kansas program and its hallowed home court long before working his first game there. He makes a special effort during pregame activities or while at a time out to notice the banners, the band and the famous "Rock, Chalk, Jayhawk" chant. It is a ritual he shares with many of his peers.

The legendary broadcast duo of Al McGuire and Dick Enberg experience Allen Fieldhouse, with McGuire joining in the "Rock, Chalk, Jayhawk" chant.

Photo provided by KU Sports Information

Scott Thornley, whose first game at Allen Fieldhouse was in the 1985-86 season, says the emotion builds well before he hits the court.

"It starts when you begin driving in from the airport," Thornley said. "Then it elevates when you turn onto campus and drive up to the building. You see all the traffic and the long lines of people waiting for the doors to open—and it's still almost two hours before the game. After I park my car, I like to walk around outside and see the fans and soak it in. I think the one thing that stands out for me is the energy I feel when I walk into the building."

The longstanding traditions and the people who are a part of the Allen Fieldhouse experience also make officiating a game there a special experience.

"I got to know many of the people who made the history and tradition," said Rick Wulkow, who called games in Allen Fieldhouse from 1979-80 to 1995-96. "I was on a first-name basis with custodians, security and even some vendors. It was one of my favorite places to work a game.

"The fans are so supportive and loyal. But they are also very knowledgeable," Thornley said. "They understand the game. It seems like the same people have been there forever. "

"It's not unusual for someone to recognize you at a game," Reynolds said. "But I remember having dinner with my son at a game in Lawrence and I had people who came right up to me and know who I was. One time I was buying ice in a convenience store in Pueblo, Colorado, and a man with a KU shirt came up to me and said, 'Hey, aren't you Stanley Reynolds, the basketball official?' Kansas fans know everything about the game."

James Naismith Court may be the tightest in college basketball. Media are packed within an arms reach of the floor, as are the team benches and scorer's table. It might make calling a game more difficult, but the officials wouldn't have it any other way.

Photo provided by Jeff Jacobsen

Allen Fieldhouse under the moonlight.

"It makes it a bit more challenging when you don't have as much room to work," 21-year officiating veteran Ed Hightower said. "But that adds to the ambience. The fans are on top of you and you are on top of the play. It is not a distraction."

Speaking of distraction, game officials are in agreement that no amount of history or crowd support compromises the integrity of their work. They do contend, however, that crowd noise can make it more challenging.

"Your crew communicates with hand signals and eye contact for the most part," Hightower said. "But it gets so loud at Allen Fieldhouse you can't hear the other officials even when they yell. Sometimes you can't hear their whistles, even when you are close to them."

"Part of the administration of the game is to talk to the players and coaches, explaining something to them while play is going on," Thornley said. "But at Allen Fieldhouse you can't always do that. It gets so incredibly loud. You can't have much of a conversation.

"When I work with officials who have not been to Allen Fieldhouse before, I explain to them that they cannot get caught up in the emotion," Hightower says. "It's always easier said than done. It's a great crowd, it's a great environment and it's a great opportunity. But we all know we have a job to do. And to do it in Allen Fieldhouse is special."

Photo provided by Jeff Jacobsen

Season-by-Season Allen Fieldhouse Win-Loss Records

Season	W-L	Season	W-L
1954-55	2-0	1964-65	7-3
1955-56	7-2	1965-66	10-0
1956-57	10-0	1966-67	12-1
1957-58	7-2	1967-68	9-3
1958-59	5-5	1968-69	10-2
1959-60	8-2	1969-70	13-0
1960-61	7-3	1970-71	14-0
1961-62	1-9	1971-72	11-3
1962-63	5-6	1972-73	7-7
1963-64	8-2	1973-74	12-1
		1974-75	11-2

Season	W-L	Season	W-L
1975-76	8-6	1998-99	10-3
1976-77	12-2	1999-00	13-1
1977-78	14-1	2000-01	13-1
1978-79	11-2	2001-02	13-0
1979-80	11-3	2002-03	15-1
1980-81	14-1	2003-04	13-1
1981-82	12-4	Totals	551-101 (.845)
1982-83	8-6		
1983-84	14-2		
1984-85	16-0		
1985-86	15-0		
1986-87	15-0		
1987-88	11-3		
1988-89	10-4		
1989-90	15-1		
1990-91	15-0		
1991-92	13-1		
1992-93	13-2		
1993-94	13-3		
1994-95	14-0		
1995-96	13-0		
1996-97	15-0		
1997-98	16-0		

Photo provided by Jeff Jacobsen

Women's Basketball
Finds a Home

Basketball already had a rich and storied tradition on the men's side at Kansas when the doors to Allen Fieldhouse opened in 1955. Almost 20 years later, the women's team also began calling the facility home.

A new coach had been hired at Kansas in the spring of 1972. Marian Washington made her debut by conducting tryouts for the team in October 1973 in Allen Fieldhouse rather than Robinson Gymnasium, where the women's practices and games had been staged since the program's inception in 1968-69. The Jayhawks and Washington made their Allen Fieldhouse debut December 12, 1973, against crosstown opponent Haskell Indian Nations University, (Haskell College, as it was known at that time), winning 69-29. Washington and the Jayhawks finished the season a respectable 11-8.

Tradition had a role in attracting Washington to Kansas, but it had nothing to do with the basketball program or Allen Fieldhouse. An outstanding multi-sport athlete, she grew up in West Chester, Pennsylvania, in a modest family setting that espoused high morals and dignity. Her opportunity was through athletics, competing primarily in track and field and basketball.

"I found out I was a gifted athlete and realized all I needed was an opportunity at the starting line," she said. "There it didn't matter how much money I had, what color my skin was. Sports gave me a real sense of worth."

Her big break came in high school in the early 1960s when she had an opportunity to work with a world-class discus thrower from the University of Kansas, Al Oerter. A four-time Olympian, Oerter suggested that if Washington ever had the chance, she should go to Kansas to work with legendary coach Bill Easton. Basketball, however, would be her sport of choice, and she opted to attend hometown West Chester State College, the dominant women's college basketball program in the 1960s and early 1970s.

Washington excelled as a player and was named to the United States national team scheduled to compete in the 1972 Munich Olympics. She and her teammates moved to Arkansas to train, but the International Olympic Committee found the schedule was too crowded and opted to cancel the women's basketball competition. Remembering Oerter's advice, she moved to Lawrence to enroll in KU's master's program and helped out with the men's track team.

Angela Aycock and Lynette Woodard were two of Washington's prized players.

Photo provided by Jeff Jacobsen

The next year she would not only be named the women's basketball coach, but would also start the women's track and field program and tack on the title of women's athletic director.

"When the chancellor told me I had gotten the position, I went blank. All I could think was, 'What have you gotten yourself into?' They were some of the most intense, exhausting and even heartbreaking years of my life."

Washington would go on to coach at Kansas for 31 years. She made an immediate splash on the national scene with the signing of highly touted Wichita North High School phenom Lynette Woodard in spring 1977. The combination of Washington and Woodard put Kansas women's basketball on the map. Woodard, the leading scorer in all of women's college basketball to this day with 3,649 points, went on to become a four-time Kodak All-American at Kansas. Her 1,572 career field goals and 2,994 field goal attempts also still stand as the most in women's college basketball history. She still holds eight KU school records.

"I had always loved basketball," Woodard said. "But I didn't know anything about basketball. It was instinctual. I always compared it to a piano player who could play by ear, but did not know the notes. This (Allen Fieldhouse) is where I learned the notes."

Woodard won the 1981 Wade Trophy—the most prestigious award in women's sports. She also went on to be a member of the 1980 U.S. Olympic team even though the United State boycotted those Olympics; to become a captain for the 1984 U.S. Olympic team; to play professional basketball overseas in Italy and Japan; to be the first female member of the Harlem Globetrotters; to play professionally in the United States in the Women's WNBA, and then to return to Kansas as a women's basketball aide, assistant coach and interim head coach. In September 2004 she was inducted into the Naismith Basketball Hall of Fame.

Woodard succeeded Washington on an interim basis during the 2003-04 season when the legendary coach stepped down during the second half of the season for health reasons. Washington resigned following the season and finished her career at Kansas with more than 550 career victories, seven conference titles, six league tournament titles, three Kodak All-Americans, 11 NCAA tournament appearances, two NCAA tournament Sweet 16 finishes, and three conference Coach of the Year awards. She garnered a unique coaching feat when she directed her squad to the Big Eight Conference title in its last year and the Big 12 Conference title in its first year of existence. She was a member of the gold-medal winning coaching staff in the 1996 Olympic games, bringing the team to Allen Fieldhouse for an exhibition game during the 1995-96 season. Washington was also the first African-American to coach a U.S. national team against international competition.

Playing alongside Woodard was another Midwesterner who had coaching aspirations. Cheryl Burnett, Washington's first full-scholarship player and point guard, arrived on campus one year ahead of Woodard in 1977. Burnett went on to become head coach at Southwest Missouri State, where she took her team to the NCAA Final Four in 1992 and 2001. Burnett faced her alma mater in the early rounds of the 2001 NCAA tour-

KU won seven conference championships under Washington.

Photo provided by Jeff Jacobsen

nament, defeating the Jayhawks on their home floor in the first round. Burnett remembers her first impressions of Allen Fieldhouse as a recruit of the Jayahwks.

"My initial reaction was not as much to the physical nature of the building, it was the history of the building. I used to go up and sit near the top of the fieldhouse and look down and imagine the players who played there and the coaches who were on the sidelines. It was awesome," said Burnett, who took over the head coaching duties at the University of Michigan in 2003. "I remember my official visit. The field-house made an impression on me then. I had only seen the building on TV before then."

The Centralia, Missouri native quarterbacked the Jayhawks to seasons of 11-15, 22-11, 30-8 and 29-8 during her tenure at KU, winning back-to-back Big Eight titles along the way along with some big victories at home.

"Kansas State was always a big game and we had a definite home-court advantage," said Burnett. "I thought Allen Fieldhouse was always a good shooting facil-ity. Playing in Allen Fieldhouse was just a wonderful time."

Burnett's desire to become a head coach became a reality, and she was the first Washington-coached player to become a Division I head coach. The 1980 KU graduate took over the head position at Southwest Missouri State in 1987.

Burnett is the only Jayhawk in addition to Woodard to have played for the Jayhawks in Allen Fieldhouse and then coach a game on the same floor. Burnett is the only former player to sit on the opposing bench as the head coach, as she did with her Southwest Missouri State Bears.

"I can't even explain what it was like to go back there and coach," Burnett said about her first game back in Allen Fieldhouse as a head coach. "There were so many memories that came back. I get to say I played basketball with Lynette Woodard, one of the greatest players ever in women's basketball. I can't put it into words other than it was just special. It's a hallowed building in terms of memories and history. Even if you're not an alumnus, Allen Fieldhouse is a special place."

Seven professional WNBA players have performed on the hardwood in Allen Fieldhouse for Washington: Woodard, Tamecka Dixon, Angela Aycock, Lynn Pride, Charisse Sampson, Jaclyn Johnson and Nakia Sanford. Washington finished her career at Kansas with a record of 559-356 in 31 seasons. The jerseys of Woodard, Dixon and Aycock have been retired and hang in the rafters of Allen Fieldhouse.

Allen Fieldhouse Moments

2000s

February 5, 2000 – Kansas 87, Texas Tech 62

Kansas started three freshmen—Nick Collison, Kirk Hinrich and Drew Gooden—for the first time since the 1982-83 season in a win over Texas Tech.

November 25, 2000 – Kansas 99, Washburn 56

KU's 99-56 win over Washburn marked the team's 500th victory in Allen Fieldhouse ... Kirk Hinrich led the Jayhawks with 22 points.

February 5, 2001 – Iowa State 79, Kansas 77

Despite shooting 50.0 percent of its field goal attempts and outrebounding the Cyclones, No. 5-ranked Kansas fell to No. 12-ranked Iowa State before a packed house at Allen Fieldhouse.

February 21, 2001 – Kansas 91, Colorado 79

KU downed Colorado, 91-79, giving head coach Roy Williams his 349th victory; the win moved him past Ted Owens into second place among Jayhawk coaches ... the victory also represented the 18th straight over CU in Lawrence.

December 4, 2001 – Kansas 83, Wake Forest 76

The No. 4-ranked Jayhawks downed No. 23 Wake Forest as freshman Wayne Simien, returning from an injury, had 10 points and 11 rebounds and became the first KU player in the Roy Williams era to record a double-double in his debut game.

January 9, 2002 – Kansas 96, Nebraska 57

KU celebrated its new No. 1 national ranking with an impressive win over Nebraska behind 20 points from Nick Collison.

January 28, 2002 – Kansas 105, Missouri 73

Drew Gooden scored 26 and Kirk Hinrich added 23 as No. 2 ranked KU mauled No. 22 Missouri in a nationally televised game in Allen Fieldhouse.

February 18, 2002 – Kansas 102, Iowa State 66

Kansas secured at least a share of the Big 12 Conference title with a victory over Iowa State ... the Jayhawks shot a season-high 62.5 percent from the field.

January 15, 2003 – Kansas 98, Wyoming 70

KU head coach Roy Williams collected his 400th career win as the Jayhawks downed Wyoming, 98-70 ... the win marked the 24th consecutive home-court victory ... Nick Collison scored 28 points as one of five Jayhawks in double figures.

January 25, 2003 – Arizona 91, Kansas 74

KU led by as many as 20 points in the first half and held a 13-point advantage at half-time, but the Jayhawks shot an anemic 29.0 percent in the second half and were defeated by top-ranked Arizona ... Arizona made 22 of 26 free throw attempts while KU made just four of 12 ... KU would later avenge the defeat by beating the Wildcats in the regional final to advance to the Final Four.

January 27, 2003 – Kansas 90, Texas 87

Two days after losing to No. 1 Arizona, KU hosted No. 3 Texas in an *ESPN Big Monday* game in Allen Fieldhouse ... Nick Collison contributed 24 points and 23 rebounds and Kirk Hinrich added 25 points, as the Jayhawks earned the much-needed victory ... ESPN broadcaster Dick Vitale was so impressed with the performance of Collison that he stood and applauded when Collison fouled out of the game ... Kansas honored former Missouri coach Norm Stewart at halftime.

February 3, 2003 – Dixon and Aycock Jersey Retirement

Tamecka Dixon and Angela Aycock, two of the all-time great players in women's basketball history, were honored at halftime of the Kansas-Missouri men's basketball game by having their jerseys officially retired and displayed in the rafters of Allen Fieldhouse.

March 1, 2003 – Kansas 79, Oklahoma State 61

In their final game in Allen Fieldhouse, seniors Nick Collison and Kirk Hinrich combined for 43 points in leading No. 7 Kansas to a 79-61 win over No. 16 Oklahoma State ... in a great display of sportsmanship, Cowboy head coach Eddie Sutton left his bench and made a trip to the KU bench to shake the hands of Collison and Hinrich as they were removed from the lineup late in the game ... the game would also represent the final appearance of Roy Williams as head coach of the Jayhawks in Allen Fieldhouse.

November 21, 2003 – Kansas 90, UT Chattanooga 76

Keith Langford scored 24 and Wayne Simien 21 in helping Bill Self win his coaching debut, 90-76, over UT Chattanooga.

November 25, 2003 – Kansas 81, Michigan State 74

Junior forward Wayne Simien scored 28 points to lead the sixth-ranked Jayhawks to a 81-74 win over third-ranked Michigan State before a sellout crowd of 16,300.

January 31, 2004 – Lynette Woodard Coaches KU Women's Team

Assistant coach Lynette Woodard assumed the role of women's interim head coach, marking the first game since the end of the 1972-73 season that Marian Washington had not been on the KU bench as head coach ... Washington announced she was taking a medical leave two days earlier ... KU downed Oklahoma State, 74-61, in Woodard's coaching debut.

February 28, 2004 – Washington Returns For The Final Time

Marian Washington, who served 31 seasons as women's head coach at KU, returned to Allen Fieldhouse after announcing her retirement the day before ... Washington was honored in a pregame ceremony.

Former president Bill Clinton was invited to speak in Allen Fieldhouse in 2004 and was introduced by former Kansas senator and KU athlete Bob Dole.

Bill Self
Men's Basketball Head Coach

On the eve prior to the announcement that I would be named the eighth coach in the 106-year history of Kansas Basketball, I sought refuge during what had been an extremely hectic week for my family and me.

I knew just where to go.

As I opened the metal door, the click echoed throughout the cavernous building. The rhythmic cadence of leather sole meeting wooden floor pierced an otherwise peaceful silence. A bright moonlight slipped through the windows, providing just enough illumination to read the banners that hung from the ceiling.

I had been here before. But this time it was even better. I was back in Allen Fieldhouse.

My earliest memories of Allen Fieldhouse were as a youngster growing up in Oklahoma watching on television as the Jayhawks battled with their Big Eight Conference rivals. I got an even more up-close and personal experience of the fieldhouse as a player in the early 1980s at Oklahoma State. Then, perhaps the biggest break in my coaching career came when then-head coach Larry Brown offered me a graduate assistant coaching position after I worked his summer youth camp.

For one year, Allen Fieldhouse became my home away from home. I felt the passion of the fans, witnessed the loyalty of those who had played there as collegians and became engulfed by a tradition rivaled by none. I was a kid in a candy store. And to top it off, I met my future wife at the Fieldhouse; she was a cheerleader, ironically, at Oklahoma State. After all, it was important to maintain a certain level of loyalty to my alma mater!

Almost 20 years after that initial coaching experience, I was blessed with the opportunity to return as the head coach of Kansas. I hold in the highest regard those coaches, players and fans who have come before me to build a tradition and establish a standard of excellence. It is humbling to be entrusted with the honor of adding to that legacy.

Kansas basketball has been well-chronicled in books, in magazines and on video. A missing element, however, has been the story of Allen Fieldhouse. It is only fitting that *Beware of the Phog* was written to celebrate the 50th anniversary of the building's existence. The memories of this grand old building are now preserved in writing and photos for all to read and see.

I have no doubts that in another 50 years there will be much more to add to the story of Allen Fieldhouse. I am sure there will be some touch ups here and there, and other improvements will be made as necessary. But I can guarantee you the aura of the fieldhouse will not change. There is no other place that compares to Allen Fieldhouse. It is truly a treasure and a key component of the fabric of the University.

Notes and Sources

Unless otherwise noted, all direct quotes were from interviews, public speaking engagements, media conferences or personal correspondence.

Foreword
"I've spent five of the greatest" *Topeka Capital Journal,* October 19, 2003
"To this day, I have never" Jayhawk Video Series, Volume 5, 1988
"Having the 1952 team back that day" *Kansas City Star,* February 12, 1995
"People who have cared all their" *St. Petersburg Times,* December 13, 1998
"I had always loved basketball, but I didn't" *Kansas City Star,* March 10, 2004
"I compared it to being a piano player, *Kansas City Star,* September 8, 2004

Chapter 1: How Cool
"I just sat down, its was too loud" *Lawrence Journal World,* November 22, 2003
"It was awesome and every bit as good as" *Kansas City Star,* November 26, 2003
"I don't know if I have ever had more" *Lawrence Journal World,* November 26, 2003

Chapter 2: Phog's Phantasy
"You don't coach basketball" *Coach Phog Allen's Sports Stories,* 1949

Chapter 3: New Digs for the Jayhawks
"The whole future is at stake" *Kansas City Star,* March 18, 1949
"That floor was laid on concrete" *Kansas City Star,* March 18, 1949

Chapter 4: A Night for the Ages
"If this is a tradition, then lets kick a hole" *University Daily Kansan,* April 15, 1953
"Again, let me say I feel extremely" *Lawrence Journal World,* December 17, 1954
"I'll be in the dressing room" *Lawrence Journal World,* February 11, 1995
"Not to put undue pressure on" *Lawrence Journal World,* February 11, 1995
"I don't want to be in a position to ask" *Lawrence Journal World,* March 2, 1955
"Boys, as Doc told you, only a few" *Lawrence Journal World,* March 2, 1955
"Imagine going down in history" *Lawrence Journal World,* February 11, 1995
"I don't think any KU players have ever" *Lawrence Journal World,* February 11, 1995
"Boys, there is a big reason you must" *Lawrence Journal World,* March 2, 1955
"Imagine going down in history" *Lawrence Journal World,* February 11, 1995
"The best thing about all of this" *Lawrence Journal World,* February 11, 1995

Chapter 5: The Fifties
"I'm delighted gentleman, that Kansas State" *Kansas City Star,* March 18, 1949

Chapter 6: The Sixties

"There had been a little bit of a drop" *Kansas Jayhawks: History Making Basketball,* 1991

"Those things are very humbling" *Lawrence Journal World,* February 24, 1986

Chapter 7: The Seventies

"Hopeful we can come up with a plan" University of Kansas News Release, August 13, 1971

Chapter 8: The Eighties

"The current seating is the same that has been" *University Daily Kansan,* August 20, 1985

"We can put Archie out there" *Kansas City Star,* March 6, 1988

"I'd love to see him introduced" *Kansas City Star,* March 6, 1988

"It was the seniors' last home game" *Kansas City Star,* March 6, 1988

"All senior days are special, but" *Kansas City Star,* March 6, 1988

"It was like Custer's last stand" *Lawrence Journal World,* December 10, 1989

"I sat there. I'm human" *Lawrence Journal World,* December 10, 1989

"We've beat some great teams" *Lawrence Journal World,* January 31, 1988

"Among the more memorable of these" *Lawrence Journal World,* November 13, 2003

"I persist in the conviction" *Lawrence Journal World,* November 13, 2003

Chapter 9: The Nineties

"The first night walking there onto the fieldhouse court" *Lawrence Journal World,* February 26, 1995

"If there's a list, it ain't a long one" *USA Today,* November 15, 1996

"Sixteen thousand people came out" *Lawrence Journal World,* February 8, 1998

"I've learned in life that you have to" *Lawrence Journal World,* January 18, 1998

"A little over 40 years ago" *Lawrence Journal World,* January 18, 1998

"I certainly hope the young man" *Kansas Jayhawks: History Making Basketball,* 1991

"It was fabulous" Associated Press, October 15, 1985

"I could not think of a finer place, *Lawrence Journal World,* October 16, 1997

"I had been there, but never" *Lawrence Journal World,* October 16, 1988

"I've spent five of the greatest" *Topeka Capital Journal,* October 19, 2003

"It is something I always wanted to do" *Lawrence Journal World,* December 2, 1992

Chapter 10: A New Millennium

"Its going to look great" *Lawrence Journal World,* April 30, 2004

"I found out I was a gifted athlete" *Philadelphia Daily Tribune,* January 16, 2000

"When the Chancellor told me" *Philadelphia Daily Tribune,* January 16, 2000

"I had always loved basketball, *Kansas City Star,* March 10, 2004

"I compared it to being a piano player, Kansas City Star, September 8, 2004

Appendix I

Year-By-Year Results in Allen Fieldhouse

Denotes starter in leading scorer listings

Number in parenthesis indicates opponent ranking at tipoff

1954-55 Dr. Forrest C. "Phog" Allen
Record: 11-10; **Big Seven:** 5-7/5th;
Allen Fieldhouse: 2-0

Kansas State	W	77-67	Mar. 1
Oklahoma	W	71-67	Mar. 8

(U.S. Olympic Playoff)

Leading Scorers

Dallas Dobbs (5-11 Jr. G)	15.9*
Gene Elstun (6-3 So. F)	14.2*
Bill Brainard (6-3 Jr. F)	10.6*
Lew Johnson (6-6 So. C)	10.0*
John Parker (5-11 So. G)	5.0*

1955-56 Dr. Forrest C. "Phog" Allen
Record: 14-9; **Big Seven** 6-6-/5th;
Allen Fieldhouse 7-2

Northwestern	W	91-70	Dec. 5
SMU	W	62-58	Dec. 21
Oklahoma	W	77-65	Jan. 7
Iowa State (16)	W	68-63	Jan. 16
Oklahoma State	W	56-55	Jan. 31
Missouri	L	78-85	Feb. 6
Nebraska	W	80-56	Feb. 11
Colorado	W	54-44	Mar. 2
Kansas State	L	68-79	Mar. 6

Leading Scorers

Dallas Dobbs (5-11 Sr. G)	16.0*
Maurice King (6-2 Jr. F)	14.0*
Gene Elstun (6-3 Jr. F)	12.8*
Lew Johnson (6-6 Jr. C)	10.3*
Ron Johnston (6-1 Jr. G)	5.5*

1956-57 Dick Harp
Record: 24-3; **Big Seven** 11-1/First;
Allen Fieldhouse: 10-0
NCAA Tournament/Final Four: 3-1 (national runner-up)
Big Seven Conference champions
Big Seven Holiday Tournament champions

Ranked #2 (AP), #2 (UPI)

Northwestern	W	87-69	Dec. 3
Marquette	W	78-61	Dec. 8
Wisconsin	W	83-62	Dec. 22
Missouri	W	92-79	Jan. 5
Kansas State	W	51-45	Jan. 12
Iowa State	W	75-64	Feb. 2
Oklahoma State	W	62-52	Feb. 12
Oklahoma	W	76-56	Feb. 18
Nebraska	W	87-60	Feb. 23
Colorado	W	78-63	Mar. 9

Leading Scorers

Wilt Chamberlain (7-0 So. C)	29.6*
Gene Elstun (6-3 Sr. F)	11.3*
Maurice King (6-2 Sr. G)	9.7*
Ron Loneski (6-4 So. F)	9.5*
John Parker (6-0 Sr. G)	5.5*

1957-58 Dick Harp
Record: 18-5: **Big Seven:** 8-4/T2nd;
Allen Fieldhouse: 7-2
Big Seven Holiday Tournament champions
Ranked #7 (AP), #8 (UPI)

Canisius	W	66-46	Dec. 4
Washington	W	77-59	Dec. 20
Oklahoma State (14)	L	50-52 OT	Jan. 2
Colorado	W	67-46	Jan. 13
Kansas State (3)	L	75-79	Feb. 3
		2OT	
Nebraska	W	104-46	Feb. 8
Iowa State	W	90-61	Feb. 15
Missouri	W	84-69	Feb. 17
Oklahoma	W	60-59	Feb. 28
		OT	

Leading Scorers

Wilt Chamberlain (7-0 Jr. C)	30.1*
Ron Loneski (6-4 Jr. F)	13.5*
Bob Billings (5-11 Jr. G)	8.7*
Bob Hickman (6-1 So. G)	5.2*
Al Donaghue (6-4 So. F)	5.0*

1958-59 Dick Harp
Record: 11-14; **Big Eight:** 8-6/T3rd;
Allen Fieldhouse: 5-5

Rice	W	65-49	Dec. 1
Denver	L	60-73	Dec. 8
North Carolina			
State (4)	L	63-66	Dec. 20
Oklahoma State	W	58-49	Jan. 5
Colorado	L	64-66	Jan. 31
Oklahoma	W	71-44	Feb. 4
Nebraska	W	66-50	Feb. 21
Missouri	W	85-81	Feb. 23
Kansas State (2)	L	77-87	Feb. 27
Iowa State	L	62-67	Mar. 3

Leading Scorers

Ron Loneski (6-4 Sr. F)	19.0*
Bill Bridges (6-5 So. C)	12.3*
Al Donaghue (6-4 Jr. F)	10.6*
Bob Billings (5-11 Sr. G)	6.0*
Bob Hickman (6-2 Jr. G)	5.1*

1959-60 Dick Harp
Record: 19-9; **Big Eight:** 10-4/T1st;
Allen Fieldhouse 8-2
Big Eight Conference co-champion
NCAA Tournament: 1-1 (regional finals)

Texas Tech	W	85-71	Dec. 7
Kentucky	L	72-77	Dec. 14
San Francisco	W	73-42	Dec. 18
Missouri	W	79-63	Jan. 16
Oklahoma State	L	49-62	Jan. 18
Iowa State	W	70-64	Feb. 6
Kansas State	W	64-62	Feb. 10
Colorado	W	75-67	Feb. 20
Oklahoma	W	65-52	Mar. 1
Nebraska	W	79-74	Mar. 7

Leading Scorers

Wayne Hightower (6-8 So. F)	21.8*
Bill Bridges (6-5 Jr. C)	11.4*
Al Donaghue (6-5 Sr. F)	10.9
Jerry Gardner (5-11 So. G)	8.9*
Bob Hickman (6-2 Sr. G)	6.4*

1960-61 Dick Harp
Record: 17-8; **Big Eight:** 10-4/T2nd;
Allen Fieldhouse: 7-3

Northwestern	W	86-69	Dec. 3
North Carolina (5)	L	70-78	Dec. 17
Iowa State	W	90-59	Jan. 14
Oklahoma State	L	49-54	Jan. 16
Kansas State (10)	W	75-66	Jan. 20
Air Force	W	78-52	Feb. 4
Colorado	W	88-65	Feb. 6
Missouri	W	88-73	Feb. 13
Nebraska	L	68-69	Feb. 25
Oklahoma	W	81-56	Feb. 28

Leading Scorers

Wayne Hightower (6-8 Jr. F)	20.7*
Bill Bridges (6-5 Sr. C)	16.1*
Jerry Gardner (5-11 Jr. G)	10.5*
Nolen Ellison (6-1 So. G)	7.9*
Allen Correll (6-3 Jr. F)	7.9*

1961-62 Dick Harp
Record: 7-18; **Big Eight:** 3-11/T7th;
Allen Fieldhouse: 1-9

Arkansas	W	85-74	Dec. 1
St. Louis	L	65-79	Dec. 4
St. John's	L	59-64	Dec. 15
Nebraska	L	67-69	Jan. 6
Missouri	L	66-79	Feb. 5
Kansas State (14)	L	72-91	Feb. 7
Iowa State	L	72-75	Feb. 10
Colorado	L	61-65	Feb. 17
Oklahoma	L	66-67	Feb. 19
		OT	
Oklahoma State	L	37-56	Feb. 24

Leading Scorers

Jerry Gardner (5-11 Sr. G)	20.7*
Nolen Ellison (6-1 Jr. G)	18.1*
Jim Dumas (6-1 Jr. G)	8.9*
Harry Gibson (6-3 So. F)	7.2*
Loye Sparks (6-4 Jr. F)	4.5*

1962-63 Dick Harp
Record: 12-13; **Big Eight:** 5-9/T6th;
Allen Fieldhouse: 5-6
Big Eight Holiday Tournament champions

Montana	W	68-56	Dec. 1
Wyoming	W	75-57	Dec. 10
Cincinnati (1)	L	49-64	Dec. 15
Denver	W	68-43	Dec. 17
Colorado	L	57-73	Jan. 5
Nebraska	W	72-53	Jan. 19
Iowa State	L	57-69	Feb. 2
Oklahoma State	L	53-54	Feb. 11
Oklahoma	L	62-64	Feb. 16
Kansas State	L	54-67	Feb. 19
Missouri	W	72-68	Mar. 1

Leading Scorers

George Unseld (6-7 So. C)	17.2*
Nolen Ellison (6-1 Sr. G)	15.8*
Allen Correll (6-3 Sr. G)	9.8
Harry Gibson (6-3 Jr. F)	8.3*
Jim Dumas (6-1 Sr. G)	6.1*

1963-64 Dick Harp
Record: 13-12; **Big Eight:** 8-6/3rd;
Allen Fieldhouse: 8-2

Arkansas	W	73-60	Dec. 4
Texas Tech	W	73-67	Dec. 10
USC	W	60-52	Dec. 13
Nebraska	W	74-48	Jan. 14
Iowa State	W	74-51	Jan. 18
Missouri	L	58-59	Feb. 4
Oklahoma	W	84-72	Feb. 15
Kansas State	L	46-70	Feb. 22
Colorado	W	73-71	Mar. 2
		OT	
Oklahoma State	W	58-46	Mar. 7

Leading Scorers

George Unseld (6-7 Jr. F)	18.4*
Walt Wesley (6-11 So. C)	10.5
Allen Correll (6-3 Sr. G)	9.9
Steve Renko (6-4 So. F)	9.9*
Harry Gibson (6-3 Sr. F)	7.9*

1964-65 Ted Owens
Record: 17-8; **Big Eight:** 9-5/2nd;
Allen Fieldhouse: 7-3
Big Eight Holiday Tournament champions

New Mexico	W	59-40	Dec. 3
Northwestern	L	55-58	Dec. 5
Loyola (Ill.)	W	80-60	Dec. 12
Missouri	W	73-66	Jan. 9
Iowa State	L	58-64	Jan. 23
Oklahoma	W	77-68	Feb. 6
Kansas State	W	86-66	Feb. 20
Nebraska	W	71-62	Feb. 23
Colorado	W	68-62	Mar. 1
Oklahoma State	L	58-64	Mar. 6

Leading Scorers

Walt Wesley (6-11 Jr. C)	23.5*
Al Lopes (6-5 Jr. G)	11.7*
Del Lewis (6-1 Jr. G)	9.8*
Riney Lochmann (6-6 Jr. F)	6.7*
Ron Franz (6-7 So. F)	5.7*

1965-66 Ted Owens
Record: 23-4; **Big Eight:** 13-1/1st;
Allen Fieldhouse: 10-0
NCAA Tournament: 1-1 (regional finals)
Big Eight Conference champions
Big Eight Holiday Tournament champions
Ranked #4 (AP), #4 (UPI)

Arkansas	W	81-52	Dec. 1
New Mexico State	W	102-51	Dec. 7
Maryland	W	71-62	Dec. 10
Iowa State	W	82-65	Jan. 8
Oklahoma	W	89-68	Jan. 10
Kansas State	W	69-61	Jan. 22
Oklahoma State	W	59-38	Feb. 12
Missouri	W	98-54	Feb. 15
Nebraska (8)	W	110-73	Feb. 26
Colorado	W	85-65	Mar. 7

Leading Scorers

Walt Wesley (6-11 Sr. C)	20.7*
Al Lopes (6-5 Sr. G)	12.4*
Jo Jo White (6-3 Fr. G)	11.3*
Del Lewis (6-1 Sr. G)	10.9*
Ron Franz (6-7 Jr. F)	9.6*

1966-67 Ted Owens
Record: 23-4; **Big Eight:** 13-1/1st;
Allen Fieldhouse: 12-1
NCAA Tournament: 1-1
Big Eight Conference champions
Big Eight Holiday Tournament champions
Ranked #3 (AP), #4 (UPI)

Xavier	W	100-52	Dec. 3
Ohio State	W	94-70	Dec. 5
Baylor	W	68-56	Dec. 10
Pacific	W	70-54	Dec. 13
Oklahoma	W	97-73	Jan. 7
Iowa State	W	73-65	Jan. 21
Nebraska	W	84-58	Feb. 7
Oklahoma State	W	52-39	Feb. 13
Missouri	W	90-55	Feb. 25
Colorado	W	66-59	Mar. 6
Kansas State	W	74-56	Mar. 11
Houston (7)	L	53-66	Mar. 17

NCAA Tournament
(Midwest Region - First Round)

Louisville (2)	W	70-68	Mar. 18

NCAA Tournament
(Midwest Region - Consolation Game)
Leading Scorers

Rodger Bohnenstiel (6-6 Jr. F)	16.4*
Jo Jo White (6-3 So. G)	14.8*
Ron Franz (6-7 Sr. F)	12.4*
Vernon Vanoy (6-8 So. C)	8.3*
Phil Harmon (6-4 So. G)	6.3*

1967-68 Ted Owens
Record: 22-8; **Big Eight:** 10-4/2nd;
Allen Fieldhouse: 9-3
NIT: 3-1 (runner-up)
Ranked #19 (AP), #18 (UPI)

Utah State	W	84-55	Dec. 2
Louisville (3)	L	51-57	Dec. 6
Cincinnati	W	67-61	Dec. 15
Stanford	W	72-54	Dec. 18
Colorado	W	66-50	Jan. 6
Portland	W	80-37	Jan. 13
Missouri	L	66-67	Jan. 15
Oklahoma	W	72-70	Feb. 3

Oklahoma State	W	52-50	Feb. 5
Nebraska	W	71-60	Feb. 17
Kansas State	L	61-64 OT	Feb. 24
Iowa State	W	91-58	Mar. 9

Leading Scorers

Jo Jo White (6-3 Jr. G)	15.3*
Roger Bohnenstiel (6-6 Sr. F)	13.7*
Dave Nash (6-10 Jr. C)	10.0*
Phil Harmon (6-4 Jr. G)	8.1*
Bruce Sloan (6-5 Jr. F)	7.6*

1968-69 Ted Owens
Record: 20-7; **Big Eight:** 9-5/2nd;
Allen Fieldhouse: 10-2
NIT: 0-1
Big Eight Holiday Tournament champions

St. Louis	W	88-65	Nov. 30
Loyola (Ill.)	W	93-61	Dec. 7
Xavier	W	79-56	Dec. 9
Syracuse	W	71-41	Dec. 14
Murray State	W	72-59	Dec. 16
Iowa State	W	94-61	Jan. 6
Colorado (17)	W	80-70	Feb. 1
Oklahoma State	W	64-48	Feb. 3
Missouri	L	55-56	Feb. 15
Nebraska	W	79-73	Feb. 22
Oklahoma	W	83-58	Feb. 24
Kansas State	L	57-64	Mar. 8

Leading Scorers

Dave Robisch (6-10 So. C)	18.1*
Jo Jo White (6-3 Sr. G)	18.1*
Bruce Sloan (6-5 Sr. F)	7.0*
Rich Bradshaw (6-3 Jr. G)	6.9*
Pierre Russell (6-3 So. F)	6.5*

1969-70 Ted Owens
Record: 17-9; **Big Eight:** 8-6/2nd;
Allen Fieldhouse: 13-0

Marshall	W	96-80	Dec. 1
Wisconsin	W	76-60	Dec. 8
SMU	W	89-77	Dec. 19
Western Kentucky	W	104-81	Dec. 20
Iowa State	W	82-62	Jan. 10

Murray State	W	64-62	Jan. 17
Valparaiso	W	74-58	Jan. 24
Colorado	W	75-73	Jan. 31
Oklahoma	W	78-41	Feb. 2
Oklahoma State	W	69-58	Feb. 9
Nebraska	W	100-87	Feb. 17
Missouri	W	63-45	Feb. 23
Kansas State (16)	W	82-79	Mar. 7

Leading Scorers

Dave Robisch (6-10 Jr. C)	26.5*
Pierre Russell (6-3 Jr. F)	13.4*
Bud Stallworth (6-5 So. F)	12.7*
Bob Kivisto (6-1 So. G)	6.7*
Roger Brown (6-10 Jr. C)	5.8*

1970-71 Ted Owens

Record: 27-3; **Big Eight:** 14-0/1st;

Allen Fieldhouse: 14-0

NCAA Tournament: 2-2 (Fourth - Final Four)

Big Eight Conference champions

Big Eight Holiday Tournament champions

Ranked #4 (AP), #4 (UPI)

Long Beach			
State (18)	W	69-52	Dec. 1
Eastern Kentucky	W	79-65	Dec. 5
South Dakota State	W	95-59	Dec. 7
Loyola (Ill.)	W	94-62	Dec. 12
St. Joseph's	W	80-65	Dec. 18
Houston	W	89-73	Dec. 19
Oklahoma City	W	101-77	Jan. 16
Iowa State	W	83-57	Jan. 18
Oklahoma State	W	90-55	Jan. 23
Kansas State	W	79-74	Feb. 1
Colorado	W	91-67	Feb. 8
Missouri	W	85-66	Feb. 20
Oklahoma	W	54-52	Mar. 6
		OT	
Nebraska	W	59-54	Mar. 13

Leading Scorers

Dave Robisch (6-10 Sr. F)	19.2*
Bud Stallworth (6-5 Jr. G)	16.9*
Roger Brown (6-10 Sr. C)	11.2*
Pierre Russell (6-4 Sr. F)	10.3*
Aubrey Nash (6-1 Jr. G)	6.6*

1971-72 Ted Owens

Record: 11-15; **Big Eight:** 7-7/T4th;

Allen Fieldhouse: 11-3

Xavier	W	75-57	Dec. 1
Kentucky (10)	L	69-79	Dec. 4
Notre Dame	W	88-72	Dec. 8
Louisville (16)	L	65-74	Dec. 11
Brigham Young (6)	W	83-67	Dec. 17
USC (10)	L	77-87	Dec. 18
Oklahoma State	W	85-58	Jan. 15
Kansas State	W	66-63	Jan. 17
		2OT	
Iowa State	W	74-71	Jan. 24
Nebraska	W	57-77	Jan. 29
		OT	
Georgia Tech	W	93-65	Feb. 7
Oklahoma	W	77-74	Feb. 12
Colorado	W	71-59	Feb. 21
Missouri (14)	W	93-80	Feb. 26

Leading Scorers

Bud Stallworth (6-5 Sr. F)	25.3*
Tom Kivisto (6-3 So. G)	8.9*
Randy Canfield (6-9 Jr. C)	7.6*
Aubrey Nash (6-1 Sr. G)	6.7*
Wilson Barrow (6-6 Jr. F)	6.4*

1972-73 Ted Owens

Record: 8-18; **Big Eight:** 4-10/6th;

Allen Fieldhouse: 7-7

Vanderbilt	L	64-72	Dec. 2
Indiana	L	55-72	Dec. 5
Murray State	W	69-63	Dec. 7
Iowa	L	56-69	Dec. 9
Xavier	W	61-54	Dec. 11
Texas Tech	W	67-51	Dec. 15
San Francisco	W	60-58	Dec. 16
Colorado	W	67-58	Jan. 13
Kansas State (18)	L	68-77	Jan. 23
Oklahoma	W	76-69	Feb. 3
Nebraska	L	46-59	Feb. 10
Oklahoma State	W	75-66	Feb. 17
Missouri	L	63-79	Feb. 27
Iowa State	L	65-89	Mar. 10

Leading Scorers

Rick Suttle (6-9 So. F)	16.3*
Dale Greenlee (6-2 So. G)	9.0*
Tom Kivisto (6-2 Jr. G)	8.6*
Danny Knight (6-10 So. C)	8.8*
Tommie Smith (6-4 So. F)	7.2*

1973-74 Ted Owens
Record: 23-7; **Big Eight:** 13-1/1st;
Allen Fieldhouse: 12-1
NCAA Tournament: 2-2 (Fourth - Final Four)
Big Eight Conference champions
Ranked #7 (AP), #10 (UPI)

Murray State	W	103-71	Dec. 1
Kentucky (10)	W	71-63	Dec. 3
Northern Iowa	W	94-60	Dec. 8
Washington State	W	66-51	Dec. 14
Oregon	W	67-49	Dec. 15
Nebraska	W	79-64	Jan. 12
Oklahoma State	W	68-66	Jan. 19
Notre Dame (1)	L	74-76	Jan. 22
Colorado	W	81-66	Feb. 4
Iowa State	W	72-57	Feb. 16
Oklahoma	W	98-80	Feb. 18
Kansas State	W	60-55	Mar. 6
Missouri	W	112-76	Mar. 9

Leading Scorers

Danny Knight (6-10 Jr. C)	12.4*
Roger Morningstar (6-6 Jr. F)	12.3*
Dale Greenlee (6-2 Jr. G)	11.8*
Norm Cook (6-8 Fr. F)	11.4*
Rick Suttle (6-10 Jr. C)	11.3

1974-75 Ted Owens
Record: 19-8; **Big Eight:** 11-3/1st;
Allen Fieldhouse: 11-2
NCAA Tournament: 1-1
Big Eight Conference champions
Big Eight Holiday Tournament champions

NE Missouri State	W	65-50	Nov. 30
Augustana (S.D.)	W	85-50	Dec. 2
Indiana (3)	L	70-74	Dec. 4
		OT	

Iowa	W	89-54	Dec. 7
Fordham	W	78-74	Dec. 13
Washington	L	64-74	Dec. 14
Missouri	W	91-86	Jan. 18
Oklahoma State	W	71-60	Jan. 25
Colorado	W	81-59	Jan. 29
Nebraska	W	72-44	Feb. 5
Iowa State	W	76-62	Feb. 12
Kansas State	W	91-53	Feb. 22
Oklahoma	W	74-63	Mar. 8

Leading Scorers

Rick Suttle (6-10 Sr. C)	14.6*
Roger Morningstar (6-6 Sr. F)	11.1*
Norm Cook (6-8 So. F)	10.3*
Dale Greenlee (6-3 Sr. G)	9.3*
Danny Knight (6-10 Sr. C)	8.5

1975-76 Ted Owens
Record: 13-13; **Big Eight:** 6-8/T4th;
Allen Fieldhouse: 8-6

Murray State	W	72-56	Nov. 29
St. Louis	W	70-64	Dec. 6
Notre Dame (9)	L	64-72	Dec. 8
Boise State	W	61-56	Dec. 11
Kentucky (14)	L	48-54	Dec. 13
Yale	W	63-54	Dec. 19
LaSalle	W	74-73	Dec. 20
Iowa State	W	68-60	Jan. 20
Kansas State	W	62-57	Jan. 31
Oklahoma	L	63-64	Feb. 7
Oklahoma State	W	70-60	Feb. 14
Missouri (14)	L	60-61	Feb. 18
Colorado	L	66-68	Feb. 28
Nebraska	L	58-62	Mar. 3

Leading Scorers

Norm Cook (6-8 Jr. F)	14.8*
Clint Johnson (6-2 So. G)	11.0*
Ken Koenigs (6-10 So. F)	10.7*
Herb Nobles (6-7 Jr. F)	10.8
Paul Mokeski (7-1 Fr. C)	10.6*

1976-77 Ted Owens
Record: 18-10; **Big Eight:** 8-6/4th;
Allen Fieldhouse: 12-2

Montana State	W	104-47	Nov. 27
Murray State	W	81-66	Dec. 1
Central Mo. State	W	74-52	Dec. 4
Oral Roberts	W	79-69	Dec. 6
Mankato State	W	87-74	Dec. 17
Arkansas (19)	L	63-67	Dec. 18
Missouri	W	77-72	Jan. 8
Oklahoma State	W	62-60	Jan. 12
Iowa State	W	73-62	Jan. 18
Colorado	W	79-70	Jan. 29
Oklahoma	W	91-81	Feb. 5
Kansas State	L	83-86	Feb. 12
Nebraska	W	74-66	Feb. 19
Nebraska	W	61-58	Feb. 26

(Big Eight Conference Tournament)
Leading Scorers

John Douglas (6-2 Jr. G)	19.2*	
Herb Nobles (6-7 Sr. F)	14.8*	
Ken Koenigs (6-10 Jr. F)	10.9*	
Clint Johnson (6-2 Jr. G)	8.9*	
Donnie Von Moore (6-9 Jr. F)	7.1*	

1977-78 Ted Owens
Record: 24-5; **Big Eight:** 13-1/1st
Allen Fieldhouse: 14-1
NCAA Tournament: 0-1
Big Eight Conference champions
Big Eight Holiday Tournament champions

Central Mo. State	W	121-65	Nov. 28
Fordham	W	99-67	Nov. 30
SMU	W	107-71	Dec. 2
Murray State	W	106-71	Dec. 5
Fairleigh Dickinson	W	88-54	Dec. 7
Kentucky (1)	L	66-73	Dec. 10
St. Louis	W	85-65	Dec. 17
Oklahoma	W	91-61	Jan. 14
Kansas State	W	56-52	Jan. 21
Colorado	W	85-56	Jan. 28
Oklahoma State	W	83-65	Feb. 1
Missouri	W	72-52	Feb. 8
Iowa State	W	80-70	Feb. 15

Nebraska	W	75-70	Feb. 18
Colorado	W	82-66	Feb. 28

(Big Eight Conference Tournament)
Leading Scorers

Darnell Valentine (6-2 Fr. G)	13.5*	
John Douglas (6-2 Sr. G)	12.7*	
Ken Koenigs (6-10 Sr. F)	11.1*	
Donnie Von Moore (6-9 Sr. F)	10.7	
Paul Mokeski (7-1 Jr. C)	9.3*	

1978-79 Ted Owens
Record: 18-11; **Big Eight:** 8-6/T2nd;
Allen Fieldhouse: 11-2
Big Eight Holiday Tournament champions

Fairleigh Dickinson	W	91-68	Nov. 29
Murray State	W	81-66	Dec. 2
Boise State	W	82-68	Dec. 4
Oral Roberts	W	90-77	Dec. 7
SMU	W	71-64	Dec. 16
Missouri	L	55-58	Jan. 17
Iowa State	W	80-71	Jan. 24
Colorado	W	56-51	Jan. 31
Oklahoma State	W	82-71	Feb. 2
Oklahoma	W	74-62	Feb. 10
Kansas State	L	56-58	Feb. 17
Nebraska	W	66-59	Feb. 21
Iowa State	W	91-70	Feb. 27

(Big Eight Conference Tournament)
Leading Scorers

Darnell Valentine (6-2 So. G)	16.1*	
Paul Mokeski (7-1 Sr. C)	14.1*	
John Crawford (6-7 So. F)	10.2*	
Wilmore Fowler (6-1 So. G)	9.2*	
Tony Guy (6-5 Fr. G)	9.2*	

1979-80 Ted Owens
Record: 15-14; **Big Eight:** 7-7/T3rd;
Allen Fieldhouse: 11-3

Nevada-Reno	W	93-75	Dec. 1
San Diego State	W	79-66	Dec. 8
California-Bakersfield	W	93-53	Dec. 10
Kentucky (5)	L	56-57	Dec. 12

Birmingham-Southern	W	90-64	Dec. 22
Wisconsin-Oshkosh	W	109-72	Jan. 5
Missouri (12)	W	69-66	Jan. 9
Kansas State	L	52-61	Jan. 19
Colorado	W	75-61	Jan. 26
Iowa State	W	72-61	Feb. 2
Nebraska	L	56-61	Feb. 5
Oklahoma	W	69-66	Feb. 13
Oklahoma State	W	84-74 OT	Feb. 23
Colorado	W	75-65	Feb. 26

Big Eight Conference Tournament

Leading Scorers

Darnell Valentine (6-2 Jr. G)	16.5*
Ricky Ross (6-6 Fr. G)	11.7*
Tony Guy (6-6 So. G)	10.9*
John Crawford (6-8 Jr. F)	7.9*
Booty Neal (6-5 Jr. G)	5.8

1980-81 Ted Owens
Record: 24-8; **Big Eight:** 9-5/T2nd;
Allen Fieldhouse: 14-1
NCAA Tournament: 2-1
Big Eight Tournament champions
Ranked #19 (UPI)

Pepperdine	W	81-67	Dec. 1
Michigan	L	52-64	Dec. 3
Oral Roberts	W	90-66	Dec. 6
Morehead State	W	90-56	Dec. 8
USC	W	91-68	Dec. 20
Rollins	W	102-47	Dec. 30
Iona	W	94-64	Jan. 10
Iowa State	W	70-58	Jan. 14
Missouri	W	63-55	Jan. 21
Colorado	W	66-59	Jan. 24
Oklahoma	W	96-67	Feb. 7
Kansas State	W	58-50	Feb. 18
Nebraska	W	75-49	Feb. 25
Oklahoma State	W	80-65	Feb. 28

(Big Eight Conference Tournament)

Oklahoma State	W	96-69	Mar. 3

Leading Scorers

Tony Guy (6-6 Jr. G)	15.8*
Darnell Valentine (6-2 Sr. G)	15.6*
David Magley (6-7 Jr. F)	9.5*

John Crawford (6-7 Sr. F)	8.1
Victor Mitchell (6-9 Jr. C)	8.1*

1981-82 Ted Owens
Record: 13-14; **Big Eight:** 4-10/7th;
Allen Fieldhouse: 12-4

Arizona State	W	63-62	Nov. 30
Texas Southern	W	67-65	Dec. 2
Michigan State	W	74-56	Dec. 5
Arizona	W	86-57	Dec. 7
Kentucky (2)	L	74-77 OT	Dec. 12
SMU	W	81-71	Dec. 19
Evansville	W	72-65 OT	Jan. 6
Rollins College	W	82-69	Jan. 9
Oklahoma State	W	77-72	Jan. 16
Alcorn State	W	72-60	Jan. 25
Colorado	W	74-60	Jan. 27
Oklahoma	W	55-53	Jan. 30
Missouri (4)	L	41-42	Feb. 9
Nebraska	W	66-63	Feb. 13
Kansas State (18)	L	53-63	Feb. 20
Iowa State	L	61-63	Feb. 27

Leading Scorers

David Magley (6-8 Sr. F)	17.3*
Tony Guy (6-6 Sr. G)	14.9*
Kelly Knight (6-7 So. C)	12.3*
Jeff Dishman (6-5 Jr. F)	9.3*
Tyke Peacock (6-1 Jr. G)	4.7

1982-83 Ted Owens
Record: 13-16; **Big Eight:** 4-10/T7th;
Allen Fieldhouse: 8-6

U.S. International	W	91-74	Nov. 27
Bowling Green	W	97-68	Nov. 29
Mississippi Valley	W	63-51	Dec. 2
St. Louis	W	83-69	Dec. 4
Memphis State	L	58-64	Dec. 18
Alcorn State	W	86-74	Dec. 20
Maine	W	79-68	Jan. 15
Missouri (13)	L	63-76	Jan. 26
Iowa State	W	75-69	Feb. 2

Colorado	L	74-75	Feb. 10
Oklahoma State	L	69-75	Feb. 12
Oklahoma (19)	W	55-53	Feb. 19
Kansas State	L	63-70	Feb. 26
Nebraska	L	58-60	Mar. 2

Leading Scorers

Carl Henry (6-5 Jr. G)	17.4*
Kerry Boagni (6-8 Fr. F)	14.1*
Kelly Knight (6-8 Jr. C)	12.3*
Calvin Thompson (6-6 Fr. F)	7.9*
Jeff Dishman (6-6 Sr. F)	5.7

1983-84 Larry Brown
Record: 22-10; **Big Eight:** 9-5/2nd;
Allen Fieldhouse: 14-2
NCAA Tournament: 1-1
Big Eight Tournament champions

Morehead State	W	75-57	Dec. 3
Jackson State	W	89-57	Dec. 5
Kentucky (2)	L	50-72	Dec. 10
Fla. Southern	W	85-73	Dec. 17
Oral Roberts	W	65-64	Dec. 19
Fla. International	W	99-47	Jan. 7
Texas Southern	W	101-64	Jan. 11
Colorado	W	53-48	Jan. 14
Missouri	W	73-56	Jan. 18
Nebraska	W	77-61	Jan. 25
Kansas State	W	65-54	Jan. 28
Wichita State	W	79-69	Feb. 5
Iowa State	W	80-72	Feb. 11
Oklahoma (8)	L	82-92	Feb. 22
Oklahoma State	W	91-70	Mar. 3
Oklahoma State	W	75-58	Mar. 6
(Big Eight Conference Tournament)			

Leading Scorers

Carl Henry (6-5 Sr. G)	16.8*
Kelly Knight (6-8 Sr. F)	11.4*
Calvin Thompson (6-6 So. G)	11.3*
Greg Dreiling (7-1 Sr. C)	9.7*
Ron Kellogg (6-5 So. G)	6.7*

1984-85 Larry Brown
Record: 26-8; **Big Eight:** 11-3/2nd;
Allen Fieldhouse: 16-0
NCAA Tournament: 1-1

Detroit	W	86-64	Dec. 1
South Dakota State	W	85-72	Dec. 4
Abilene Christian	W	84-72	Dec. 8
South Carolina State	W	81-54	Dec. 10
Houston	W	87-75	Dec. 15
Texas Southern	W	78-74	Jan. 3
Western Carolina	W	79-62	Jan. 7
Iowa State	W	76-72	Jan. 17
Missouri	W	70-68	Jan. 22
Colorado	W	88-69	Feb. 4
Oklahoma State	W	84-72	Feb. 6
Memphis State	W	75-71	Feb. 9
Kansas State	W	75-64	Feb. 20
Oklahoma (5)	W	82-76	Feb. 24
Nebraska	W	70-65	Feb. 28
Nebraska	W	74-69	Mar. 5

Leading Scorers

Ron Kellogg (6-5 Jr. F)	17.6*
Danny Manning (6-11 Fr. F)	14.6*
Calvin Thompson (6-6 Jr. G)	13.7*
Greg Dreiling (7-1 Jr. C)	13.1*
Cedric Hunter (6-0 So. G)	6.7*

1985-86 Larry Brown
Record: 35-4; **Big Eight:** 13-1/1st;
Allen Fieldhouse: 15-0
NCAA Tournament: 4-1 (Tie Third -Final Four)
Big Eight Conference champions
Big Eight Tournament champions
Ranked #2 (AP), #2 (UPI)

SIU-Edwardsville	W	86-71	Dec. 3
Western Carolina	W	101-79	Dec. 4
South Alabama	W	72-48	Dec. 9
Kentucky (9)	W	83-66	Dec. 14
Arkansas	W	89-78	Dec. 21
George Washington	W	94-71	Dec. 23
SMU	W	72-56	Jan. 11
Oklahoma State	W	95-72	Jan. 18
Oklahoma (5)	W	98-92	Jan. 21
Louisville	W	71-69	Jan. 25

Colorado	W	100-64	Feb. 5
Missouri	W	100-66	Feb. 11
Nebraska	W	79-61	Feb. 15
Kansas State	W	84-69	Feb. 22
Iowa State	W	90-70	Mar. 1

Leading Scorers

Danny Manning (6-11 So. F)	16.7*
Ron Kellogg (6-5 Sr. F)	15.9*
Calvin Thompson (6-6 Sr. G)	13.4*
Greg Dreiling (7-1 Sr. C)	11.6*
Cedric Hunter (6-0 Jr. G)	9.1*

1986-87 Larry Brown
Record: 25-11; **Big Eight:** 9-5/T2nd;
Allen Fieldhouse: 15-0
NCAA Tournament: 2-1
Ranked #20 (AP)

Tennessee-Martin	W	88-69	Nov. 29
Southern	W	87-69	Dec. 1
Washington	W	82-68	Dec. 4
Colorado	W	59-56	Dec. 13
Texas Tech	W	82-52	Dec. 20
The Citadel	W	74-71	Dec. 22
Temple (8)	W	67-64	Jan. 8
Miami	W	82-47	Jan. 17
Missouri	W	71-70	Jan. 20
Nebraska	W	86-65	Jan. 22
Iowa State	W	72-48	Jan. 27
Oklahoma State	W	88-63	Feb. 7
Notre Dame	W	70-60	Feb. 8
Oklahoma (8)	W	86-84	Feb. 14
Kansas State	W	84-67	Feb. 19

Leading Scorers

Danny Manning (6-11 Jr. F)	23.9*
Cedric Hunter (6-0 Sr. G)	11.6*
Kevin Pritchard (6-3 Fr. G)	9.6*
Chris Piper (6-8 Jr. F)	6.6*
Mark Turgeon (5-11 Sr. G)	5.0*

1987-88 Larry Brown
Record: 27-11; **Big Eight:** 9-5/3rd;
Allen Fieldhouse: 11-3
NCAA Tournament: 6-0 (Champions)

Pomona-Pitzer	W	94-38	Dec. 1
St. John's	W	63-54	Dec. 5
Appalachian State	W	73-62	Dec. 7
Rider	W	110-72	Dec. 12
American	W	90-69	Jan. 6
Missouri	W	78-74	Jan. 9
Hampton	W	95-69	Jan. 16
Kansas State	L	61-72	Jan. 30
Oklahoma (7)	L	65-73	Feb. 3
Colorado	W	73-62	Feb. 6
Iowa State	W	82-72	Feb. 13
Nebraska	W	70-48	Feb. 16
Duke (6)	L	70-74 OT	Feb. 20
Oklahoma State	W	75-57	Mar. 5

Leading Scorers

Danny Manning (6-11 Sr. C)	24.8*
Milt Newton (6-4 Jr. F)	11.6*
Kevin Pritchard (6-3 So. G)	10.6*
Chris Piper (6-8 Sr. F)	5.1*
Jeff Gueldner (6-5 So. G)	3.9*

1988-89 Roy Williams
Record: 19-12; **Big Eight:** 6-8/6th;
Allen Fieldhouse: 10-4

Seattle	W	98-65	Dec. 1
Loyola-Chicago	W	100-80	Dec. 3
Pacific Lutheran	W	112-61	Dec. 7
Northern Arizona	W	109-59	Dec. 12
Brown	W	115-45	Jan. 3
Iowa State	W	127-82	Jan. 7
SMU	W	90-82 OT	Jan. 9
Wichita State	W	86-66	Jan. 25
Kansas State	L	70-71	Jan. 28
Missouri (5)	L	66-91	Feb. 1
Oklahoma State	L	81-87	Feb. 8
Oklahoma (1)	L	89-94 OT	Feb. 15
Colorado	W	111-83	Feb. 25
Nebraska	W	80-71	Mar. 1

Leading Scorers

Milt Newton (6-4 Sr. F/G)		17.7*
Mark Randall (6-9 So. F)		16.0*
Kevin Pritchard (6-3 Jr. G)		14.5*
Mike Maddox (6-7 So. F)		10.9*
Freeman West (6-5 Jr. F)		9.2*

1989-90 Roy Williams
Record: 30-5; **Big Eight:** 11-3/T2nd;
Allen Fieldhouse: 15-1
NCAA Tournament: 1-1
Ranked #5 (AP), #5 (UPI)

Alabama-Birmingham	W	109-83	Nov. 15
Idaho	W	87-58	Nov. 30
Md-Baltimore Co.	W	86-67	Dec. 2
Tennessee-Martin	W	103-48	Dec. 4
Kentucky	W	150-95	Dec. 9
Pepperdine	W	98-73	Dec. 16
Arizona State	W	90-67	Dec. 22
Winthrop	W	94-51	Jan. 6
Oklahoma State	W	91-77	Jan. 13
Elizabeth City State	W	132-65	Jan. 18
Colorado	W	90-69	Jan. 31
Oklahoma (9)	W	85-74	Feb. 3
Missouri (2)	L	71-77	Feb. 13
Nebraska	W	94-67	Feb. 17
Kansas State	W	70-58	Feb. 24
Iowa State	W	96-63	Mar. 3

Leading Scorers

Kevin Pritchard (6-3 Sr. G)		14.5*
Mark Randall (6-9 Jr. F)		13.3*
Rick Calloway (6-6 Sr. F)		13.1*
Terry Brown (6-2 Jr. G)		11.0
Jeff Gueldner (6-5 Sr. G)		10.7*

1990-91 Roy Williams
Record: 27-8; **Big Eight:** 10-4/T1st;
Allen Fieldhouse: 15-0
NCAA Tournament: 5-1 (national runner-up)
Big Eight Conference co-champions
Ranked #12 (AP), #12 (UPI)

Marquette	W	108-71	Dec. 1
SMU	W	80-60	Dec. 4
Rider	W	103-51	Dec. 15
Texas-San Antonio	W	101-69	Dec. 22
North Carolina St.	W	105-94	Jan. 5
Md-Baltimore Co.	W	97-46	Jan. 10
Miami	W	73-60	Jan. 16
Missouri	W	91-64	Jan. 19
Wichita State	W	84-50	Jan. 23
Colorado	W	95-62	Jan. 26
Nebraska (15)	W	85-77	Feb. 6
Oklahoma State	W	79-69	Feb. 9
Kansas State	W	68-67	Feb. 16
Oklahoma	W	109-87	Feb. 23
Iowa State	W	88-57	Feb. 26

Leading Scorers

Terry Brown (6-2 Sr. G)		16.0*
Mark Randall (6-9 Sr. C)		15.0*
Adonis Jordan (5-11 So. G)		12.5*
Alonzo Jamison (6-6 Jr. F)		10.4*
Mike Maddox (6-7 Sr. F)		7.4*

1991-92 Roy Williams
Record: 27-5; **Big Eight:** 11-3/1st;
Allen Fieldhouse: 13-1
NCAA Tournament: 1-1
Big Eight Conference champions
Big Eight Tournament champions
Ranked #2 (AP), #2 (UPI)

Maryland-Baltimore Co.	W	122-58	Nov. 23
Arkansas-Little Rock	W	91-80	Nov. 26
Central Mo. State	W	83-54	Nov. 30
DePaul	W	104-75	Dec. 14
Seattle Pacific	W	97-62	Dec. 21
Pepperdine	W	79-73 OT	Jan. 2
Louisville	L	78-85	Jan. 11

Nebraska	W	103-78	Jan. 25
Kansas State	W	80-58	Feb. 3
Iowa State	W	91-60	Feb. 12
Colorado	W	82-45	Feb. 15
Oklahoma	W	84-65	Feb. 24
Oklahoma			
State (14)	W	77-64	Mar. 2
Missouri (11)	W	97-89	Mar. 8

(Big Eight Conference Tournament)

Leading Scorers

Rex Walters (6-4 Jr. G)	16.0*
Adonis Jordan (5-11 Jr. G)	12.8*
Richard Scott (6-7 So. F)	10.1*
Alonzo Jamison (6-6 Sr. F)	10.0*
Eric Pauley (6-10 Jr. C)	9.0*

1992-93 Roy Williams
Record: 29-7; **Big Eight:** 11-3/1st;
Allen Fieldhouse: 13-2
NCAA Tournament: 4-1 (Tie Third - Final Four)
Big Eight Conference champions
Ranked #9 (AP), #4 (Coaches)

Georgia	W	76-65	Dec. 1
Emporia State	W	91-56	Dec. 7
East Tennessee St.	W	86-83	Dec. 19
North Carolina St.	W	84-64	Dec. 21
Wichita State	W	103-54	Jan. 6
Iowa State	W	78-71	Jan. 9
Oral Roberts	W	140-72	Jan. 14
Long Beach State	L	49-64	Jan. 25
Rollins	W	103-56	Jan. 30
Missouri	W	86-69	Feb. 1
Oklahoma State	W	84-72	Feb. 10
Oklahoma (19)	L	77-80	Feb. 17
Kansas State	W	77-64	Feb. 20
Colorado	W	72-68	Feb. 27
Nebraska	W	94-83	Mar. 3

Leading Scorers

Rex Walters (6-4 Sr. G)	15.3*
Adonis Jordan (5-11 Sr. G)	12.1*
Eric Pauley (6-10 Sr. C)	11.9*
Richard Scott (6-7 Jr. F)	10.6*
Steve Woodberry (6-4 Jr. G-F)	10.1

1993-94 Roy Williams
Record: 27-8; **Big Eight:** 9-5/3rd;
Allen Fieldhouse: 13-3
NCAA Tournament: 2-1
Ranked #13 (AP), #12 (Coaches)

Western Michigan	W	69-50	Nov. 17
California (6)	W	73-56	Nov. 19
Temple (7)	L	59-73	Dec. 1
Washburn	W	82-68	Dec. 6
Arkansas-Little Rock	W	98-63	Dec. 11
Furman	W	101-60	Dec. 20
Indiana (22)	W	86-83	Dec. 22
		OT	
UNC Asheville	W	90-44	Jan. 5
SMU	W	91-59	Jan. 8
Oklahoma	W	94-84	Jan. 10
Kansas State	L	64-68	Jan. 17
Oklahoma State	W	62-61	Jan. 26
		OT	
Nebraska	W	94-87	Feb. 6
Missouri (12)	L	74-81	Feb. 20
Colorado	W	106-62	Feb. 26
Iowa State	W	97-79	Mar. 3

Leading Scorers

Steve Woodberry (6-4 Sr. G)	15.5*
Richard Scott (6-7 Sr. F)	13.7*
Greg Ostertag (7-2 Jr. C)	10.3*
Jacque Vaughn (6-1 Fr. G)	7.8*
Sean Pearson (6-4 So. G-F)	7.6

1994-95 Roy Williams
Record: 25-6; **Big Eight:** 11-3/1st;
Allen Fieldhouse: 14-0
NCAA Tournament: 2-1
Big Eight Conference champions
Ranked #5 (AP), #10 (Coaches)

San Diego	W	83-65	Nov. 26
Coppin State	W	91-69	Dec. 5
Florida (6)	W	69-63	Dec. 7
Santa Clara	W	80-75	Dec. 20
Rice	W	71-57	Dec. 22
Fort Hays State	W	93-55	Dec. 31

East Tennessee St.	W	106-73	Jan. 3
Kansas State	W	78-74	Jan. 18
Nebraska	W	84-67	Jan. 23
Colorado	W	99-77	Jan. 31
Iowa State (11)	W	91-71	Feb. 4
Oklahoma	W	93-76	Feb. 11
Missouri (14)	W	88-69	Feb. 25
Oklahoma State	W	78-62	Mar. 5

Leading Scorers

Jerod Haase (6-3 So. G)	15.0*
Raef LaFrentz (6-11 Fr. F)	11.4*
Scot Pollard (6-10 So. C)	10.2
Jacque Vaughn (6-1 So. G)	9.7*
Sean Pearson (6-4 Jr. F)	9.6*
Greg Ostertag (7-2 Sr. C)	9.6*

1995-96 Roy Williams
Record: 29-5; Big Eight: 12-2/1st;
Allen Fieldhouse: 13-0
NCAA Tournament: 3-1 (regional finals)
Big Eight Conference champions
Ranked #4 (AP), #5 (Coaches)

UCLA (23)	W	85-70	Dec. 1
Pittsburg State	W	103-48	Dec. 18
Cornell	W	100-46	Jan. 2
East Tennessee State	W	108-73	Jan. 4
SMU	W	83-61	Jan. 6
Saint Peter's	W	85-71	Jan. 15
Oklahoma	W	72-66	Jan. 22
Oklahoma State	W	84-66	Jan. 31
Kansas State	W	72-62	Feb. 4
Iowa State (21)	W	89-70	Feb. 7
Colorado	W	85-70	Feb. 14
Nebraska	W	81-71	Feb. 19
Missouri	W	87-65	Feb. 26

Leading Scorers

Raef LaFrentz (6-11 So. F)	13.4*
Paul Pierce (6-6 Fr. F)	11.9*
Jacque Vaughn (6-1 Jr. G)	10.9*
Jerod Haase (6-3 Jr. G)	10.8*
Scot Pollard (6-10 Jr. C)	10.1*

1996-97 Roy Williams
Record: 34-2; Big 12: 15-1/1st;
Allen Fieldhouse: 15-0
NCAA Tournament: 2-1
Big 12 Conference champions
Big 12 Tournament champions
Ranked #1 (AP), #5 (Coaches)

San Diego	W	79-72	Dec. 1
George Washington	W	85-56	Dec. 11
UNC Asheville	W	105-73	Dec. 15
North Carolina State	W	84-56	Dec. 21
Washburn	W	90-65	Dec. 30
Brown	W	107-49	Jan. 2
Texas (19)	W	86-61	Jan. 6
Niagara	W	134-73	Jan. 9
Iowa State (8)	W	80-67	Jan. 13
Texas A&M	W	89-60	Jan. 22
Nebraska	W	82-77 OT	Feb. 1
Oklahoma State	W	104-72	Feb. 12
Colorado (15)	W	114-74	Feb. 15
Missouri	W	79-67	Feb. 17
Kansas State	W	78-58	Feb. 22

Leading Scorers

Raef LaFrentz (6-11 Jr. F)	18.5*
Paul Pierce (6-6 So. F)	16.3*
Jerod Haase (6-3 Sr. G)	12.0*
Scot Pollard (6-11 Sr. C)	10.3*
Jacque Vaughn (6-1 Sr. G)	10.2*

1997-98 Roy Williams
Record: 35-4; Big 12: 15-1/1st;
Allen Fieldhouse: 16-0
NCAA Tournament: 1-1
Big 12 Conference champions
Big 12 Tournament champions
Preseason NIT champions
Ranked #2 (AP), #8 (Coaches)

Santa Clara	W	99-73	Nov. 14
Rice	W	88-61	Nov. 17
Western Kentucky	W	75-62	Nov. 19
UNLV	W	92-68	Nov. 21
Emporia State	W	102-50	Dec. 4
Massachusetts	W	73-71	Dec. 10

Middle Tennessee St.	W	103-68	Dec. 13
Pepperdine	W	96-83	Dec. 18
Nebraska	W	96-76	Jan. 3
Colorado	W	111-62	Jan. 7
Kansas State	W	69-62	Jan. 17
Texas Tech	W	88-49	Jan. 24
Baylor	W	94-47	Jan. 28
Missouri	W	80-70	Feb. 8
Iowa State	W	71-54	Feb. 21
Oklahoma	W	83-70	Feb. 23

Leading Scorers

Paul Pierce (6-6 Jr. F)	20.4*
Raef LaFrentz (6-11 Sr. F)	19.8*
Billy Thomas (6-4 Sr. G)	13.6*
Ryan Robertson (6-5 Jr. G)	8.3*
Lester Earl (6-8 So. F)	7.6

1998-99 Roy Williams
Record: 23-10; Big 12: 11-5/T2nd;
Allen Fieldhouse: 10-3
NCAA Tournament: 1-1
Big 12 Tournament champions
Ranked #22 (AP), #23 (Coaches)

Gonzaga	W	80-66	Nov. 13
Fort Hays State	W	91-67	Nov. 21
Iowa	L	81-85	Dec. 8
USC	W	107-78	Dec. 12
DePaul	W	74-66	Dec. 17
Texas A&M	W	95-57	Jan. 2
Iowa State	W	74-60	Jan. 9
Texas	W	76-67	Jan. 18
Missouri	L	63-71	Jan. 24
Colorado	W	77-74	Jan. 30
Nebraska	L	59-64	Feb. 10
Kansas State	W	62-47	Feb. 17
Oklahoma State	W	67-66 OT	Feb. 22

Leading Scorers

Eric Chenowith (7-0 So. C)	13.5*
Ryan Robertson (6-5 Sr. G)	12.8*
Kenny Gregory (6-5 So. G-F)	11.3*
Jeff Boschee (6-1 Fr. G)	10.9*
Nick Bradford (6-6 Jr. F)	9.2*

1999-00 Roy Williams
Record: 24-10; Big 12: 11-5/5th;
Allen Fieldhouse: 13-1
NCAA Tournament: 1-1

Fairfield	W	97-71	Nov. 19
Pepperdine	W	76-61	Dec. 2
Pittsburg State	W	96-71	Dec. 11
Ohio State (12)	W	80-67	Dec. 16
Princeton	W	82-67	Dec. 22
Pennsylvania	W	105-59	Jan. 4
Kansas State	W	87-79	Jan. 12
Nebraska	W	97-82	Jan. 15
Colorado	W	89-74	Jan. 24
Texas Tech	W	87-62	Feb. 5
Iowa State (14)	L	62-64	Feb. 16
Oklahoma (20)	W	53-50	Feb. 20
Baylor	W	80-70	Feb. 26
Missouri	W	83-82	Mar. 5

Leading Scorers

Kenny Gregory (6-5 Jr. G-F)	12.8*
Drew Gooden (6-9 Fr. F)	10.6
Nick Collison (6-9 Fr. F)	10.5*
Jeff Boschee (6-1 So. G)	10.0*
Luke Axtell (6-10 Jr. G-F)	8.7

2000-01 Roy Williams
Record: 26-7; Big 12: 12-4/T2nd;
Allen Fieldhouse: 13-1
NCAA Tournament: 2-1
Ranked #12 (AP), #7 (Coaches)

North Dakota	W	92-61	Nov. 17
Boise State	W	101-61	Nov. 20
Washburn	W	99-56	Nov. 25
Middle Tennessee	W	92-66	Nov. 27
Illinois State	W	80-61	Nov. 30
Tulsa	W	92-69	Dec. 16
Nebraska	W	84-62	Jan. 17
Texas A&M	W	100-70	Jan. 20
Kansas State	W	92-66	Jan. 27
Texas	W	82-66	Feb. 3
Iowa State (12)	L	77-79	Feb. 5
Oklahoma State	W	77-61	Feb. 10
Colorado	W	91-79	Feb. 21
Missouri	W	75-59	Mar. 4

Leading Scorers

Drew Gooden (6-10 So. F)	15.8*
Kenny Gregory (6-5 Sr. G-F)	15.6*
Nick Collison (6-9 So. F)	14.0*
Kirk Hinrich (6-3 So. G)	11.5*
Jeff Boschee (6-1 Jr. G)	11.1*

2001-02 Roy Williams
Record: 33-4; Big 12: 16-0/1st;
Allen Fieldhouse: 13-0
NCAA Tournament: 4-1 (Tie Third -
Final Four)
Big 12 Conference champions
Ranked #2 (AP), #2 (Coaches)

Pittsburg State	W	105-62	Nov. 28
Wake Forest (23)	W	83-76	Dec. 4
UMKC	W	79-68	Dec. 8
South Carolina State	W	106-73	Dec. 15
Valparaiso	W	81-73	Jan. 2
Nebraska	W	96-57	Jan. 9
Oklahoma (5)	W	74-67	Jan. 19
Missouri (22)	W	105-73	Jan. 28
Colorado	W	100-73	Feb. 2
Texas Tech (24)	W	108-81	Feb. 9
Baylor	W	87-72	Feb. 16
Iowa State	W	102-66	Feb. 18
Kansas State	W	103-68	Feb. 27

Leading Scorers

Drew Gooden (6-10 Jr. F)	19.8*
Nick Collison (6-9 Jr. F)	15.6*
Kirk Hinrich (6-3 Jr. G)	14.8*
Jeff Boschee (6-1 Sr. G)	13.4*
Wayne Simien (6-8 Fr. F)	8.1

2002-03 Roy Williams
Record: 33-4; **Big Eight:** 14-2/1st;
Allen Fieldhouse: 15-1
NCAA Tournament: 5-1 (National Runner-up)
Big 12 Conference champions
Ranked #6 (AP), #2 (Coaches)

Holy Cross	W	81-57	Nov. 19
UNC Greensboro	W	105-66	Nov. 22
Central Mo. State	W	97-70	Dec. 4
Emporia State	W	113-61	Dec. 14
UCLA	W	87-70	Dec. 21
UNC Asheville	W	102-50	Jan. 2
Nebraska	W	92-59	Jan. 11
Wyoming	W	98-70	Jan. 15
Kansas State	W	81-64	Jan. 18
Arizona (1)	L	74-91	Jan. 25
Texas (3)	W	90-87	Jan. 27
Missouri (21)	W	76-70	Feb. 3
Iowa State	W	70-51	Feb. 16
Colorado	W	94-87	Feb. 19
Texas A&M	W	85-45	Feb. 26
Oklahoma State (16)	W	79-61	Mar. 1

Leading Scorers

Nick Collison (6-9 Sr. F)	18.5*
Kirk Hinrich (6-3 Sr. G)	17.3*
Keith Langford (6-4 So. G)	15.9*
Wayne Simien (6-9 So. F)	14.8
Aaron Miles (6-1 So. G)	8.9*

2003-04 Bill Self
Record: 24-9; Big 12: 12-4/T2nd;
Allen Fieldhouse: 13-1
NCAA Tournament: 3-1
Ranked #16 (AP), #9 (Coaches)

UT Chattanooga	W	103-73	Nov. 21
Michigan State	W	81-74	Nov. 25
Fort Hays State	W	80-40	Dec. 10
Binghamton	W	78-46	Dec. 29
Villanova	W	86-79	Jan. 2
Kansas State	W	73-67	Jan. 14
Richmond	L	68-69	Jan. 22
Colorado	W	78-57	Jan. 25
Missouri	W	65-56	Feb. 2
Texas Tech	W	96-77	Feb. 7
Baylor	W	74-54	Feb. 18
Iowa State	W	90-89 OT	Feb. 21
Oklahoma	W	79-58	Feb. 29
Nebraska	W	78-67	Mar. 3

Leading Scorers

Wayne Simien (6-9 Jr. F)	17.8*
Keith Langford (6-4 Jr. G)	15.5*
J.R. Giddens (6-5 Fr. F)	11.3*
Aaron Miles (6-1 Jr. G)	9.1*
David Padgett (6-11 Fr. C)	6.5*

Appendix II
Allen Fieldhouse Records

INDIVIDUAL

Most Points — 56, Oscar Robertson, Cincinnati, vs. Arkansas, 1958 NCAA Tournament, March 15, 1958

Most Points By A Kansas Player — 52, Wilt Chamberlain, vs. Northwestern, December 3, 1956

Most Field Goals — 21, Oscar Robertson, Cincinnati, vs. Arkansas, 1958 NCAA Tournament, March 15, 1958

Most Field Goals By A Kansas Player — 20, Wilt Chamberlain, vs. Northwestern, December 3, 1956

Most Free Throws — 18, Wilt Chamberlain, vs. Nebraska, February 8, 1958

Most Free Throws By A Visiting Player — 16, Gene Phillips, SMU, vs. UTEP, 1970; 16, Kresimir Cosic, BYU, vs. Cincinnati, 1972

Most Free Throws By A Kansas Opponent — 15, Don Tomlinson, Missouri, February 15, 1969; 15, Damon Bailey, Indiana, December 22, 1993

Most Three-Point Field Goals — 11, Terry Brown, Kansas vs. N.C. State, January 5, 1991; 11, Randy Rutherford, Oklahoma State, vs. Kansas, March 5, 1995

Most Three-Point Field Goals By A Visiting Player — 11, Randy Rutherford, Oklahoma State, vs. Kansas, March 5, 1995

Most Rebounds — 36, Wilt Chamberlain, Kansas vs. Iowa State, February 15, 1958

Most Rebounds By A Visiting Player — 23, Tom Robitaille, Rice, vs. Kansas, December 1, 1958

TEAM

Most Points — 150, Kansas, vs. Kentucky, December 9, 1989

Most Points By A Visiting Team — 107, Kansas State, vs. Houston, 1970

Most Points By A Kansas Opponent — 95, Kentucky, December 9, 1989

Fewest Points — 37, Kansas, vs. Oklahoma State, February 24, 1962; 37, Portland, vs. Kansas, January 13, 1968

Most Rebounds — 72, Kansas, vs. Colorado, February 26, 1994

Most Field Goals — 52, Kansas, vs. Kentucky, December 9, 1989 (85 attempts); 52, Kansas, vs. Elizabeth City State, January 18, 1990 (83 attempts)

Fewest Field Goals — 11, Kansas, vs. Oklahoma State, February 24, 1962

Fewest Field Goals By A Visiting Team — 12, Syracuse, vs. Kansas, December 14, 1968

Most Free Throws — 38, Kansas, vs. Niagara, January 9, 1997 (52 attempts); 38, Kansas, vs. Missouri, February 17, 1958 (52 attempts); 38, Kansas, vs. Western Kentucky, December 20, 1969 (42 attempts)

Most Free Throws By A Visiting Team — 37, Oklahoma City, vs. Kansas, January 16, 1971

Fewest Free Throws — 2, Kansas, vs. San Francisco, December 16, 1972

Most Fouls — 37, American, vs. Kansas, January 6, 1988

Most Fouls By Kansas — 31, vs. Oklahoma City, January 16, 1971

Fewest Fouls — 8, Kansas, vs. Murray State, January 17, 1970

Fewest Fouls By A Visiting Team — 9, Nebraska, vs. Kansas, January 6, 1962; 9, Portland, vs. Kansas, January 13, 1968

Appendix III

Allen Fieldhouse Attendance

(Since 1964-65)

Year	Attendance	G	Avg.	Season Record	Home Record
1964-65	84,642	10	8,464	17-8	7-3
1965-66	124,300	10	12,430	23-4	10-0
1966-67	171,750	13	13,208	23-4	12-1
1967-68	171,924	12	14,327	22-8	9-3
1968-69	167,949	12	13,996	20-7	10-2
1969-70	150,972	13	11,613	17-9	13-0
1970-71	187,750	14	13,411	27-3	14-0
1971-72	175,050	14	12,504	11-15	11-3
1972-73	160,200	14	11,442	8-18	7-7
1973-74	158,550	13	12,196	23-7	12-1
1974-75	166,025	13	12,771	19-8	11-2
1975-76	146,220	14	10,444	13-13	8-6
1976-77	145,488	14	10,392	18-10	12-2
1977-78	182,250	15	12,150	24-5	14-1
1978-79	195,980	13	15,075	18-11	11-2
1979-80	186,703	14	13,335	15-14	11-3
1980-81	198,329	15	13,222	24-8	14-1
1981-82	152,293	16	9,518	13-14	12-4
1982-83	132,251	14	9,447	13-16	8-6
1983-84	185,400	16	11,587	22-10	14-2
1984-85	212,828	16	13,301	26-8	16-0
1985-86	213,034	15	14,202	35-4	15-0
1986-87	233,800	15	15,587	25-11	15-0
1987-88	216,650	14	15,475	27-11	11-3
1988-89	202,488	14	14,463	19-12	10-4
1989-90	242,225	16	15,139	30-5	15-1
1990-91	230,600	15	15,373	27-8	15-0
1991-92	219,550	14	15,682	27-5	13-1
1992-93	235,000	15	15,667	29-7	13-2
1993-94	241,000	16	15,063	27-8	13-3
1994-95	218,300	14	15,593	25-6	14-0
1995-96	204,500	13	15,731	29-5	13-0
1996-97	242,100	15	16,140	34-2	15-0
1997-98	256,436	16	16,027	35-4	16-0
1998-99	211,600	13	16,277	23-10	10-3
1999-00	227,800	14	16,271	24-10	13-1
2000-01	226,500	14	16,179	26-7	13-1
2001-02	211,700	13	16,285	33-4	13-0
2002-03	260,800	16	16,300	30-8	15-1
2003-04	228,200	14	16,300	24-9	13-1
Total	**7,778,837**	**561**	**13,866**	**925-347**	**491-70**

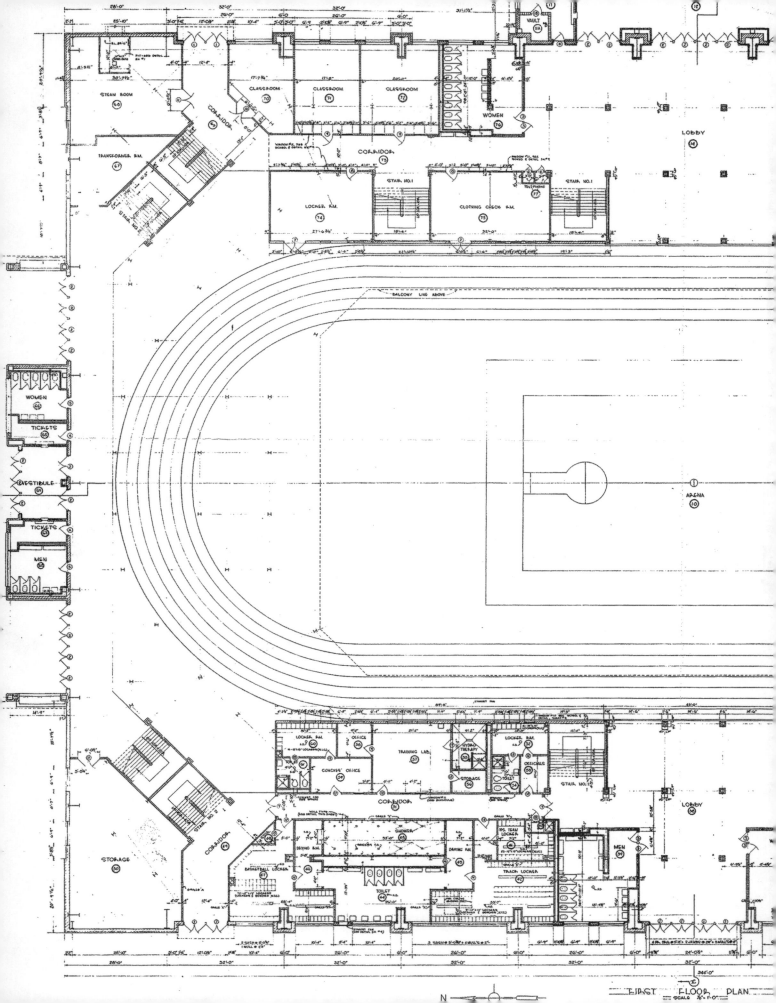

FIRST FLOOR PLAN
SCALE 1/8"=1'-0"

N